D1105949

WITNESS TO EXTINCTION

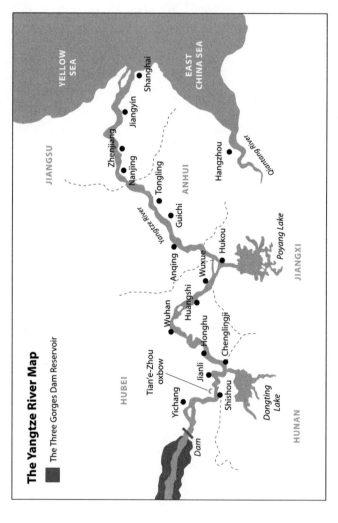

Map showing the middle-lower Yangtze region, featuring locations described in the text. The baiji formerly occurred from the lower Three Gorges region of the main Yangtze channel (immediately upstream of Yichang) to the estuary, as well as in Dongting and Poyang Lakes and in the neighbouring Qiantang River to the south.

WITNESS TO EXTINCTION

How we failed to save the
Yangtze River Dolphin

~

SAMUEL TURVEY

OXFORD
UNIVERSITY PRESS

OXFORD
UNIVERSITY PRESS

Great Clarendon Street, Oxford OX2 6DP

Oxford University Press is a department of the University of Oxford.
It furthers the University's objective of excellence in research, scholarship,
and education by publishing worldwide in

Oxford New York

Auckland Cape Town Dar es Salaam Hong Kong Karachi
Kuala Lumpur Madrid Melbourne Mexico City Nairobi
New Delhi Shanghai Taipei Toronto

With offices in

Argentina Austria Brazil Chile Czech Republic France Greece
Guatemala Hungary Italy Japan Poland Portugal Singapore
South Korea Switzerland Thailand Turkey Ukraine Vietnam

Oxford is a registered trade mark of Oxford University Press
in the UK and in certain other countries

Published in the United States
by Oxford University Press Inc., New York

British Library Cataloguing in Publication Data

Data available

Library of Congress Cataloging in Publication Data

Data available

Typeset by SPI Publisher Services, Pondicherry, India
Printed in Great Britain
on acid-free paper by
CPI Antony Rowe, Chippenham, Wiltshire

ISBN 978-0-19-954947-4

1 3 5 7 9 10 8 6 4 2

For Leigh
because not many other people deserve much credit in this story

On the dark brown banks of the Yangtze,
the future has already arrived.

Paul Theroux
Sailing through China

Contents

~

Contents

Author's Note

~

B efore we start, it is necessary to provide a few brief lines of explanation about the nature and transliteration of Chinese names, and the method of standardization that has been used in the text of the pages that follow. Two main points must be made. Firstly, Chinese personal names consist of a one-syllable family name and a typically two-syllable personal name. Unlike in English, the family name is placed before the personal name. Secondly, different transliteration methods have been used by sinologists over the years for expressing Chinese words in the Roman alphabet. The transliteration system used almost exclusively here is the modern pinyin system (which gives the capital of China as Beijing), which over the last few decades has taken over from the older Wade-Giles system (full of more breathy aspirations, apostrophes, and hyphens, in which the capital was called Peking). The only deliberate exception is the name of the river at the heart of the book, which I have given as 'Yangtze' due to personal preference, but which should strictly be transliterated as the somewhat uglier 'Yangzi'. However, it's actually called 'Chang Jiang' in Chinese anyway, so it's not as though it really matters.

As a final, unrelated point, I would like to quote a line from the preface written by Qian Zhongshu to his great twentieth-century Chinese novel, *Fortress Besieged*: 'In writing about these people, I did not forget they are human beings, still human beings with the basic nature of hairless, two-legged animals.' That sums up my opinions, I think, as well as anything that I can say myself.

Prologue

~

It sometimes happens that a single chance occurrence
alters the whole trend of a man's life and career.

Charles Hoy
The 'white-flag' dolphin of the Tung Ting Lake

It all started for me when I was 21. I had just completed an undergraduate degree in Zoology, and after a heady, unforgettable summer spent on a research station in Asiatic Russia, I was now beginning my doctoral research project, an investigation into the fossil deposits of the Yangtze Basin. I had to fly out to the old Guomintand capital Nanjing in early October, right at the start of my doctoral studentship—before I had been able to give much consideration to what the subject of my research was actually supposed to be, let alone make even a feeble attempt to learn any Chinese—in order to tag along as the only Westerner on a three-month field project being carried out by my Chinese supervisor and his team close to the city of Yichang, one of the major ports on the Yangtze River.

That first visit to China was one of the hardest trips I have ever taken. As we came in to land, the thick layer of smog that was spread over the entire country wrapped itself around us. Stepping from the plane, the end of the runway disappeared into a yellowish grey haze, and wherever we went the air remained choked with pollution—only the most obvious indication of the extreme assaults being waged across the country on its natural environment as part of the national drive for greater industrialization.

In the hills to the north of Yichang, I slowly gathered together a large collection of fossils that would provide me with information for my thesis on the faunal relationships between southern China and other geographical regions many millions of years ago. But although my research gradually progressed, my Chinese language skills did not advance at the rate I had blithely and naively predicted. I quickly learnt the characters for 'man' and 'woman'— invaluable for deciding which bathroom to use—but even though my elderly supervisor was kind and gentle, and gave me as much support as possible, my ability to converse with the other members of the palaeontological research team remained limited. My days were spent gathering fossils in silence, and then retreating to my hotel room to read the stack of novels I had brought with me. It was an odd, lonely existence, and contrasted starkly with my magical summer in Yekaterinburg—where I had spent my evenings gabbling away in ropey Russian, sharing home-made vodka around the camp fire, and feeling *alive*.

After a few weeks of successful fieldwork and lots of fossils, the Chinese researchers decided that we had earned a short break. We were not far from the Three Gorges, one of China's most famous and beautiful visitor attractions, where the Yangtze rushes over rapids between a series of narrow forested cliffs. However, it was decided instead that it would be more educational to visit the country's greatest industrial development, situated immediately downstream from the rapids. The Three Gorges Dam was first envisioned by Sun Yat-Sen, the founder of modern China, decades before the Communist Party came to power, but construction on the project had not begun until 1994, twenty years after a smaller-scale dam had already been built downstream at Gezhou. It was to be the largest hydro-electric power station in the world, as well as controlling the seasonal floods which had devastated the lower Yangtze region throughout China's history, but over a million inhabitants of Hubei Province and Chongqing Municipality to the west were to be displaced by its 600-kilometre-long reservoir. Its statistics were meaningless; they were too vast to comprehend.

The dam would not be finished until 2006, but by now construction had already been under way for four years.

The dam site was on a scale I had never encountered before. The entire landscape from one horizon to the other was filled by an immense grey wall of concrete, crawling with cranes and construction workers all along its rim. Girders sprouted everywhere from half-finished columns and buttresses, like strange new plants growing in front of our eyes and replacing the life that had been stripped away from the valley in front of the dam. The dark brown air rang with noise, and was thick with dust and smoke.

We climbed the hill overlooking the dam site, and entered the small visitor centre to escape the pounding roar of construction. The main display area was taken up by a large model showing what the dam would look like when complete, set in a landscape painted in bright greens and blues as if trying to pretend that these colours still existed outside. The construction continued on relentlessly behind the smoked glass walls.

Beside the model stood a young attendant, her hands held firmly together in front of her white uniform. She looked like an airline hostess, and smiled when I spoke to her.

There was only one thing I wanted to know. 'What effect will this dam have on the baiji?' I asked.

She paused, her smile tightening. She frowned slightly.

'Ah . . . the baiji.' Her voice had a gentle, musical lilt. Then her smile grew. 'The baiji . . . the baiji will be *fine*.'

Part One

THE BEGINNING

1

THE GODDESS
OF THE YANGTZE

The dolphin is the most remarkable animal in the world.

Calligraphy presented to Professor G. Pilleri
by the finger writer Tang Wenri, Yueyang, 1979

Once upon a time, so the story goes, lived a beautiful and kind-hearted girl on the south bank of the Yangtze. She had lost her parents and lived with her stepfather, a mean-spirited man who showed her no love and beat her regularly. As she grew up into a slim, graceful maiden, she longed to be free of her cruel guardian, but he realized that she would fetch a good price if he sold her to a trader in women on the north bank. He concocted a story to lure her into accompanying him over the river, but when their boat was halfway across, they were caught in a sudden storm and became drenched with rain. The old man, seeing the outline of his stepdaughter's young body through her thin wet dress, felt a wave of lust and forced himself upon her. Managing to break free, and realizing the fate that awaited her when they arrived at the shore, she threw herself into the fast-flowing river. As she fell into the water and disappeared beneath the waves, she was changed miraculously into a beautiful white dolphin which swam happily away, free at last. The storm reached new heights of anger, and the stepfather was flung into the river by a mighty wave; the waters closed over his head. As he fell into the depths, he also became changed, but this time not into an elegant dolphin but a 'river pig' or ugly porpoise.

At least, that is how the story is told in the provinces of Jiangsu and Anhui. Further upstream, between Dongting Lake and the city of Wuhan, the local people tell of a dark general who was called away to war, and who longed to return home to see his daughter. One evening, he met a young lady in an inn beside the Yangtze. After spending the night together, the girl told the general that her father was also a soldier, but he had left home when she was very small. The general was gripped by dread; he asked her quickly where she had grown up, and she spoke the name of the general's own village. Yelling out his grief and shame, the general flung himself into the waters of the Yangtze. His daughter ran after him and drowned herself in the river as well. The general was changed by magic into a porpoise, and his daughter, pure in spirit, turned into a shining white dolphin.

There are many stories like this along the Yangtze—of drowned daughters and grieving fathers, of landlords banning their lovesick daughters from falling in love with poor farm labourers, and even of lazy fishwives drowned by their relatives—but all have the same ending, a strange metamorphosis that allows these victims to overcome a grief that is too great to bear. Echoes of Ovid and the magical sea-changes of Prospero ripple down the Yangtze's waters. The white dolphin swims on in the river, the stories say, reunited now with her father or swimming forever ahead of her stepfather, and continues to show her kindness and purity by warning fishermen of coming storms. Many old Chinese texts, such as the Tang Dynasty *Ben Cao Shi Yi* and the Ming Dynasty *San Cai Tu Hui*, report that the boat people watched dolphins in order to predict the weather, calling the animal 'the worshipper of the wind', because when they were seen diving up and down in the waves it meant that strong winds or tidal waves were coming.

How can you know when ships are threatened by danger, and what makes you aware of the will of heaven even before the oracle, asked the Song Dynasty poet Kong Wuzhong in his *Jiangtun Shi*, 'Ode to the River Dolphin'—surely it is affection that you show for humans? Local fishermen along the Yangtze called the dolphin the 'Lord of the Waves and Billows', according to Mao Sheng in the 'Collected Reports of the Kind Deeds of Water Animals', written during the Song Dynasty (AD 960–1279). The reincarnated maiden was revered as the Goddess of the Yangtze, and had many names—*jiangma* or river horse, *taipai*, *qiangji*, the *chan* fish or the well fish (the last name having arisen because its blowhole was thought to resemble a well shaft). Most often, though, it was simply known as the white dolphin, or *bai ji*.

～

Baiji have been known and written about by Chinese authors for thousands of years. The oldest known reference to the river dolphin of the Yangtze is found in the *Er Ya*, an early philological work—a kind of dictionary, defining the correct usage of Chinese characters in the past and the present—that can be traced back with certainty at least as far as the early Han Dynasty, between 206 BC and AD 8. Different theories suggest that it may actually date back to the beginning of the Zhou Dynasty over 3,000 years ago, or may have been compiled by Confucius or his pupil Pu Shang in the fifth century BC; or it may simply be a compilation of fragments written by different scholars at different times. Whoever wrote the *Er Ya* made a wrong guess about what kind of animal the baiji actually was—unsurprising for someone writing almost three millennia before Carl Linnaeus formalized the classification of the natural world—but otherwise provided a surprisingly accurate and detailed description of the creature:

> The *ji* is a kind of shark. Its body is similar to that of a sturgeon. Its tail is like that of the *qin* fish. It has a large stomach. Its snout is small and pointed. The long upper incisor teeth grow in a single row. When it presses its upper and lower jaws together, it can hold an

object in its mouth. The nose is situated on the forehead. The *ji* can make noises. Its body consists of a great many bones but very little flesh. It gives birth to live young. It is very fond of eating small fish. It is slightly more than a chang in length. It is common in rivers. [1]

Throughout Chinese history, baiji have been the subject of both scholarly and popular interest, featuring in encyclopaedias and academic texts as well as poems, stories, and legends. However, for some reason they were never physically portrayed in classical Chinese paintings, ceramics, or sculptures, unlike other animals with symbolic significance in Chinese culture such as tigers or cranes, or even other freshwater species such as fish, shrimps, and prawns, which had great economic importance and were frequently represented in visual media. A few of the classical texts that mention dolphins include simple, largely inaccurate illustrations, but probably the first ever detailed, artistic representation of a baiji in Chinese art may have been the watercolour painted by Ren Zhongnian, which was presented to the Swiss cetacean researcher Giorgio Pilleri in Wuhan in 1979.

This lack of available paintings, sculptures, or translations of the many Chinese texts that mentioned the baiji meant that, although Chinese authors had been familiar with the species for millennia, its recognition by the West took a long time to occur. It seems that the first European to record the presence of freshwater cetaceans in the Yangtze was Lord George Macartney, the first British envoy to China. During his famous visit to the country in 1793, during which he refused to kowtow to Emperor Qianlong, insulted a jade gift, and failed to negotiate any British trading requests, he crossed the Yangtze at Zhenjiang when travelling south on the Grand Canal that links Beijing with the southern provinces. Macartney's diarist noted that during their Yangtze crossing 'the waves rolled like the sea, and porpoises are said to be sometimes leaping amongst them'. [2] This brief account was ignored by the Western scientific establishment, as was that of Robert Swinhoe almost 100 years later. Swinhoe, an industrious English naturalist fluent in both Mandarin and local Chinese dialects, journeyed up the Yangtze to Chongqing to assess the navigability of steamships in the river in his secondary capacity as a 'roving consul' for the British plenipotentiary in China for Great Britain. In his 'Catalogue of the Mammals of China (south of the River Yangtze) and of the Island of Formosa', published in the *Proceedings of the Zoological Society of London* in 1870, Swinhoe reported that 'white porpoises' could be seen as far up the Yangtze as Hankou (then an independent town which was called 'Hankow' by the British, but now absorbed into the sprawling conurbation of Wuhan). Above that port, and upstream as far as Yichang, Swinhoe noticed what seemed to him to be a smaller and apparently different form of white porpoise. While an extremely observant and talented naturalist, Swinhoe was in error in this instance, as his two types of white porpoises were actually the same kind of animal. Furthermore, he did not attribute much importance to his sightings. Instead, he assumed that the animals he had seen—or those downstream from Wuhan, at least—were merely Indo-Pacific humpback dolphins, a whitish or pale pink marine dolphin species that was first documented over a century earlier and had just been fully described by William Henry Flower, and which superficially resembles the baiji but is actually only distantly related. In fact, Swinhoe reported that 'South-China white porpoises', as he called the humpback dolphins, were 'to be seen in all the rivers of South China'; his sightings in the Yangtze were therefore considered to be of no special significance. Swinhoe's report of white dolphins in the Yangtze remained forgotten by zoologists until 1938, when its historical importance was appreciated by Glover M. Allen, a mammalogist at Harvard University's Museum of Comparative Zoology.

It was not until almost half a century after Swinhoe's sightings that the baiji was finally recognized as a distinct species by scientists in the West, thanks to the efforts of an American teenager named Charles Hoy. The 17-year-old son of the principal of a Christian seminary near the town of Chenglingji, Hoy was passionate about natural history and spent much of his time on nearby Dongting Lake, one of the large lake systems appended to the main channel of the Yangtze. He was familiar with the freshwater dolphins found in the region, having encountered them on several occasions, and later wrote that they were often seen in shallow water working up the mud in their search for fish; 'the sudden appearance of a school of these whitish dolphins close to a small boat is very startling.'[3]Hoy believed that the animal was only found in large numbers around the mouth of Dongting Lake, which emptied into the main river near Chenglingji, as although he had lived in China for several years he had never seen dolphins except in the lake and the channel that connected it to the Yangtze. During winter, the lake's level fell so low that it scarcely contained more water than in the river. 'In spite of its large size, Tungting Lake suffers, like many human beings of big proportions, from chronic indecision; it is unable to make up its mind whether to be lake or mud flat,' wrote the American zoologist Clifford Pope, who visited Dongting in 1921.[4]During the winter low-water season, Hoy observed that baiji were easily seen and occurred in 'great numbers', usually in groups of three or four individuals, but occasionally of as many as ten or fifteen.

On 18 February 1914,[5]Hoy was on a duck hunt in the shallow channel near Chenglingji when his party passed through a school of baiji, and he managed to shoot one of the dolphins at a distance of 70 yards. The author of the *Er Ya* was correct in stating that 'the *ji* can make noises'; Hoy later wrote that 'when shot it gave a cry like that of a water-buffalo calf... The Chinese say that a peculiar roaring noise, that is often heard at night on the lake, is due to these dolphins, and, judging from the noise that the one I secured made, this would probably seem to be the case.'[6]His prize was too heavy to lift into the boat, so one of the boatmen grabbed the animal by its long snout, allowing the others to slip a rope around its wounded body and row to shore 'with the dead monster in tow'. An unintentionally chilling photo taken shortly after the group's triumphant return shows Hoy crouching over the dead baiji close to the lake shore, holding his shotgun with pride;

blood oozes from the side of the dolphin, its mouth propped open with a stick. Great excitement surrounded the capture, and Hoy even sampled some of the animal's meat, which reminded him of a mixture of beef and liver: 'though I found it excellent, it was just a trifle coarse in fibre, though quite tender.'[7] Hoy kept the skull and cervical vertebrae, and on his return to the United States shortly afterwards, he sold them to the United States National Museum of Natural History—part of the Smithsonian Institution in Washington, DC—where they were studied by Gerrit S. Miller Jr. To his surprise, Miller found that the white Chinese river dolphin was not a specimen of humpback dolphin, but instead something altogether different. He described it as a new genus and species of cetacean, *Lipotes vexillifer*, in the museum's in-house journal, *Smithsonian Miscellaneous Collections*, in 1918. It was one of the last large mammals ever to be described by science.

The scientific binomial that Miller erected for the animal is based on a persistent misunderstanding. In his letter accompanying the specimen, Hoy wrote that 'the natives give it the name *Peh Ch'i*, which they tell me means "white flag", because the dorsal fin, which they liken to a flag, is so prominent when the animal comes to the surface to breathe'.[8] Miller accordingly gave his new species the specific name *vexillifer*, derived from the Latin for 'flag bearer'. But Hoy, like many Westerners before and after him, had been confused by the subtle distinctions of the Chinese language. The word *qi*, meaning flag or banner and pronounced with a soft, breathy 'ch' sound, is extremely similar to the untrained ear to the word *ji*, meaning dolphin, and Hoy had simply misinterpreted the animal's standard name 'baiji'. To add further to the confusion, the Chinese word *qi*, meaning fin, also sounds very similar and has an identical transliteration into the Roman alphabet, and this led to the baiji's name becoming doubly mistranslated from the Western 'white flag' into 'white fin' in *Names of Vertebrates*, a standard Chinese scientific text compiled in the mid-1950s by the National Committee for Unifying Academic Terms. Thus entrenched in the formal scientific literature of both China *and* the English-speaking world, these mistakes were only highlighted by the Chinese cetacean specialist Professor Zhou Kaiya in 1977. Despite this, the baiji is still frequently referred to erroneously as the 'white-flag dolphin' in Western news reports or popular accounts of the species today.

But it is the story of what happened to Charles Hoy after he shot his dolphin that provides the first whispered warning of what fate also had in store for the baiji. Impressed by his knowledge of natural history and clear aptitude for collecting specimens of unusual new animals, Miller arranged for Hoy to be employed by the Smithsonian Institution to collect mammals in Australia. Hoy travelled widely across the continent over a three-year period from June 1919 to April 1922, eventually collecting 1,179 mammals as well as almost 1,000 birds and various other zoological specimens. But what Hoy saw during his time in Australia disturbed him greatly. Wherever he went, he found that the country's native mammals were experiencing a decline that was catastrophic in both magnitude and speed. He was continually frustrated by the difficulty of procuring specimens to send to the Smithsonian, when only a few years earlier the same species had been abundant. One old kangaroo trapper told him that 'as late as two years ago he was sure of *at least* six or seven dozen wallaby skins a week while this year he hasn't seen even one!'[9] The driving factor for these population collapses remains the subject of debate; Hoy himself considered that they had been caused by a combination of overhunting, land clearance for agriculture and stock grazing, increased predation by introduced foxes and feral cats, competition by introduced rodents, poison baiting to control rabbits, and disease epidemics. He became increasingly discouraged about the future survival of the country's mammals, and wrote in 1920 that 'it is only a matter of time before the Australian fauna is extinct and if nothing is done now it will soon be too late'.[10]

But worse was to come. The same 1923 issue of *The China Journal of Science & Arts* that published Hoy's account of his capture of 'the "white-flag" dolphin of the Tung Ting Lake' featured an article on the Oriental blood fluke. This flatworm parasitizes the mesenteric veins and causes schistosomiasis, a debilitating chronic infection that damages the liver and intestines, and 'which in heavily infected districts of the Yangtze Valley causes the death of thousands of human beings each year'.[11] The article's author warned that, although foreigners in China did not normally contract the disease, the flood lands and backwaters of the Yangtze Valley were a constant source of danger for infection, and it affected almost 10 per cent of the inhabitants of the country around Dongting Lake. Hoy had been one of the few foreigners unlucky enough to develop schistosomiasis, possibly as a direct result of his explorations around the lake—as Clifford Pope later put it, Hoy contracted his infection 'from the very waters that had yielded to him their great secret'.[12] When he returned to China in 1922 Hoy was also unlucky enough to develop appendicitis, which was aggravated by the intestinal damage and associated residual effects of his boyhood fluke infection. Within a few years of discovering the baiji, Hoy was dead.

∽

Most people don't realize that dolphins can live in rivers. Several typically marine species of dolphins and porpoises, including not only the Indo-Pacific humpback dolphin in Asia but also the familiar bottlenose dolphin ('Flipper' from the television show), can sometimes be found in the estuaries of rivers such as the Thames, and may even venture further upstream. In the seventeenth century, for instance, harbour porpoises were sometimes to be found in the canals of Amsterdam, and one animal swam up the Seine as far as Paris. But a number of other species of cetacean—the mammal group including all dolphins, porpoises, and whales— are far more dependent upon freshwater habitats.

The first group, the facultative river dolphins, consists of three species with populations that occur in both marine and freshwater. The tucuxi (pronounced 'tucu-shee') is a small grey dolphin that occurs along the coast of eastern Central and South America, and is also found inland throughout the Amazon and Orinoco river basins. The Irrawaddy dolphin, an unusual-looking animal with a rounded, beakless face that is actually closely related to the killer whale, is found in coastal waters in the Bay of Bengal and southeast Asia, and also in the Ayeyarwady (Irrawaddy), Mekong, and Mahakam rivers. The third species has already been mentioned in the legends of the baiji—this is the Yangtze finless porpoise, locally called *jiangtun* or *jiangzhu*, the latter name meaning 'river pig'. This distinctive dark porpoise, which lacks not only a beak but also a dorsal fin, occurs in a geographically narrow ribbon of shallow water that traces the outline of the Asian continent eastward from the Persian Gulf around southeast Asia (where it is known locally as 'bowl head') as far as the Inland Sea of Japan and also south to Java, as well as in the lower and middle reaches of the Yangtze.

Although none of the freshwater populations of these species migrate into marine habitats, they have not been isolated from their sea-going relatives for very long on the geological timescale. Riverine Irrawaddy dolphin populations appear to have left the sea extremely recently, maybe in the order of a few hundred thousand years ago, and the major population division within this species is actually between animals from the northern and southern parts of its southeast Asian range. The marine and freshwater populations of both tucuxi and finless porpoise are distinguished by more genetic and physical differences, and freshwater tucuxis are sometimes considered to be a separate species from coastal animals, but they still left the sea relatively recently. Finless porpoises appear to have only entered the Yangtze river system between 0.72 and 1.08 million years ago,[13] and the Yangtze population is only classified as a separate subspecies rather than as a distinct species.

The evolutionary story is quite different for the second group of freshwater dolphins, the obligate river dolphins—the group to which the baiji belongs, together with the boto or famous pink Amazon River dolphin, the susu or Ganges River dolphin, the bhulan or Indus River dolphin, and the franciscana or La Plata

River dolphin. Out of these species, all but the franciscana are restricted entirely to freshwater environments; the franciscana is also found along the coastline of Brazil and Argentina. Interestingly, this lineage started off marine, later became adapted for freshwater, and then secondarily re-evolved the ability to occupy the marine environment.

The obligate river dolphins are an extremely unusual group of cetaceans, and despite their name they look very different from the familiar 'Flipper'. They have very long, thin beaks lined with large numbers of tiny teeth that give them almost crocodile-like faces—taken to an extreme in the Ganges and Indus dolphins—as well as reduced, almost hump-like dorsal fins, rounded paddle-like flippers, and flexible necks, which together give them a very different profile to the streamlined appearance of their marine namesakes. They also all have small eyes—about the size of a fingernail—and reduced vision, and whereas the Yangtze and Amazon dolphins still have limited powers of sight, the Ganges and Indus dolphins do not even have lenses in their eyes. They are effectively blind and only able to detect the presence and direction of light. This is compensated for by enhanced powers of sonar, which allows the animals to echolocate in murky riverine environments. More unusual alternative ways of detecting prey have also been developed by the Ganges and Indus species, which often swim on their sides and feel along the river bottom with flippers that have scalloped, finger-like trailing edges.

The obligate river dolphins have traditionally been grouped together by scientists in a single mammal family, the Platanistidae, because it has usually been assumed that the distinctive characteristics shared by all of these species must indicate that they are closely related to one another. These dolphins have also been widely interpreted as ancient 'living fossils', which found competition from more 'modern' dolphins in marine environments too great and were forced to find refuge in river systems. Such attitudes are highlighted by Miller's original description of the baiji: the genus name *Lipotes* means 'left behind'. But recent genetic studies[14]have shown that the obligate river dolphins actually consist of two distinct and only distantly related lineages. The most ancient of these is the evolutionary line represented today by the Ganges and Indus dolphins, which separated from all other cetaceans around 30 million years ago—very soon after the evolutionary division between the toothed whales and the huge filter-feeding baleen whales. These dolphins are related to a widely varied range of extinct marine species which also possessed elongated beaks, so it seems that this character is not a specific adaptation for living in rivers. The other obligate river dolphins—the baiji, boto, and franciscana—are more closely related to one another, and their similarities to the Ganges and Indus dolphins are largely due to the independent development of similar adaptations to cope with the common challenges of their riverine environments—a process known as convergent evolution. The last common ancestor of these latter species probably lived in the Pacific Ocean around 20 million years ago, during the Miocene Epoch. During this time interval, the Amazon flowed westwards, into the Pacific, rather than eastwards into the Atlantic as it does today, before the rise of the Andes forced it to switch direction. The ancestral river dolphin population must have independently colonized the two major river systems on either side of this great ocean basin, with the lineages leading to the Amazon River dolphin and the franciscana subsequently separating from each other a few million years later. To set this ancient evolution into context, genetic studies have also revealed that the forty or more species of marine dolphins and porpoises all diverged from each other within the past 10 million years or so. Although the marine relatives of river dolphins decline and disappear from the fossil record at around the same time, the franciscana is today able to coexist with a range of 'modern' marine dolphin species along the Atlantic seaboard of South America, which suggests that simple competition may not be the whole story behind the original disappearance of river dolphins from the sea.

The ancestors of the baiji not only survived as their habitat shifted from marine to freshwater, but thrived in the proto-Yangtze and its associated waters for well over 100 times the period that human beings have existed on the planet. There is very little fossil evidence of freshwater dolphins in China to throw any light on this long period of evolution. The fragmentary fossilized snout of an animal that has been named *Prolipotes*—literally meaning 'before the baiji'—was discovered in sediments near the Yujiang River delta in southern China that may be around 10 million years old, although it is too incomplete to tell how closely related it is to modern baiji. But by the start of the historical era, the baiji enjoyed a wide distribution across southeast China.

As late as the 1970s, Western scientists followed Charles Hoy and Clifford Pope in believing that the species was restricted to an 'astonishingly confined range'[15] limited to Dongting Lake and the channel leading to the Yangtze—supporting their view of the animal as a living fossil unable to adapt to modern environmental conditions. In fact, its distribution stretched from the Yangtze delta upstream as far as Yichang, as Swinhoe first correctly noted. This would always have marked the natural geographic limit of both the baiji and the finless porpoise in the main Yangtze channel, as above Yichang the river becomes a series of rocky rapids through the famous Three Gorges region that are inhospitable for both species. Baiji also occurred in the lower Yangtze's many tributaries and the series of large lake systems associated with the river that were permanently or seasonally connected to the main channel, notably Dongting and Poyang Lakes. Its range can be thought of as following the 'W' pattern of the middle and lower reaches of the Yangtze, where Yichang, Wuhan, and Nanjing sit at the top of the three branches from west to east, with the river resting its elbows in Dongting and Poyang Lakes to the south. The dolphin was also found in the neighbouring Qiantang River, which flows into the East China Sea a few hundred kilometres to the south, and which was formerly connected to the Yangtze by southerly-flowing channels that emptied into the delta near the city of Hangzhou until thirteen centuries ago.

Using comparisons with river dolphin population densities in areas of the Amazon Basin that remain relatively undeveloped today, researchers have speculated that the baiji's historical range may once have been able to support several thousand animals. Less than 2,000 years ago, the lower stretches of the Yangtze were described as 'teeming' with dolphins by Guo Pu, a scholar of the Jin Dynasty (AD 265–420). But this situation was not to last. The baiji's fortune was about to change for the worse.

2

THE AMAZON
OF THE EAST

When we ask the river to yield the way, it must yield!

Mao Zedong

The Yangtze is one of the world's most important freshwater ecosystems. It is the longest river in Asia and the
third longest in the world; its headwaters rise high on the Tibetan
Plateau, and 6,300 kilometres downstream almost a thousand
billion cubic metres of water finally flow into the East China
Sea every year. Its English name derives from a local term meaning 'son of the sea' used for the lower reaches of the river near
Zhenjiang, and which may be derived from the name of the nearby
ancient city of Yangzhou, which is mentioned as being close to a
once more westerly situated delta in the earliest Chinese records.
But in China it is more commonly called the Chang Jiang, which
simply means 'long river'.

The Yangtze has a biological heritage to match these imposing
statistics. Over 350 species of fish have been recorded from the
river basin, 177 of which are endemic—they are found nowhere
else in the world. These include two species of ancient armour-
plated sturgeons and their distant relative the Yangtze paddlefish, so-called because it has a tremendously elongated snout

which—with some stretching of the imagination—resembles a boat's paddle. This snout is more than just a garish ornamentation, as it allows its owner to act like an underwater sniffer dog—it is studded with remarkable receptors that can detect subtle electric currents generated by the smaller animals on which the paddlefish feeds. All three of these species can grow to several metres long, but the paddlefish is the real record-breaker; one individual caught near Nanjing measured over 7 metres in length, making it the largest freshwater fish in the world. The only other species of paddlefish is a much smaller river-dweller found in the Mississippi and neighbouring parts of the southeastern United States.

The Yangtze and its associated waterways are also home to many other remarkable species. The Yangtze giant soft-shelled turtle is probably the largest freshwater turtle in the world. The river's rich wetlands boast the only species of alligator found outside North America, although these are much smaller beasts than their more famous Florida cousins. The wetlands that line the river channel are also a critical wintering ground for huge numbers of waterbirds and waders that breed further north in Siberia. These include five species of cranes, the most beautiful of which, the brilliant white Siberian crane, formerly also wintered further west in India and around the Caspian Sea, but has now been reduced to a few thousand birds that spend several months of the year around Poyang Lake. The river basin was also once lined with lush forests that were home to a wide range of large mammals—elephants, rhinos, tigers, tapirs, and gibbons—which are today largely restricted to the balmy conditions of tropical Asia, but which were once also able to survive in the Yangtze Basin's unique ecosystem of scorching summers and freezing, snowy winters. Although there is nothing quite like it still around today, in many ways the Yangtze ecosystem—a river basin containing tremendous, globally significant levels of aquatic and terrestrial biodiversity—was once the Amazon of the East.

It isn't much like the Amazon any more, though. Eastern China today has very little to show of its past biological riches, as a result

1. The baiji, or Yangtze River dolphin (*Lipotes vexillifer*). The species displays 'classic' river dolphin characteristics, such as a long, thin beak, tiny eyes, and a reduced dorsal fin, giving it a very different appearance to typical marine dolphins.

2. A remarkable postage stamp issued in 1958, celebrating the destruction of China's forests during the Great Leap Forward—a period during which at least 10 per cent of the country's remaining forests were cut down in a few months. The text at the bottom of the stamp reads 'Using petrol saws to cut down trees'.

3. A stylised depiction of a baiji swimming in the waves of the Yangtze (identifiable by its white colouration and long snout), from an eighteenth century Qing Dynasty manuscript.

4. The teenage Charles Hoy posing next to the baiji he shot in February 1914 in the shallow channel connecting Dongting Lake to the main Yangtze. The head and cervical vertebrae of this individual were later sent to the United States National Museum of Natural History, and represent the holotype specimen upon which the species *Lipotes vexillifer* is based.

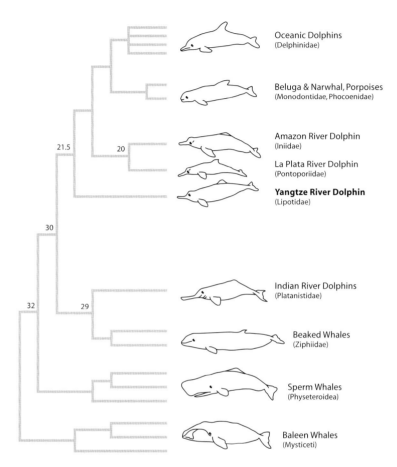

5. A phylogeny or family tree of the cetaceans, showing the interrelationships of the modern groups of whales, dolphins and porpoises. Although the different species of river dolphin were once grouped together by scientists, recent studies have shown that they are only distantly related to one another. The lineage that eventually evolved into the baiji is estimated (on the basis of genetic analysis) to have diverged from all other cetaceans around 20 million years ago, and represents a distinct mammal family, the Lipotidae. Estimated divergence dates in millions of years are indicated at several key points in the phylogeny.

6. Qi Qi, the famous captive baiji who was caught in a rolling hook long-line at the mouth of Dongting Lake in 1980 and lived at the Institute of Hydrobiology in Wuhan for over 22 years before dying of old age, shortly after the last ever verified sighting of a wild baiji. Nearly all of the photographs ever taken of baiji are of Qi Qi.

7. A typical view of surveying conditions in the main Yangtze channel during the 2006 baiji survey. In the 1,669 kilometres between Yichang and Shanghai, we counted a minimum of 19,830 large shipping vessels in the river—more than one every 100 metres.

of thousands of years of environmental exploitation, transformation, and degradation by a constantly growing human population that saw the landscape as a resource to support the continued expansion of society and technology, a powerhouse to fuel what would become one of the world's great empires. Deforestation for land clearance, building timber, and fuel began in the region during prehistory, and rice cultivation, which developed in the fertile lands along the middle and lower stretches of the Yangtze over 7,000 years ago, has supported extremely high human population densities for the past three millennia. Timber exports rose to meet demand in Beijing and northern China during the growth of the empire, and a medieval economic revolution more than a thousand years ago led to further increases in population growth, deforestation, and intensive rice farming across the Yangtze Basin; some cities had by now already reached populations of over a million inhabitants, and timber shortages began to be reported from across the region. More intensive environmental degradation followed the large migration of people from northern China into the lowland Yangtze region during the Qing Dynasty (AD 1644–1912), which led to a population explosion during the eighteenth and nineteenth centuries and a huge increase in conversion of the river's floodplain into agricultural fields. Increased soil erosion, expansion of the Yangtze delta as a result of increased amounts of sediment running off the land into the river, and regional-scale changes to rainfall patterns and water quality were readily apparent by the late Imperial period.

Unsurprisingly, these escalating demands on China's environment led to unsustainable human-wildlife conflicts. Two species of rhinoceros may once have occurred in the Yangtze region, and they were apparently so numerous that historical records report that hunting expeditions would round them up by the scores or even hundreds at a time. Their tough hides were used as standard protective armour by soldiers for more than a millennium during the Archaic period. However, persecution for rhino horn for use in Chinese traditional medicine led to the disappearance of rhinos from eastern China by early Imperial times, and the animals finally died out in southwest China in the nineteenth century. Demand for rhino horn continued, and trade during the Tang Dynasty (AD 618–907) is now believed to be a major factor responsible for the global decline of the Javan and Sumatran rhinoceros species, which are both now among the rarest and most threatened mammals on earth. Elephants were still present in the lower Yangtze valley until around AD 600, and along the middle stretches of the river and in southeast China until about a thousand years ago, but they eventually disappeared due to a combination of ongoing deforestation and human persecution, by farmers defending their crops and hunters targeting them for ivory and for their trunks (which were considered a delicacy). The plaintive song of the gibbon once characterized the Yangtze Gorges and became a poetic symbol of the melancholy of travellers far from home, but it has not been heard in central and eastern China for several hundred years. These species today only survive in southeast Asia, with Chinese populations of elephants and gibbons restricted to the tropical forests of Xishuangbanna in the far southwest of the country (a separate and extremely endangered species of gibbon also survives—although as only a handful of individuals—on Hainan Island off southern China). Giant pandas are at least still familiar today as a Chinese animal, but they are now only found in the mountains of Gansu, Shaanxi, and Sichuan. They once had a much wider range across eastern China, but they finally disappeared from the forests of Shennongjia, their last stronghold in the Yangtze region, over 100 years ago.

The most extreme example of the historical disappearance of Chinese wildlife is that of the milu, an unusual deer species also known as Père David's deer, which is adapted for living in marshlands in the Yangtze valley. The deer was almost extinct in the wild as early as AD 200, but a semi-captive herd was maintained for the pleasure of the Emperor in the Imperial Hunting Lodge outside Beijing, protected by a 72-kilometre long wall and armed guards. Père Armand David, the French Catholic missionary and zoologist

who first revealed the existence of the giant panda to the Western
world, discovered the herd when he peeked over the park walls in
1865, and eventually persuaded the Emperor to send a few pairs to
Europe. It was just in time: in 1894, catastrophic floods destroyed
much of the Imperial Hunting Lodge, and nearly all of the Chinese
herd of deer was eaten by starving farmers and Chinese troops
during the Boxer Rebellion a few years later. The last of the deer
from the Imperial Hunting Lodge died in a menagerie in Beijing
some time between 1917 and 1921. The species was only saved
from extinction by the survival of the small European population.
Eighteen animals were sent from zoos around Europe to Woburn
Abbey, where the Duke of Bedford managed to establish a herd
from the handful of animals that succeeded in breeding; apparently this herd was descended from 'a single fine old stag in the
original consignment of six deer from Paris which refused to allow
any other stags near the hinds as long as he lived'.[1] The global
population of Père David's deer now stands at over 2,000 animals
thanks to these exhaustive conservation efforts. This was not to be
the only time that intensive captive breeding using just a handful
of surviving animals was proposed to save a highly threatened
Chinese mammal from extinction; however, the plan would not
turn out to be so successful in the future.

∽

Many popular accounts of the baiji have assumed that the almost
sacred status in which the animal was held by the fishing communities of the Yangtze ensured that it was traditionally kept
free from persecution. For example, Clifford Pope, who paid
the fishermen at Dongting Lake twenty-five dollars in 1921 for
a baiji that was later hung from the ceiling of the American
Museum of Natural History, was unable to secure a second animal no matter how much he advertised. 'One suggestion for
the failure of the fishermen to help further', wrote Pope, 'was
that they hold the dolphin in awe, believing that ill fortune
descends on those who molest it. The individual that they brought

me may have been merely a compromise with fate; or perhaps they had been threatened by their guild.'[2] In the words of Simon Winchester in *The River at the Centre of the World*, 'fishermen regarded the animals as simply too godlike to catch. If one turned up in their nets, they let it free. That was the rule, obeyed by all.'[3]

However, this idealistic view of the past, as is so often the case, falls sadly short of what we actually know about historical events. China's rural population is not noted for treating its country's wildlife with undue respect, but instead have a rather more practical attitude; the famous saying about the people of southern China states that they eat anything with four limbs except tables, anything that flies except aeroplanes, and anything that swims except ships, and the baiji was unfortunately awarded no special treatment by the voracious locals. Indeed, Charles Hoy's original account of his capture of a baiji in 1914 clearly reveals that the local people around Dongting viewed the animal as a resource as well as a goddess, as they 'came from far and wide to beg for the blubber and flesh. It seems that the natives consider the blubber to be of considerable medicinal value, using it for coughs and colds both externally and internally.'[4] The older Chinese historical records that provide early descriptions of baiji also reveal the surprisingly wide range of economic uses for dolphins over the past 2,000 years.

Despite Hoy's fairly positive description of the taste of baiji meat, Chinese commentators expressed differing opinions over its culinary properties. Some authors reported that the dolphin was not edible, and complained that its bones were hard and its flesh was fatty, whereas the famous Tang Dynasty doctor Chen Zangqi considered that the meat tasted like water buffalo, although it was slightly salty and foul smelling. Hoy's correspondents told him that it was almost as good as beef, and strips of baiji blubber hung in the air would keep for years without going rancid. Chen Zangqi recommended that this dried baiji meat should be eaten for the treatment of a range of medieval maladies, including poisoning, miasma, malaria, and demonic possession. However, probably the most widespread reason for exploiting baiji for much of China's history was to obtain fat to produce oil for lamps. Although dolphin oil was a valued resource for poor people along the Yangtze, it apparently only generated a very dim light, which was used for lighting rooms where peasants did their weaving at looms; it was also used to provide light for the old parlour game of Shu Fu, and for additional lighting at banquets and feasts. However, dolphin oil was too dim to be of any use for reading or studying, and Chen Zangqi wrote that it was commonly believed that this was the reason that Chinese women were so lazy. Dolphin fat could also be used to kindle a fire even with a contrary wind, and when mixed with lime it was excellent for caulking boats. The flammable properties of baiji fat led to a remarkable new use for the animal during the Wan Li period of the Ming Dynasty (AD 1573–1619), when the Ministry of War issued an order that its fat should be collected for use in the making of pyrotechnical weapons of attack.

Although Hoy apparently believed the rather unlikely story that Yangtze fishermen only made use of baiji that they captured by accident, because of the superstitions surrounding the animal, in fact early Chinese records show that river dolphins were actively exploited throughout the country's history. Fishermen regarded baiji as being extremely cunning, and knew that it was impossible to catch them using bait. However, they could be ambushed by throwing nets over them, and could also be snared using fishhooks, which caught in their throats or between their teeth. The most ingenious technique was to catch young dolphins and hold them in the water, which would lure the frantic mother baiji close to the fishermen so that she too could be caught. The *Yueyang Feng Fu Zhi*, a topographical gazetteer of the town of Yueyang written during the Song Dynasty, went so far as to lament the excessive exploitation of baiji by fishermen in this region, but its authors were resigned to the fact that 'once people have got into the habit of doing something, it is quite impossible to stop them'.[5] They were not writing because of concerns over the status of the species, though, but instead felt that limiting the local utilization of baiji 'would be especially desirable as it is difficult to get used to the evil smelling meat of the river dolphin'.[6] In some regions, hunting baiji was instead even further encouraged because the animal was regarded not as a deity but as a pest, thanks to its 'evil deeds'[7] in competing with local people for fish.

It is impossible to determine the extent to which these traditional methods of exploitation impacted baiji populations across the Yangtze region before the modern historical period. Giorgio Pilleri, the first Western scientist to study the animal in its natural habitat rather than trying to kill it, considered that there was absolutely no doubt that the precarious status of the species by the late twentieth century was the direct result of two millennia or more of persecution.[8] Possible support for this idea comes from Clifford Pope's colourful account of his attempts to obtain baiji specimens for the American Museum of Natural History in 1921, his last instructions 'to get Lipotes even if I had to fish for it with a thousand-foot net'.[9] Even at this early date it took the fishermen working for Pope a full month to find an individual in Dongting Lake, then thought to be the stronghold of the species, and as we have seen, no more could be located despite Pope's best efforts. However, although this may indicate that baiji were already in decline, it may instead simply reflect seasonal movements made by the animals to and from the lake. Such behaviour had been noted earlier by Charles Hoy, who was told by his Chinese correspondents that the dolphins would migrate into the various streams that flow into the lake to breed. Hoy himself had seen baiji in one of these streams in May, and also observed that the dolphins could never be found in the clear part of the lake or far below its mouth. Perhaps Pope was simply looking for baiji in the wrong place; we will never know for sure.

Whether or not the baiji was already in decline by the start of the twentieth century, though, the decades following Hoy and Pope's attempts to capture dolphins at Dongting were to see tremendous political and social upheavals in China, which brought about disastrous new changes for both the country's rural human population and its native species. After years of bitter internal conflict following the collapse of the Qing Dynasty, in October 1949 the Chinese Communist Party finally succeeded in defeating its rivals to power and proclaimed the establishment of the People's Republic of China. Less than ten years later, after the Party had already made its mark by implementing major collectivist land reforms and the first of its purges of intellectuals and free-thinkers, Chairman Mao Zedong initiated his Second Five Year Plan, better known as the Great Leap Forward. Mao's aim was to transform China almost overnight from the agrarian economy supported by countless millions of peasant farmers that it had existed for thousands of years into an industrial society able to compete with other world powers—believing that his country's lack of technological expertise could be compensated for by harnessing the revolutionary fervour of the people to mobilize massive amounts of manual labour. But the backyard steel furnaces set up in every commune across the country, fuelled by household goods and national propaganda, were able to produce only useless pig iron; crops were often left untended and rotted in the fields, and pseudoscientific attempts to force the land to yield more grain all failed. Local authorities tried to save face by inventing increasingly preposterous claims of steel production and record harvests, but this strategy backfired, leading in turn to higher and higher demands from the central authorities for grain and rice to be exported from the countryside. This pathetic sequence of events led, inevitably, to tragedy, as China was driven into one of the worst famines ever recorded. It is estimated that as many as 40 million Chinese farmers may have died of starvation during the 'Three Bitter Years' between 1959 and 1962.

The appalling—and completely avoidable—national catastrophe triggered by the Great Leap Forward inevitably had major impacts on China's natural environment. Forest destruction escalated as peasants tried to obtain charcoal to fuel their useless furnaces, and although meaningful statistics from this period remain almost impossible to obtain, at least 10 per cent of the country's remaining forests were cut down in a few months. Mao even went so far as to declare a surreal war against sparrows—in practice targeting all small birds—that only made the famine worse as locusts and other insect pests skyrocketed in numbers. Starving families were driven to eat anything they could find, including baiji, which could now no longer be venerated under Mao's aggressively secular regime. As reported by Simon Winchester, one Hong Kong journalist observed that 'the goddess of the Yangtze became lunch'.[10] In his travels through the Yangtze region, Winchester was told by fishermen that they now felt responsible for hunting baiji during the Great Leap Forward:[11]

> 'Back in the sixties we needed to eat. I took a lot of the dolphins out, and I sold them, or took the meat for my family. It didn't matter that we had once called them goddesses. We didn't care…
>
> 'Yangtze fishermen have good hearts, you know. We love this river. We love the fish. We love the dolphin and we revere her. But back then—back then it was very different. It was very difficult. Mao did some terrible things. We had to eat. We thought we had no choice. It was the dolphins, or it was our children. Which would you choose?'

However, several years before Simon Winchester interviewed this fisherman, Douglas Adams had received a letter from a couple who had been working in China, who had heard a radio programme he had presented on the plight of the baiji in the late 1980s. 'We enjoyed the Yangtze dolphin programme,' they wrote, 'but listened with a touch of guilt! We recently spent three months working in a number of factories in Nanjing. We had a wonderful time with the people and ate well. To honour us when we left, one of them cooked a Yangtze dolphin…PS Sorry, it was two dolphins—my husband reminds me that he was guest of honour and had the embryo.'[12] Whether this shocking story refers to baiji or, maybe more likely, finless porpoises (as most people are unaware that there are two different species in the Yangtze), it shows that Chinese cetaceans were venerated in a somewhat more pragmatic way than we might like to imagine.

Increasing persecution for food was only one of many dangers facing the baiji by the middle years of the twentieth century. A much more shocking threat during this period was reported by Zhou Kaiya, who recalls reading in the local newspapers during the Great Leap Forward about a factory that was set up at Zhenjiang in the lower Yangtze valley to use baiji leather for the production of bags and gloves. In his book *Baiji: The Yangtze River Dolphin and other Endangered Animals of China*, Professor Zhou described how notices were put up in front of purchasing stations along the river, informing fishermen that baiji and finless porpoises would be bought in large numbers for five to ten cents a kilo.[13] However, this leather factory was inevitably short-lived, because the raw materials it required were soon exhausted throughout the Zhenjiang region.

Professor Zhou's striking account of the leather factory has been widely reproduced in popular and scientific accounts of the decline of the baiji. However, the grand claim of a factory that used river dolphins as its raw material must be considered in the context of the many ludicrous stories that were put forward during the madness of the Great Leap Forward—a time when Chairman Mao proclaimed that 'Man must conquer nature', and when the Communist Party had not only made it possible for fields to produce more than ten times their former yield, but also for roosters to lay eggs, sheep to give birth to five lambs at once, pigs to breed with cows, and pumpkins to grow as large as people. The supposed leather 'factory' may in fact have been completely fictitious, or could have been a local fisheries production company that may have opportunistically made a few baiji leather products from animals that were found dead or had been caught accidentally in fishing gear.

Whether or not the baiji leather factory ever really existed, though, Mao's attempts to conquer the natural world through the might of Communist labour had other dire consequences for the dolphin. Following Mao's call to arms against the environment, the first important campaign during the Great Leap Forward was the 'battle' to build large hydropower stations. The construction of huge dams to harness the power of the country's main rivers, often led by people with little or no previous experience in such projects, became an ongoing struggle in China to force nature into obedience under the might of the Communist Party.

The detrimental impact on the baiji of these dam-building projects—which fragmented dolphin populations and accidentally killed many animals during heavy construction work, as well as preventing the migration of fish to their spawning grounds and drastically changing the river flow and water conditions—soon became apparent. Despite the massive political changes that followed the establishment of the People's Republic of China, scientific research had been able to start developing within the country, for a few years at least. Although the increasing exclusion of the outside world by the new Communist regime made it all but impossible for outside scientists to study China's wildlife—with Western cetacean researchers in the 1970s still forced to rely entirely on Hoy and Pope's limited English-language observations from fifty years earlier—Chinese-led baiji research was becoming established to fill this role instead by the 1950s. Zhou Kaiya, then a young scientist based in Nanjing, conducted the first research on baiji in the lower Yangtze mainstem, and also documented the presence of the species in the smaller Qiantang River to the south. He was told by fishermen in Fuyang County that dozens of baiji could be seen in the Fuchun River, a tributary of the Qiantang, in the mid-1950s. One was even caught and exhibited in the Zhejiang Provincial Museum in Hangzhou; this preserved specimen is featured today on the museum's website.[14] However, the Qiantang River and its tributaries became the target of one of Mao's huge-scale water development projects in the late 1950s, to construct a dam for the Xinanjiang hydropower station and reinforce the main river bank by block filling. Baiji have not been seen in the river since.

Although the scale of the national catastrophe caused by the Great Leap Forward was downplayed strongly in China, Mao was forced to take much of the blame for the Second Five Year Plan's acknowledged economic failures. He fought his way back to dominance by promoting his cult of personality and encouraging a new phase of nationwide purges that pushed the country dangerously close to civil war. Most Western audiences have no frame of reference with which to understand the atmosphere of ideology, tyranny, and indoctrination that engulfed China during the Cultural Revolution of the 1960s and 1970s, and all academic research ground to a halt as 'counter-revolutionary' intellectuals across the country were persecuted, tortured, and sent for 're-education'. Scientific institutions were only able to begin slowly re-establishing themselves following Mao's death in 1976 and the subsequent denouncement and arrest of the Gang of Four, the aggressive critics of Mao's political opponents.

Despite the restrictions against academic research in China during the middle years of the twentieth century, investigations on baiji were able to continue throughout this period on a modest local scale. Zhou Kaiya continued to document all baiji reports in the Nanjing region throughout the 1960s and 1970s, recording that fifteen animals were captured by fishermen between 1956 and 1974; he was able to secure five of these individuals as specimens for the collections of Nanjing Normal University. He also conducted interviews with fishermen along many parts of the middle and lower Yangtze to gather more data on the distribution of baiji in the river. Now middle-aged, Zhou was finally able to return to active baiji research in the late 1970s—but although baiji were still to be found in the main channel of the Yangtze, he found that they had not only died out in the Qiantang River but were now also disappearing from other parts of their former range. Although the dolphins continued to be seen in the channels leading to the river, they were no longer to be seen in the main waters of either Poyang and Dongting Lake, once thought to be the only refuge of the species. It remains unclear what caused the dolphins to vanish from these large bodies of water, which both still contain populations of finless porpoises. Although both lakes have always experienced large seasonal fluctuations in water depth, they have also become much shallower over the past few decades, due to increased siltation caused by ongoing deforestation and agricultural development along their shores from the time of the Great Leap Forward onwards. However, other human activities are also likely to have contributed to the decline of the baiji in the lakes. During his visit to Dongting in the 1920s, Clifford Pope observed prophetically that 'there were thousands of fishermen actually straining creatures of all sizes from the rapidly vanishing lake, and it seemed that the dolphin must soon fall victim to one of their innumerable methods of separating the water from everything in it but the mud'.[15]

~

Zhou Kaiya and his colleagues started surveying baiji populations in the Yangtze for the first time in 1978, a year after I was born, and further work also began to be carried out further upstream by the River Dolphin Research Group that was set up at the Institute of Hydrobiology (IHB) in Wuhan in the same year. Despite having worked on baiji for decades, studying animals that had been stranded or killed by fishing gear and documenting local knowledge about the species that he gathered from fishermen along the river, the crippling checks on scientific research in China during the Cultural Revolution meant that Professor Zhou had never actually been able to charter a survey vessel and observe live baiji in their natural environment. It was not until April 1979 that he finally got his chance to see them, when his team found a small family group of baiji in the river just downstream of Tongling in Anhui Province. He later wrote that his joy was 'beyond description'.[16]

These surveys provided the few other bits and pieces of information we now have about baiji ecology. In particular, the dolphins were usually seen in quiet stretches of water, either just downstream of islets and sandbars in the channel, where the water formed counter-current eddies that acted as refuges from the fast flow of the river, or—as Charles Hoy had observed decades earlier—in the mouths of side-channels where tributaries or lakes emptied into the main Yangtze, such as the Balijiang river section at the mouth of Poyang Lake.

But soon, a much more startling discovery also became apparent to the Chinese researchers. The first surveys by Zhou's team, which focused on the 250-kilometre stretch of river between the cities of Nanjing and Guichi in the lower Yangtze, estimated that there were up to 60 baiji living in this region, and the researchers extrapolated from this figure to estimate that there may have been about 400 baiji left throughout its range in the main channel. This was not a lot of animals, especially given modern estimates that the Yangtze may have been able to support several thousand dolphins in the recent past. And successive surveys revealed that even this remnant population was dwindling away fast. Whereas the Nanjing-Guichi surveys reported that baiji were usually found in the river in groups of six to ten, and sometimes as many as seventeen, by the mid-1980s groups of only two or three animals were all that were usually found, with larger groups of up to seven animals only rarely to be seen. No groups of more than ten baiji were seen after 1988. New surveys carried out in 1985–6 from Yichang downstream to Jiangyin, a 1,512-kilometre stretch encompassing most of the baiji's historical range, still saw 42 different baiji groups and generated a population estimate of 300 animals, but only a couple of years later, new Chinese surveys from Yichang all the way to the estuary near Shanghai conducted between 1987 and 1990 saw far fewer animals, and estimated that only 200 baiji were now left. It looked like the last population of baiji left in the world had halved in number in less than a decade.

Estimating the rate of the baiji's decline on the basis of these different surveys is not an exact science. Even counting the number of dolphins in a group at the best of times can be tricky, as aquatic mammals only come to the surface relatively briefly to breathe and spend far more time below the surface; in large groups, it's likely that there will be many more animals underneath the water than are visible at any one time, and observers can easily be misled into underestimating the number of animals present. The likelihood of spotting animals also varies according to a number of other factors, most obviously how far away the animals are and the viewing conditions when they are observed. A number of statistical 'distance sampling' techniques are now available to try to get beyond the vagaries imposed by conditions in the field, and use survey data to calculate mathematically how many animals might actually be present in a population of a rare or poorly known species.

However, the different baiji surveys that were conducted from the 1970s until the 1990s were simply too varied to provide results that can be compared in a meaningful way. A total of ten surveys were carried out during this period, and these differed not only in the numbers of baiji seen and estimated, but also in the numbers of observers involved in each survey, whether they used large research vessels or small fishing boats—which have different clearances above the water, and so allow observers to see for different distances—and whether these were single boats or a series of boats, operating either alongside each other or along different sections of the river simultaneously. Sometimes researchers simply looked for animals from the river bank instead. Some researchers surveyed short sections of the river (from 170-kilometre stretches upwards) and extrapolated their population estimates across the whole of the baiji's range, often applying fairly arbitrary 'correction factors', whereas others attempted to assess the baiji's status from Yichang all 1,669 kilometres of the way downstream to the estuary. Sometimes single surveys were used as the basis for population estimates, in other cases the results of multiple surveys were combined and averaged out. The actual methods of looking for animals also differed wildly. Some surveys travelled along the river at a fairly constant rate (although often at different speeds between different surveys), whereas others concentrated their efforts along sand bars and banks where baiji were known to occur, and looked for other signs such as fishing activities and circling gulls which might indicate the presence of fish shoals that would also attract baiji. Only a few research teams actually used binoculars, and one group proudly described how they improved survey techniques by looking for baiji from both sides of the boat.

Later researchers recognized that no adequate or reliable estimates exist for the numbers of baiji left in the Yangtze during this period. It was likely that many animals—perhaps a substantial proportion of the total remaining baiji population—were missed during these various survey attempts. However, despite all of these major research problems, a pattern still seemed clear. Successive surveys, however they were carried out, continued to find fewer and fewer baiji left in the river. It certainly seemed that the baiji population was continuing to fall precipitously as the years passed. And given that this was the only information that was actually available to anybody, it looked like something had to be done. But before any baiji conservation could be attempted, one problem remained. What was actually causing the disappearance of the baiji in the main channel of the Yangtze? The Chinese researchers had, in fact, already gathered some of the pieces to solve the puzzle. During their surveys, they had not only seen diminishing numbers of living baiji in the river, but had also found lots of dead baiji, either floating downstream or washed up on banks or sandbars. This was obviously a pretty bad sign for the future of the species. But the worst of it was that these animals had been killed by lots of different things.

∼

In October 1988, when there were only about 200 baiji—as a best guess—left in existence, Douglas Adams visited the Yangtze in search of river dolphins. Following on from the mega-success of *The Hitchhiker's Guide to the Galaxy*, Adams was now working on another radio series called *Last Chance to See*, which was again to be subsequently converted into book form. Together with the zoologist Mark Carwardine, he was travelling around the world in an attempt to find several highly endangered species—including the aye-aye, Komodo dragon, and kakapo—while documenting their plights. Unlike many of the increasing flood of celebrities who try to increase their marketability by making a token programme about the environment, beneath his trademark humour Adams was clearly concerned about the future of the animals whose stories he was telling. *Last Chance to See* was the first, and probably the only real time that the baiji got a boost of international publicity when there was still an opportunity to do anything to help it, and it is telling that it came from a comedy author and his media production crew rather than a conservation organization.

In one of the most memorable passages of the book, Adams and the production team travelled across Shanghai trying to find condoms to put over their microphone in order to make it waterproof. The reason they wanted to do this was to record the sounds that the baiji could hear when the animals were trying to echolocate. After the inevitable trials and tribulations of a foreigner in the ancient, alien culture that is China (with an equally inevitable heavy dose of added sexual humour), Adams and co. found some condoms and eventually managed to lower their microphone into the Yangtze.

> The sound we heard wasn't exactly what I expected. Water is a very good medium for the propagation of sound and I had expected to hear clearly the heavy, pounding reverberations of each of the boats that had gone thundering by us as we stood on the deck. But water transmits sound even better than that, and what we were hearing was everything that was happening in the Yangtze for many, many miles around, jumbled cacophonously together.
>
> Instead of hearing the roar of each individual ship's propeller, what we heard was a sustained shrieking blast of pure white noise, in which nothing could be distinguished at all.[17]

By the 1980s, the twentieth century had taken its toll on the Yangtze, and showed no signs of letting up. The 'Golden Channel' had always been a vital highway for shipping and trade, but before 1949, when the People's Republic was founded, there were only around 500 Chinese and foreign vessels combined in operation on the river. However, following the industrialization of Mao's China, vessel traffic began to double every decade, and tens of thousands of ships were moving up and down the river by the time of Zhou Kaiya's renewed baiji surveys. The four cities of Nanjing, Zhenjiang, Nantong, and Zhangjiagang in Jiangsu Province became open to foreign ships in 1984, with 41 deep-water berths for 10,000-ton ocean-going freight vessels put into operation within a decade. More international ports were being established along the middle and lower stretches of the Yangtze every year. By 1992, there were 221 ports along the Yangtze, 37 of which could handle over 1 million tons of cargo a year. These unprecedented levels of vessel traffic had a massive effect on baiji; the constant 'blast of pure white noise' that swamped the complex auditory environment in which they navigated and hunted with echolocation had made them effectively blind, and they surfaced into boats, staving their heads open and disembowelling them-selves on propellers. Up to a third of all dead baiji found in the lower stretches of the river during the 1980s may have been killed by collisions with boats: the dolphins were becoming road-kill. Further baiji deaths occurred during channel maintenance, with six dolphins killed in 1974 alone by explosives used to clear navi-gation channels.

But the escalating levels of vessel traffic were only one of the new threats now facing the baiji. Communist China's onslaught against the environment led to huge quantities of untreated water loaded with industrial and agricultural pollutants, sewage, and other waste products pouring into the Yangtze. By 1985, waste water emissions along the river totalled almost 130 billion tons. Metal works, chemical companies, and power plants lining the Yangtze released untreated waste rich in petroleum by-products, phenols, cyanides, heavy metals such as mercury, chromium, and cadmium, and synthetic organic chemicals into the river. Large stretches of river became covered with oily films. These pollu-tants impacted the dolphins in a number of ways. The fish on which they fed were killed off, with die-offs of poisoned fish sometimes reported to smell of kerosene. Massive chemical spills, although usually unreported and covered up, are known to have killed many of the river's cetaceans directly—for example, a 5-ton truck carrying yellow phosphorus fell into the river in 1989, and soon afterwards several dead baiji were found floating near the scene of the accident. The constant pernicious inflow of pollutants also had many other hugely harmful effects on dolphins. We now know that marine mammals will bioaccumulate heavy metals and other pollutants, notably persistent organic chemicals such as polychlorinated biphenyls (PCBs) and tributyl tin (used widely in anti-fouling paint on boats), up the food chain from their prey. These pollutants are extremely long-lived, very resistant to metabolism or biodegrading in the environment, and their lethal toxicity has almost no bounds: they can retard growth, cause physical deformities, damage organs such as the brain and the liver, encourage the development of cancers, trigger neurological and behavioural impairment, and suppress hormones and the immune system. They may even be able to alter the balance of chloride ions in the outer hair cells of the dolphin's ear, deafening the animals and making echolocation impossible; this could make baiji swim into ships, starve to death, or strand themselves on the river bank. Maybe worst of all, pollutant loads carried by dolphin mothers can be passed onto their unborn young, and kill embryos, foetuses, and newborns, so that animals living in polluted water may not even be able to reproduce. China's industrial growth was leaving a deadly legacy for its freshwater princess.

However, it seems that even this wasn't what was really killing all of the baiji. A hundred years ago there were 'only' (I use the word advisedly) one billion people on our planet. Now, despite Deng Xiaoping's belated attempts to control population growth in China by introducing the one-child policy in 1979, there are almost that many people living in the drainage basin of the Yangtze alone. The country's staggering levels of overpopulation are summed up in the well-known Chinese phrase, *ren shan ren hai*: 'people mountain people sea'. The fertile plains and valleys of southeastern China support one of the highest human population densities on the planet, and there isn't much room left for nature any more. People's daily needs conflict sharply with the needs of the pitiful remnants of the region's wildlife, and direct overexploitation of the environment by local people up and down the river has hit the Yangtze ecosystem hard. The real problem for the baiji came from fishing. Combined with the added effects of pollution and the construction of dams, sluices, locks, and floodgates that blocked migration routes, overfishing caused fish stocks in the river to crash. The record high fish catch in the Yangtze of 458,000 tons in 1954 had declined to less than 200,000 tons by the 1970s, and dropped again to an average of only 100,000 tons a decade or so later. Several key economic species suffered further catastrophic declines. In particular, the harvest of the Chinese anchovy or *fengweiyu* (the 'phoenix-tailed fish') averaged 400,000 tons in the 1970s and was the mainstay of many local fisheries, but the annual catch along the river had fallen to only 115 tons by 1985. Another species favoured by fishermen, Reeves' shad or *shiyu*, had an annual catch before the 1970s of around 500 tons, which peaked at an unsustainable 1,500 tons in 1974, and which then crashed during the 1980s and 1990s. The official Red Data book of Chinese fishes indicates that the shad catch fell to as little as 10 tons across the entire country, but the story in the Yangtze is even grimmer: there have not even been any confirmed reports of this well-known species in China's largest river for the past decade. Many other sought-after fish species, such as the Yangtze pufferfish or *hetun* (a name which ironically means 'river dolphin'), have also undergone massive declines in recent years. Although any statistics from the time of the Great Leap Forward and the Cultural Revolution have to be interpreted with caution, there is still no doubt that the Yangtze's once-rich fisheries have now collapsed.

It wasn't just overfishing that was the problem, though. As well as removing the baiji's supply of fish, the fishermen were accidentally killing baiji directly, too. Whereas almost all of the other large animals that humans have driven to extinction were actively targeted—either hunted for food, or persecuted because of the perceived threat they posed to people or livestock—the baiji was now rapidly becoming an incidental casualty of attempts to hunt other species. It is estimated that there are over 160 different kinds of fishing gear in the Yangtze River, and many of these had the unfortunate side-effect of killing dolphins as well as catching fish. Free-floating gill nets and fixed 'hedges' of fyke nets set in shallow water along the river bank both took their toll—in fact, gill nets are the main cause of death in most populations of small shallow-water cetaceans around the world today, as dolphins and porpoises get their beaks or flippers entangled in the mesh, struggle, and drown, and the fixed nets are known to have killed over 15 per cent of all dead baiji found in the lower stretches of the Yangtze. The worst culprit, however, was rolling hook long-line fishing, called *gon gou* in Chinese. This fishing technique first started in the Yangtze around fifty or sixty years ago. The long-lines are almost 100 metres long, are armed with about a thousand vicious, close-set, unbaited hooks, and are either held behind the fishing boat to drift in the current or are anchored to the river bed with stones but roll along the bottom—hence the name 'rolling hook'—and often float free. Fishermen leave the fixed long-lines in the water, returning every 12–24 hours to collect all of the fish that have become caught on the hooks. But it wasn't just fish that got hooked. Simon Winchester was shown one of these long-lines by a Yangtze fisherman he interviewed in the 1990s:

> At first he said nothing, but then as if by way of answer he slowly got up, walked to a locked box near the prow of his boat, and pulled from it a huge and tangled mess of fishing line that jangled and clanked with its several pounds of rusty ironmongery. He shook it at me, almost angrily, inviting me to take a look. But I knew what it was instantly: this was an example of the very device that had put the pathetic little Yangtze dolphin into such grave danger: it was called a rolling hook trawl, and it was every bit as vicious a device as it appeared. It didn't just catch fish: it snared them, hurt them and killed them. . . .
>
> When a dolphin was snagged on one hook, it panicked, thrashed violently around and, instead of freeing itself (as might happen

if there had been only one hook), was promptly caught on a neighbouring hook and then by more and more until it was raked with slashes and cuts and was eventually dragged from the river bleeding to death from a thousand cuts.[18]

In total, between 50 and 60 per cent of all dead baiji found by Chinese researchers in the 1970s and 1980s were riddled with dozens or even hundreds of hook marks, their skins torn and ulcerating—clear signs of having been killed by long-lines. And even this wasn't all. By the 1990s, a new form of fishing was becoming widespread in the Yangtze that was even more destructive than rolling hooks. China was experiencing a new phase of economic expansion, but, as had happened so many times before in the twentieth century, many people did not benefit from this latest country-wide restructuring. Many jobs were lost. In an attempt to keep food on the table, fishing became an alluring new option for people who had previously worked on the land. The only problem was that these novices knew nothing about how to actually catch fish. The solution? Just stick electrodes from a storage battery into the water. That will kill everything you need—indiscriminately. Even the other fishermen on the Yangtze viewed the destructiveness of these newcomers with contempt, but that didn't stop them, or the new threat they clearly posed to the baiji. The electro-fishermen operated at night, using gear produced in illegal underground factories and lashed to bamboo poles at the head of their boats. The lethal electric charge was able to kill anything within a range of 20 metres and was left running continuously in the water as the boats drifted along the river, leaving death and devastation in their wake. Chinese researchers estimated that about 40 per cent of all known baiji deaths in the 1990s were caused by electro-fishing—this was now apparently the biggest threat to baiji survival.

Looking back over the past few decades, despite all of the various reports about dead dolphins collected by Chinese scientists, we still have relatively little meaningful information that can help us to disentangle how important each of these different threats was to the survival of the baiji. Sadly it turned out that socialist societies were not immune to environmental damage, no matter what their leaders said. However, the bottom line is that quite simply so much happened to the Yangtze ecosystem in the twentieth century, and the baiji was forced to suffer so many different indignities, that we may never know which of these human impacts really killed the most dolphins, or whether it was the joint effect of fishing, pollution, boat traffic, and maybe all sorts of other factors as well that together pushed the species towards the edge. Ironically, almost the only thing we do know is that the Three Gorges Dam—the one Chinese environmental issue that Westerners love to hate—had almost nothing to do with the disappearance of the baiji; it was simply built too late to have any real added effect. We don't even know why the baiji appeared to decline so much more rapidly than the finless porpoise, which was still reported in relatively large numbers in the Yangtze into the 1990s. Maybe the baiji was more of a bottom-feeder, and so could have been more vulnerable to rolling hooks on the river bed. The stomach of the dolphin caught all those years ago by Charles Hoy contained 1.9 litres of a species of long, eel-like catfish that inhabits the mud at the bottom of Dongting Lake, which lends some support to this idea. Maybe the fact that the baiji was a larger animal than the porpoise, and reached reproductive maturity slightly later, meant that female dolphins had more time to accumulate harmful pollutants that could kill their unborn offspring. Maybe both species were similarly affected by all of these different human threats, but the porpoise could reproduce more quickly—or maybe the porpoise population in the river was just higher to begin with. We simply have no idea. Despite all of this uncertainty and all of these problems, though, as the twentieth century drew to a close, it was clear that something had to be done to try to save the baiji. Fast.

3

THE AQUATIC PANDA

The gravity of the situation represents both hope and opportunity. But if we fail to make the correct choices now, the last pandas will disappear, leaving us with the nostalgia of a failed epic, an indictment of civilization as destroyer. We cannot recover a lost world.

George Schaller
The Last Panda

In the years following the death of Chairman Mao and the end of the Cultural Revolution, Western scientists were able to venture back into China for the first time in decades. The first cetacean biologist to have the opportunity to work with Chinese researchers in this brave new world was Professor Giorgio Pilleri from the Institute of Brain Anatomy in Berne, who was privileged to be able to help Zhou Kaiya and his team with their dolphin surveys in the lower reaches of the Yangtze around Nanjing. Pilleri was not only able to observe several baiji in their natural habitat, but was also impressed by the concerns already being widely voiced in China about the need to try to conserve the species. He observed in 1979 that 'as I was able to see for myself from talks with authorities during my stay in China in a number of Chinese institutes, all the responsible officials and all the scientists working with dolphins are without exception aware of the dangerous position of *Lipotes* today, and are doing everything in their power to try and save the species'.[1] In the 1980s the Chinese government elevated the baiji to the First Order of Protected Animals, the highest level of national conservation protection (the finless porpoise only made it to the Second Order, partly because it was more abundant than the baiji, and partly because it was generally thought to be the reincarnation of an incestuous rapist, and so did not really have public support on its side), and the Chinese Wild Animal Protection Law prohibited people from catching baiji. Fishermen received hefty prison sentences for killing dolphins,[2] and even scientists had to gain approval from the Chinese Ministry of Agriculture—the government body that deals with all freshwater issues within China—before they could try to capture any for research or conservation.

The dangers posed by rolling hook long-lines and fyke nets were also appreciated early on, and the increasing reports of incidental baiji deaths associated with these fishing methods led the Chinese authorities to ban their use in the Yangtze. A series of river sections at Shishou, Honghu, Tongling, and Zhenjiang were officially designated over the next few years as national and provincial reserves specifically aimed to protect the baiji, with the Chinese State Council offering to invest 12 million yuan (about a million pounds) into a special baiji conservation fund in 1992, aimed partly to develop the 135-kilometre Xin-Luo National Baiji Reserve at Honghu. In these river sections, it was proposed that fishing would be completely banned, pollution would be stringently controlled, and other human activities, notably boat traffic, would be reduced as much as possible, with all freight vessels forced to travel at slow speeds to minimize the risk of colliding with baiji. A further series of 'protection stations' were set up along the river at Jianli, Chenglingji, Hukou, Anqing, and Zhenjiang, where it was intended that reserve staff would make daily patrols to monitor baiji populations, control fishing restrictions, rescue injured, sick, or stranded animals, and generally educate local people about the importance of baiji conservation. This would ultimately form part of a larger-scale conservation network that would extend along the entirety of the baiji's range in the middle and lower stretches of the Yangtze. And anyway, the fishermen themselves realized what they were doing to the dolphins, and were also becoming increasingly concerned about baiji conservation—or so Simon Winchester's informant claimed:[3]

> 'But then as the years went by they became more and more difficult to find. We all'—and here he gestured to the other fishermen, who had gathered their skiffs around his and were listening to him, nodding themselves—'we all slowly realized what was happening. We were killing them off, and by doing so we were helping to kill the river. And soon our attitude changed. Every time a baiji came out, cut to pieces by the hooks, we felt we had lost a little more. So we stopped using these rolling hooks. We went back to nets. And if we ever find a baiji—and I haven't seen one for six or seven years now—we throw it back. It's the rule again.'

It would be nice to believe that little fable. Unfortunately, things didn't quite work out like that in reality. China has among the highest amount of environmental laws and regulations in the world, but this impressive legislation won't change the country's environmental problems one jot if it isn't acted on; however, it has been estimated that as little as 10 per cent of these laws are actually ever enforced.[4] To the jaundiced eyes of many people in the international conservation community, making environmental laws in China often seems to be little more than a case of ticking the boxes on a 'to do' list, just another example of saving face rather than actually doing anything useful for endangered species. The baiji reserves are unfortunately a perfect example of 'paper parks'—parks that exist solely on paper rather than conveying any benefits or protection to the species they are supposed to conserve. A lot of people still seem to be employed in them, but it remains difficult to work out what any of the reserve staff actually do. Certainly they didn't seem to be particularly interested in controlling illegal fishing, which continued on despite the blanket ban on rolling hooks, fyke nets, and later on for electro-fishing as well; all three fishing practices remain alive and well in the Yangtze today, unlike the cetaceans they caught by accident. Although rolling hooks have now been phased out in several regions of the Yangtze, this was actually carried out by the fishermen themselves because the gear became less effective at catching fish following the decline of many key species, rather than because of any kind of official crackdown on their use.[5] Local fisheries authorities will cheerfully acknowledge that rolling hooks are still the main kind of fishing gear being used in many sections of the river even today, and seem oblivious to the need for any enforcement. I was told by one reserve staff member, who at least acknowledged that there was a problem, that the illegal fishermen were just too clever for them: the officials only worked from nine to five but the fishermen came out in the early morning or at night. They couldn't find any way to get round that, they said. It's hard to see how conservation can be made to work in the face of this sort of attitude. Indeed, the researchers and officials I have worked with in China invariably follow the local custom of having to eat dinner at exactly 6.30 p.m., robotically and rigidly, during which they down copious volumes of beer and potent local rice wine that tastes of nail varnish remover: work is impossible after such a performance, and it's hard to appreciate just how much of a hurdle this is to getting anything done until you have had to endure several frustrating months of such banquets. I would imagine that nothing is known about any nocturnal animals in China, and astronomy must be a difficult science to practice.

But even if the reserve staff had been as diligent and attentive as possible, this *in situ* conservation strategy also suffered from more intractable problems, which presented a barrier to any realistic chances of protecting baiji in the river. Was it really likely that the Chinese authorities would—or even could—exert the kind of firm control on the escalating economic development seen all along the Yangtze that was really required to save the baiji in its natural habitat? Even at the time, it must have seemed naive to believe that conservation concerns were going to have any effect on China's rapidly growing economy. In retrospect it is certainly hard to see how levels of vessel traffic could have been prevented from increasing along the Yangtze, one of China's main trade arteries, no matter what may have been felt about the baiji by a small minority of scientists. And even if vessel speed was somehow regulated within the reserves, limiting the likelihood of baiji being killed by ship strikes, there would still be nothing to stop pollutants and free-floating rolling hooks from drifting downstream into the protected river sections. Maybe worst of all, one of the few things that we actually do know about baiji behaviour is that several different studies during the 1980s and 1990s showed that they swam up and down the river rather than staying put in a particular place. Photo-identification studies found that one group of baiji that could be identified by distinctive scratches and scrapes on their backs moved 100 kilometres upriver in only three days, and another animal photographed in 1989 was identified a year later over 200 kilometres further upstream. Why, then, would baiji be likely to stay in a river section that had been designated as a reserve, rather than just swimming in and out into unprotected areas? Ultimately, it seems as though the entire Yangtze downstream from the Three Gorges would have had to receive similar stringent levels of protection in order to have any real effect at conserving a wide-ranging species like this—and, sadly but surely, this was never going to happen.

In the light of these fundamental concerns, Douglas Adams and increasing numbers of conservationists recognized that 'there is probably little hope of saving the dolphins in the Yangtze river itself, despite all the time and effort invested in protecting them'.[6] So what could be done? Was there another solution, or was the baiji doomed?

~

Maybe, however, there was something else that could be done—a possible solution that was in some ways even more extreme than trying to clean up almost 2,000 kilometres of the Yangtze at impossibly short notice. The first time that this alternative conservation strategy was suggested in print was by Giorgio Pilleri after his visit to China in the late 1970s. He noted in 1979 that 'it seems to me that one solution would be to breed the river dolphin on a large scale in the safety of captivity. Clearly the task will not be an easy one. The Chinese have, however, achieved success in far more difficult enterprises. Moreover they have an enormous experience of breeding both land and water animals, having developed skills which are seldom to be found in other countries. If they succeed in saving *Lipotes vexillifer* in this way, it will certainly be a splendidly original achievement.'[7]

Pilleri was a great fan of keeping unusual cetaceans in captivity. He himself had first managed to transport a pair of wild-caught Indus River dolphins by air from west Pakistan to his Brain Anatomy Institute in 1969, and over the years that followed managed to maintain six others in Berne as well. However, it seemed that the Chinese had indeed been thinking along the same lines. Less than a year after Pilleri's suggestion, on 11 January 1980 the staff of the River Dolphin Research Group at Wuhan's Institute of Hydrobiology received a call from the Yueyang Institute of Aquatic Products (a typically functionally named Chinese institution) that two dolphins had been accidentally caught by fishermen at the mouth of Dongting Lake, Charles Hoy's old stomping ground. By the time a group of scientists led by Professor Chen Peixun arrived after the eight-hour drive from Wuhan, one of the dolphins, a female, had already died. The other animal, a young male no more than a year old, had also been badly injured by rolling hooks; in addition to numerous cuts and bruises, he had two large connected wounds almost ten centimetres deep cut into the back of his neck. It seemed unlikely that he would survive. Although he made it back to Wuhan alive, covered with wet cloth on a mattress of cotton and straw, after a few days his wounds became seriously infected and his health began to fade. In a novel approach, presumably because of a lack of either alternative treatments or any prior expertise with cetaceans, the research group staff applied a poultice of traditional

Chinese medicines, a white powder from Yunnan Province called *baiyao*, to the dolphin's wounds. Luck was on Professor Chen's side; against all odds, the young animal pulled through. They decided to call him 'Qi Qi', a Chinese name which initially appears intimidating but which is in fact pronounced quite simply: 'chee chee'.

Qi Qi's early days at Wuhan remained challenging. Together with Chongqing and Nanjing, Wuhan is known as one of the 'ovens of China', where the continental climate is extremely cold in winter but unbearably hot during the summer. Qi Qi was kept in an unfiltered outdoor pool full of tap water, in which water temperatures fluctuated from nearly freezing to over 35°. He was often found barely moving, in obvious discomfort and with purple rashes all over his body. To begin with, the research staff were also clearly confused about what he actually ate. Wei Zhuo, later the research group's chief ecologist, described the early attempts to feed him in his idiosyncratic book *Save the Yangtze River's Endangered Animals: We are all the Yangtze's Children*:[8]

> In the beginning, we didn't even know what you ate, so we had to experiment cautiously. First we tried giving you steamed bread, which you didn't eat; then we tried normal bread, which you also didn't like; next we tried fruit, but you refused that too; you weren't very interested in pork or beef, either; next we tried to feed you fish, which you just ate randomly without showing much interest; finally, having tried everything, we moulded those foods into different shapes and found that you were interested in fish-shaped food. I don't remember how many times we failed, but we were very careful and after a lot of research we finally figured out that your food was freshwater fish.

One might think that this embarrassing exercise would have been covered up by the Chinese researchers, but no. They often mentioned in subsequent papers how they had tried to feed Qi Qi with apples and vegetables,[9] and even Zhou Kaiya later reported that 'once they tried to feed him steamed bread in the shape and colour of a fish. Qi Qi, waving his head and tail, swam away from the imitation fish. The experiment clearly shows that animal's strong ability in differentiation.'[10]

It almost beggars belief that fish came only a poor sixth in the list of possible food items that the scientists at the country's official baiji research facility tried to feed to Qi Qi. Over 2,000 years earlier, the author of the *Er Ya* was already well aware of what baiji ate, as were all of the villagers living along the Yangtze, who had persecuted the species for millennia because it competed with them for fish. This didn't really bode well; it seemed that the finer points of baiji conservation were going to be something of an uphill struggle.

However, Qi Qi was tenacious, whether he ate fruit or not. Once the research staff started trying to control the temperature of his outdoor pool by putting a roof up over it and throwing ice blocks into the water during the summer, and once they started actually feeding him fish, he became strong and healthy. The world's first captive baiji, he became a national celebrity, visited by tourists and dignitaries from across China. He also provided the staff of the River Dolphin Research Group with a tremendous opportunity for scientific study. Over the years that followed, the Wuhan team churned out reams of scientific papers describing his anatomy, physiology, and captive behaviour. Hours of film footage exists showing Qi Qi hoisted out of the water by the side of his pool, looking somewhat nonplussed and surrounded by Chinese researchers covering him with blue antiseptic ointment and reading off reels of ticker-tape. They also tried repeatedly to cryogenically store his sperm, but although Qi Qi was masturbated with electrodes so often that, I'm told, towards the end of his life he would swim over excitedly, roll over, and show his penis to any visitors coming into his enclosure—an unfortunate kind of 'Pavlov's baiji' response—the Wuhan team never managed to preserve any sperm successfully despite the endless rounds of dolphin electro-ejaculation.

Despite their success with Qi Qi, though, Chinese researchers would not be so lucky with any other attempts to maintain baiji in captivity. Only a year after Qi Qi was brought to Wuhan, another male dolphin was captured, again close to Dongting Lake. Named Rong Rong—after Huarong County in Hunan Province, where he was caught—he was put into Qi Qi's pool to keep him company. However, this new animal was not as sturdy as Qi Qi; the temperature fluctuations in the outdoor pool proved too much for him, and he froze to death in February 1982, as the unmanaged water temperature dropped towards zero. But the staff at the Institute of Hydrobiology were persistent—they were determined to try to find a mate for Qi Qi. If there was any hope of conserving baiji in captivity, they had to be able to breed.

A few years later, in March 1986, an official capture expedition made up of twenty-two rented fishing boats led by a scientific research vessel set off towards the mouth of Dongting Lake to try to find more baiji to bring to Wuhan. After a false start, when a group of nine dolphins was encircled by nets but the strong current made it impossible to pull them in, the team achieved success, and two baiji—a male and a female—were caught from another large group and transported safely back to Wuhan by helicopter, where they were placed together into a separate outdoor pool. But once again, tragedy struck. Within a couple of months the male animal, named Lian Lian, became ill, and had difficulty in rising to the surface. The young female, named Zhen Zhen—a Chinese diminutive meaning treasured and rare—would dive beneath him and lift him to the surface, apparently to help him breathe, and swam close to the walls of the pool to prevent him from colliding with them, but it was no good; Lian Lian died in June 1986, only seventy-six days after being captured. Zhen Zhen was then introduced to Qi Qi's pool; she was still young and excitable, and bit Qi Qi several times, giving him scars. Her youth was the main problem—based on field studies and autopsies of wild baiji, the staff at Wuhan estimated that she would only become sexually mature when she was 5 or 6, so they would have to wait several years to find out if she would be able to mate successfully with Qi Qi. But it was not to be. After two and a half years in captivity,

Zhen Zhen died in September 1988. That year the summer had been tremendously hot, and the research group staff had erected a temporary shelter made out of old sheets of corrugated iron to shield the dolphins in their unregulated outdoor pool from the harsh sun; but Zhen Zhen ate some of the chunks of rusting iron that fell from the shelter into her pool, and was killed. She would be the last baiji ever to be brought into captivity. Qi Qi remained alone for the rest of his life.

Other than the IHB's surprise success with Qi Qi—probably more a matter of good luck than anything else—it was clear that the track record for keeping baiji in captivity in China was pretty bad. Indeed, two other animals, Su Su and Jiang Jiang, that were caught or found by fishermen further downstream in 1981 and were put into holding pools in Nanjing by Zhou Kaiya's team, also only lasted for a few weeks—maybe not surprisingly, given that Su Su had already narrowly avoided being boiled up for pig feed by the fishermen that found her, had been left to thrash around on the ground in a village for several hours, and was then put in a small pond where children threw clods of earth at her and jabbed her with bamboo poles.[11] Although the name 'Su Su' has been artfully transliterated as meaning 'brought back from the jaws of death'[12] (rather unfortunate for an animal that survived for only seventeen days in captivity after arriving at Nanjing), it didn't look like this approach would be able to bring the baiji back from the jaws of extinction.

～

But maybe there was still another way to try to save the baiji, something far more novel than either the seemingly impossible task of cleaning up the Yangtze or alternatively putting a few solitary animals into concrete tanks. This third way was also first suggested in the early 1980s, and by February 1985 the plans were already under way. If the challenge of protecting a section of the main Yangtze channel was proving insurmountable, then why not set up a baiji reserve somewhere else, not in the river itself but in an associated or neighbouring body of water, where human impacts could be managed much more effectively? Instead of a natural reserve within the boundaries of the baiji's dwindling range, why not protect them instead in a 'semi-natural' reserve?

The first attempts to try to set up a semi-natural reserve were carried out by Zhou Kaiya and his team. The scientists from Nanjing identified a thin channel, 1.5 kilometres long and between 40 and 200 metres wide, running between two islands in the river near the town of Tongling in Anhui Province which they thought was an appropriate location for such a reserve. Initial plans to control the water level in the channel with sluice gates and pumps proved to be too expensive, and the channel was instead separated from the flow of the main river with metal and bamboo barriers at either end, but the team went ahead with earth-moving operations to increase water depth in the reserve and to build up the height of the bordering dykes. A lot of money was poured into the operation. A laboratory with holding pools, hospital pools, a fish farm, and living quarters for scientists, and even a holiday complex for the anticipated influx of tourists, were built alongside the channel. Huge Communist-style shining metal statues of stylized baiji cresting the waves adorned the banks and arched over the road alongside the reserve.

Everyone in Tongling got very excited—the baiji was going to put their town on the map. More government money was spent on erecting more baiji statues. The local guesthouse changed its name to the 'Baiji Hotel'. The local brewery even started making its own official 'Baiji Beer', with '*Lipotes vexillifer*' printed on the bottle cap—probably the only beer in the world to carry a scientific name. When Douglas Adams visited in 1988, although he reported that 'Tongling was not beautiful'[13] (I can vouch that this is something of an understatement), he was impressed and astonished by the range of baiji-related branding that would hopefully help to bring more money into the reserve. The town sold baiji shoes, baiji cola, baiji computerized weighing scales, baiji toilet paper, baiji phosphorus fertilizer, and baiji bentonite—'a mining product used in the production of toothpaste, iron and steel casting, and also as an additive for pig food. Baiji Bentonite was a very successful product.'[14]Adams left Tongling feeling uplifted and hopeful for the future of the baiji. Inevitably, this meant that things weren't going to work out as planned.

In the end, no baiji were ever introduced into the Tongling semi-natural reserve, despite all of the money that was effectively wasted in developing the infrastructure for the project, and in making the town 'baiji-friendly'. Although the project was being coordinated by Zhou Kaiya, the world's most established and senior baiji researcher, the Nanjing research group was lacking the crucial trump card in a power struggle that was developing within China—it didn't have any captive baiji. The River Dolphin Research Group in Wuhan, on the other hand, had Qi Qi, and for over two years had Qi Qi's ill-fated 'child bride' Zhen Zhen as well. These animals conferred Wuhan with all the prestige it needed to be recognized as the national focus for baiji research and conservation, and Nanjing's importance was slowly eclipsed throughout the 1980s. By the time Douglas Adams was being impressed by the facilities at Tongling during his 1988 visit, the Wuhan team had already proposed an alternative location for a semi-natural baiji reserve, further upstream in Hubei Province. Even more unfortunately for Zhou Kaiya, this second proposed baiji reserve—an oxbow lake called the Tian'e-Zhou (or Swan) oxbow, adjacent to the main channel of the Yangtze near the town of Shishou—was considerably more impressive than the site at Tongling. It was 21 kilometres long and had only been cut off from the main river in 1972, and was still connected during the summer months when water levels were high, allowing fresh through-flow of water to prevent the oxbow from stagnating. Unlike the reserve at Tongling, it also contained a plentiful supply of fish, with an estimated annual yield of over 1,000 tons—easily enough to support a breeding group of dolphins, maybe up to 50 or even 80 animals.[15]Even more importantly, finless porpoises were also frequently seen in the oxbow, suggesting that it would also be a suitable home for baiji.

The Wuhan team described Tian'e-Zhou as being 'like a miniature Yangtze'[16]—in effect, it represented what the pre-industrial Yangtze ecosystem should be like, free of heavy boat traffic and in a situation where other human impacts such as fishing and pollution could be minimized. By the early 1990s, the oxbow had been designated as a National Baiji Reserve by the Chinese Ministry of Agriculture, and was later nominated for inclusion on the Ramsar List of Wetlands of International Importance, an international conservation convention that aims to protect the world's key wetland sites. If the baiji recovery programme was going to involve intensive *ex situ* conservation, this was potentially the perfect habitat for establishing a closely managed dolphin population. However, the real environmental situation at Tian'e-Zhou was not necessarily as rosy as it had been painted. Furthermore, the decision over which of the various suggested recovery strategies stood the best chance of saving the baiji was not only up to China. The wider world was watching, and had also become involved.

4

EAST MEETS WEST

*'I am sick of meetings; cannot a man turn his head
without he have a meeting?'*

Arthur Miller
The Crucible

In 1981, shortly after Qi Qi had taken up residence with the
River Dolphin Research Group in Wuhan, Professor Chen
Peixun was invited to attend a conference on marine mammals
in the United States. In order to repay the favour, she provided
her host, Bill Perrin, with a reciprocal invitation to visit Wuhan.
Although he didn't manage to spot any wild baiji during the brief
boat trip he took along the Yangtze, his experiences in China
and discussions with Professor Chen alerted him to the huge gap
in Western scientific knowledge about the river system and its
dolphins—unstudied by outside researchers for sixty years—and
also to the major limitations to understanding cetacean biology in
China only a few years after the end of the Cultural Revolution. As
chairman of the Cetacean Specialist Group for the International
Union for the Conservation of Nature (IUCN), Perrin was well
placed to try to rectify this mutual shortfall. Together with his
colleague Bob Brownell Jr—a cetacean biologist at the US Fish
and Wildlife Service, who had been awarded his doctoral thesis from the University of Tokyo for research into the enigmatic

franciscana or La Plata River dolphin—Perrin managed to tackle the formidable logistics of organizing an international conference in China, and in October 1986 the first ever workshop on the biology and conservation of river dolphins was held at the Institute of Hydrobiology in Wuhan. Perrin and Brownell hoped that the meeting would bring all of the world's river dolphin experts together to compare their knowledge of different species, and to identify the common problems that these dolphins were facing. In particular, they felt that it was important to expose the Chinese researchers who were looking at baiji to the kinds of studies that were being carried out in other countries.

Talking to Perrin, Brownell, and other researchers who attended this historic conference today, it seems that the international participants came to the meeting feeling quite optimistic about the baiji's prospects to begin with. China was then very much a closed country, and there had been little indication to the outside world that the species was particularly threatened. However, the sober findings of the Nanjing and Wuhan research teams started to come out at the workshop. It soon became clear to everyone that the dolphins were being killed by a range of different human activities in the Yangtze, and that their habitat was rapidly being lost. The situation was clearly worse than everyone had thought, and the Westerners became more and more pessimistic as the workshop went on. For their part, the two different Chinese factions both presented their suggestions for *ex situ* baiji conservation in the Tongling and Tian'e-Zhou semi-natural reserves and in the Wuhan dolphinarium. Out on the river, the international participants saw for themselves that rolling hook fishing, which they had been told was banned, was still being widely carried out throughout the baiji's range, and they were further shocked by the levels of heavy ship traffic in the main channel. It certainly seemed as though the baiji had little chance of survival in its natural habitat.

Despite this, however, the Western scientists decided that the best chance to save the baiji would be the drastic enforcement of protective measures in the river, rather than moving any animals to establish a breeding programme away from the main channel. It seemed pretty clear, Perrin and Brownell said, that pitifully little was being done by the Chinese authorities to preserve the baiji's habitat or to actually get any harmful fishing gear out of the water, despite the existing legislation banning its use. The allegedly protected river sections should be properly patrolled, and serious efforts should be made to limit ship traffic in the main channel, or at least to alter the shipping routes away from sections of river that were favoured by baiji. If the Chinese government was serious about conserving its aquatic panda, then they would listen to the advice of these international experts and act accordingly. Then, even though the remaining baiji might be able to move up and down the river, they would hopefully recognize that harmful human impacts were decreasing in some parts of their range, and so they would begin to stay preferentially in these protected sections and avoid the more dangerous areas. That was the best way to try to save the baiji from extinction, they thought.

Looking back, it's hard to know how realistic these recommendations could have seemed even at the workshop. Certainly, there was an urgent need for more enforcement of existing conservation legislation along the river regarding fishing gear, but any wider-scale regulation of human activities in the region would clash with the first real economic growth that the country had seen since the early twentieth century. The Chinese researchers at the workshop expressed their concerns that development along the Yangtze was an essential part of that economic growth, and that it was beginning to escalate. Would anyone in power who mattered actually be prepared to follow the suggestions of a handful of international visitors—visitors from a country that only a few years earlier had been considered an enemy of China, and that was still regarded with suspicion—if that meant limiting the country's material wealth? Unfortunately, if it came down to a trade-off between saving a few dolphins that barely anyone in China had ever seen or even heard of, or allowing more people nationwide to have the 'three wheels' (sewing machine, wristwatch, and bicycle) or the 'four machines' (television, sewing machine, radio, and washing machine), which was more likely to win?

So what was wrong with the semi-natural reserve option? It seems that some of the international participants simply didn't think that the Chinese researchers had the ability to find enough baiji to form a breeding population, or—maybe more importantly—to transfer them to one of the semi-natural reserves without harming or killing them. Certainly neither of the Chinese research teams had a great track record with keeping baiji alive in captivity; but, equally, the semi-natural reserves were a completely different and far more natural environment than the unregulated concrete tanks in Wuhan or Nanjing. However, it was true that disconcertingly large numbers of people had always been actively involved in the previous baiji capture attempts, and some of the delegates were concerned that footage of the successful capture of Zhen Zhen showed that she was handled quite roughly by hangers-on who didn't really seem to have the necessary experience to be involved in such a careful operation. Maybe this had something to do with the premature deaths of Rong Rong, Lian Lian, Su Su, and Jiang Jiang, thought the American biologists, in addition to the inadequate conditions in which the dolphins were subsequently kept.

However, it has to be remembered that from the time of the Wuhan meeting onwards, the main problem with baiji conservation was the great uncertainty about every possible strategy that had been suggested. Quite simply, no one had ever tried anything like this before. There was a lot of discussion at Wuhan, and no major approach was left unconsidered. Maybe, after all, the semi-natural reserve option could—and should—form a part of the baiji recovery programme, reasoned some of the international participants. Out of the two alternative semi-natural reserves, Tian'e-Zhou certainly seemed like the better option, but before any attempts could be carried out to set up an *ex situ* baiji breeding programme there, the international group demanded that some major changes had to be made. Apparently, managing the reserve

cost about US$25,000 per year, but although a large part of this
was covered by the Shishou County authorities, the Ministry of
Agriculture and the provincial fisheries authorities, 30 per cent
of the budget was raised by fishing in the oxbow.[1] Even worse,
about 500 fishermen still lived along the banks of the reserve.
Altogether, about 650 tons of fish were being taken from the
reserve each year.[2] If the Chinese researchers were suggesting that
fishing was the principal factor responsible for killing baiji in
the Yangtze, how on earth could they then support putting all
of their efforts into a project to translocate dolphins to Tian'e-
Zhou, without making sure that the animals wouldn't be exposed
to exactly the same threats in their supposedly safe new home?
Even if the most harmful fishing techniques weren't being used
in the reserve, was the oxbow actually big enough to contain
sufficient fish to support hundreds of fishermen as well as a viable
population of baiji? In addition, the oxbow was still connected
to the main Yangtze channel for almost half of the year. The
River Dolphin Research Group at Wuhan suggested that plant-
ing a cordon of willow trees across the entrance from the main
river would keep the dolphins in,[3] but this plan didn't seem very
convincing.

The best solution, suggested some of the Westerners, was not
only to sort out these fundamental problems, but also to carry
out a 'test run' to see if the Tian'e-Zhou oxbow was actually
capable of supporting a breeding population of cetaceans, before
pulling out all the stops and actually trying to catch any more
baiji. The most obvious way to do this, they said, would be to
introduce some finless porpoises into the reserve. If the porpoises
could survive and breed, then the animals could be removed from
the oxbow and the baiji captures could begin in earnest. Removing
the porpoises was crucial, reasoned the Westerners, because they
might compete with the introduced baiji for food, and might even
pose a direct threat to the dolphins. Although most of the surveys
had reported that baiji and porpoises could often be seen feeding
in the same area, and sometimes even swimming together in

mixed groups—indeed, it was standard practice to scan porpoise groups when looking for baiji—there were also some disconcerting reports that porpoises had been seen displaying what seemed to be aggressive behaviour towards the larger dolphins. Why then increase the risks of establishing a viable baiji population in the oxbow with this unknown factor?

Was this a good suggestion? The international community clearly thought so, but in retrospect, it has some pretty major flaws. Firstly, it would take several years for an introduced population of porpoises to actually start breeding, but even by the mid-1980s it was clear that the baiji didn't have that much time left. Delaying the start of intensive conservation actions for the species would only make any eventual success even harder to achieve, and it's difficult to know why no one argued this at the time. Did the baiji realistically have several years to wait around in the degraded and dangerous main channel of the Yangtze, given that little conservation work was going on to protect it *in situ* either? However, this cautiousness serves as an important example of how, by and large, the international advisers felt that they couldn't commit themselves to any recommendations about risky conservation strategies without more robust data. The inescapable paradox was that because the baiji was already so rare and so difficult to observe in the wild, it was extremely unlikely that anyone was actually going to be able to get any meaningful new data on the animal. At some point, positive action was going to be required based on whatever knowledge was already available, rather than waiting in vain to learn something new as the species dwindled away to extinction. Maybe even more importantly, though, what did the international advisers actually think would happen if the introduced porpoise population did manage to start breeding in the reserve? This would represent the first time that a viable translocated population of cetaceans had ever been established anywhere in the world—a great scientific success. Would the Chinese then really be prepared to just put these animals straight back into the Yangtze? This was clearly a difficult situation full of difficult decisions. However, if the international advisers on the one hand were adamant that translocations to Tian'e-Zhou shouldn't start before porpoises were used as a test run, but on the other hand were also adamant that dolphins and porpoises shouldn't be kept together in the same reserve, it does seem that the baiji was damned if you do and damned if you don't with this one.

~

Even more disconcertingly, the workshop highlighted fundamental differences concerning Chinese and Western attitudes towards baiji conservation that began to set serious alarm bells ringing for the international participants. Whereas the Westerners considered that *ex situ* breeding in a semi-natural reserve could maybe constitute part of the recovery strategy for the baiji, it seemed that the Chinese felt that this approach would be all that was necessary for its conservation. Certainly trying to clean up the Yangtze was a monumental task, and may well have been impossible to manage in the time period needed to do any good for the dolphin even if concerted actions were taken, but this didn't seem to be what was making the Chinese researchers focus so heavily on alternative *ex situ* strategies. Instead, it seemed as though the Chinese preferred the *ex situ* approach because it felt more substantial and 'hands on'; because it was probably going to be easier to get internal funding to support baiji captures than to try to promote conservation in the river; and because any baiji in captivity or even semi-captivity were an extremely valuable commodity, that would attract visitors, add to the prestige of the research group that was in charge, and act as a cash cow for further funding. Maybe this attitude is not that different to those adopted by other financially challenged organizations in the West. However, the Americans felt that scarcely concealed vested interests were being combined with an apparently genuine belief that *in situ* conservation could be completely ignored and everything would still be OK for the baiji. Indeed, they felt at times that the River Dolphin Research Group seemed to act as though they were just dealing with a big fish rather than a cetacean, and that intensive, invasive techniques which worked in fish farms could just as well be applied to baiji conservation. The Western observers, who felt that any *ex situ* work had to be combined with a clear plan to try to reverse the environmental degradation in the main Yangtze channel, were also concerned by what seemed to be a lack of long-term planning on the part of the Chinese researchers and administrators. They tried to discuss what would happen if the *ex situ* efforts were successful, and it proved possible to establish a breeding population of baiji in the reserve. Would the River Dolphin Research Group and the regional authorities then be willing to reintroduce any of these animals back into the wild? Although they didn't say no flat out, I was told, there was clearly a lot of reluctance to even consider this issue.

Conflicts between Chinese and international researchers over the importance of *ex situ* conservation were by no means limited to the problems of how to save the baiji. In *The Last Panda*, George Schaller recounted that, around the same time in the mid-1980s, the Chinese participants in the famous giant panda conservation programme at Wolong Reserve felt that removal of as many pandas as possible into a poorly equipped concrete breeding facility—where animals were fed gruel rather than bamboo and panda life expectancy was frighteningly short—was the key conservation action that was required to save the species, despite outrage from the Western project participants that little was being done to study or protect the animals in their natural habitat. The Japanese cetacean researcher Toshio Kasuya, who was also present at the 1986 Wuhan baiji workshop, suggests that the main problem faced by the participants was that they lacked a common language—meaning not that some spoke Chinese and others English, but that many key words had radically different meanings depending on one's cultural background. The term 'conservation', it seems, simply meant something quite different in the West than it did in China—a country that had been overpopulated for so long that concepts of wilderness or of nature existing in its own right had little meaning or relevance any more, and where cultural appreciation of animals was largely restricted to their symbolic importance for human affairs. Maybe in this context, it becomes easier to understand why the Chinese did not seem to appreciate why the Western participants considered the Tian'e-Zhou reserve to be at most a temporary solution to the problems of trying to save the baiji, and why breeding endangered species in zoos was apparently seen as a greater conservation success in China than sustaining populations in the wild.

The meaning of what constituted 'conservation' was not the only fundamental difference between Eastern and Western thinking which became apparent at Wuhan, and which continued to cause major problems for baiji conservation over the years to come. The trauma of Chairman Mao's regime was still a recent memory for the Chinese participants at the workshop, and it had severe repercussions on the development of Chinese science. Whereas scientific thinking in the West involves testing existing hypotheses and exposing them to critical scrutiny, up until a few years earlier anyone in China who challenged the status quo could be hauled off to a labour camp for re-education. Most notoriously, Mao had actively encouraged the country's intellectuals to speak out and provide healthy criticism about government policies in 1956 and 1957 during what became known as the 'Hundred Flowers Campaign', under the slogan 'Let a hundred flowers bloom, let a hundred schools of thought contend'. But this turned into a trap to identify potential dissidents, and was rapidly followed by waves of persecution and an ideological crackdown. This intellectual despotism was in turn merely the latest manifestation of the much older Chinese system of rigid hierarchical order, in which everyone has their designated place and where authority and seniority are accorded with the highest respect, and which still underpins much of the country's cultural value system. Even today, many Chinese scientific journals do not use peer review—the process by which research is exposed to the scrutiny of other academics prior to publication—because of the need to save face, the sense of deference and unwillingness to be seen to criticize fellows or seniors, or even the perceived dangers implicit in such criticism. Although the situation is slowly changing, what constituted scientific thought in China during the 1980s and 1990s often bore little resemblance to what Western observers would think of as logical deduction. In particular, it was often impossible to ascertain whether a supposedly scientific conclusion presented by Chinese researchers was based on real data, or instead whether it represented nothing more than an untested hypothesis (and typically a hypothesis that had been proposed by a more senior researcher). Actually having a truly scientific discussion in Wuhan proved to be much harder than the Western delegates had anticipated. And to make matters worse, the Communist authorities usually allocated scientists to different research facilities irrespective of their specific training. For example, Professor Wang Ding, the current and very capable head of the Wuhan group, was originally a physicist who had little knowledge of river dolphins, or even of rivers, when he started the job. No wonder the international participants at Wuhan were frequently confused by the Chinese ideas about baiji conservation.

And, in addition to all of these hurdles, more practical problems for implementing baiji conservation measures also became apparent. At the Wuhan meeting it became clear to the wider world that no love was lost between the different research groups from Wuhan and Nanjing, and there was significant tension between the two factions throughout the workshop. The competition was both intellectual and financial, and the River Dolphin Research Group had also recently poached Nanjing's main field researcher, which only added to the acrimonious feelings. The inability of the only two organizations devoted to baiji research to pool their expertise didn't make the other workshop participants optimistic about the proposed Chinese plans to save the species, and it must be recognized as yet another issue that may have hindered conservation action during the 1980s.

The Wuhan workshop was followed during the late 1980s and 1990s by several subsequent conferences, workshops, and meetings devoted to baiji conservation, which involved both representatives from the Chinese research groups and regional authorities as well as members of the international scientific and conservation communities, with researchers from the USA, Canada, Japan, the UK, and other countries all variously taking part. However, although the Western participants always felt that each of the meetings reached a positive conclusion, which would allow Chinese and international researchers to begin working together in the right direction, the plans never seemed to be carried out when everyone returned home. The Westerners felt indignant that the Chinese participants seemed to want to do everything their own way—although they agreed to the international recommendations proposed at each meeting, afterwards they seemed to pay no attention to anything that had been said. The fact that international advice was welcomed but then seemingly ignored time and again led to the progressive deterioration of international collaborations for trying to develop a workable baiji recovery programme. Even more seriously, in the years that followed it became increasingly hard for international collaborators to avoid the suspicion that some of the Chinese institutions and organizations that were involved in the discussions may have highlighted the plight of the species to try to attract money that would then be used for other projects, such as improving their on-site research facilities. No one in the international community wrote the baiji off prematurely, I was told by Tom Jefferson, then the co-acting director of Hong Kong's Ocean Park Conservation Foundation who attended many of these meetings; however, many people certainly began to write the conservation programme off. If they had seen a genuine change in direction, they would have been very willing to re-engage—but instead there was just increasing frustration at seeing so much money and effort being spent to set up all of these meetings, only to see things going nowhere time and time again.

These problems were exemplified by the ongoing concerns felt by the Westerners about the Tian'e-Zhou oxbow. The Chinese assured the international workshop participants that the fisheries operations at Tian'e-Zhou would be relocated, but although some fishermen were moved from the vicinity, by the twenty-first century there were still around 300 fishermen living along the oxbow, their relocation apparently hampered by a lack of livelihood alternatives and shortage of funds to make compensation payments.[4] Despite this, the River Dolphin Research Group organized the capture and translocation of five porpoises into the reserve in 1990, followed by another five in 1993 and then twelve additional animals in 1995 and 1996. As the international community had feared, the project suffered a number of predictable setbacks. One of the first animals translocated in 1990 died from injuries suffered during its capture, and two other animals were killed within two years by illegal rolling hooks in the reserve. A pregnant female that had been introduced into the reserve gave birth prematurely to a dead infant as a result of the stress of her capture. Another seven animals were accidentally killed in 1993 during a botched attempt to capture them for a radio-tracking study, and then fourteen animals escaped from the reserve during the flood season in the summer of 1996, when a series of nets that had been put in place to separate the oxbow from the main Yangtze channel proved inadequate. Despite all of these deaths, there was still so much competition between the surviving animals and the fishermen who were still working in the reserve that fifteen of the remaining porpoises were then released back into the Yangtze.[5] However, several animals were still left in the reserve, meaning that, even if the horrendous track record of porpoise survival at Tian'e-Zhou could be overlooked, the oxbow still couldn't be considered a suitable *ex situ* environment for baiji.

~

At the end of the day, I was told by many of the Western participants who attended the frustrating conservation workshops held in China during the 1980s and 1990s, the reason that very little was ever actually done to conserve the baiji was because there was simply no determination to make things happen on the part of the Chinese government. Despite all the legislation, publicity, and baiji beer, everything was just lip service. Throughout the twentieth century, China has demonstrated in numerous other situations that the concerted top-down power of its government can effect social and cultural change on a massive scale; whatever those in the West may think about the human rights issues surrounding many of these actions, the international participants were right that the capacity and infrastructure was certainly there to carry out the necessary conservation actions to save the baiji either *in situ* or through translocation. But conservation is a challenge which involves sacrifices, compromises, and tough decisions. Following through with the recommendations to improve the condition of the main Yangtze channel would have required some very unpopular moves by central and regional governments, such as relocation of shipping routes and removal of fishing gear, that would have generated major conflicts with other user groups throughout the hugely populated river basin. It seems that this was not a challenge that the authorities were prepared, or even able, to take. Instead, the international community felt that the authorities were putting all of their support into captive breeding as a false security blanket, a supposedly simpler approach that would save them from having to try anything else to save the baiji; but in the end they didn't even provide much support for the semi-natural reserve option either.

And, yet, this isn't the whole story. It's easy for us to point our finger at China, and lay all the blame for the failure of baiji conservation with them. However, whereas the Chinese authorities certainly could and should have done a lot more to try to save the species, it is crucial to recognize that the conservation challenges presented by the plight of the baiji were not really embraced by any of the international experts or organizations that became involved over the years in this sorry saga either. Although we can forgive the Westerners for hoping in the beginning that the bill for baiji conservation would be picked up by the Chinese authorities, when it became increasingly clear to the outside world that this was just not going to happen, then was it really acceptable to continue standing passively on the sidelines and watch the species fade away towards extinction? I was disconcerted by the attitudes of the scientists who had attended these early meetings. While criticizing the Chinese for not considering that they should act on any international conservation recommendations, the Western advisers clearly didn't feel that it was *their* job to save the baiji, either. You have a workshop, generate a report, and then go and do something else—you can only hope that people will pay attention, I was told. We all had day jobs already. But if the Chinese authorities didn't care, then the international scientists and conservationists were the only people in the world who did. Was anybody else really likely to step in to try to do anything?

Some might say that maybe it isn't the role of scientists, concerned with specialist knowledge and theoretical abstracts, to implement practical conservation programmes in the real world—although the line has become progressively more blurred in the growing field of conservation biology, where research and action now increasingly go hand in hand. What's more inexcusable is that although some of the major international conservation organizations provided funding for meetings, surveys, and associated research, they provided no meaningful support to carry out any active baiji conservation, either. Even at the time, the international advisers didn't think that making the conditions at the Tian'e-Zhou reserve suitable for baiji would have been overly expensive, which was why they were so frustrated that the Chinese authorities didn't seem to be doing much about it. Certainly just 'throwing money' at the baiji problem would have been unlikely to do much good, given the concerns of the Western scientists that money dedicated to baiji research was being misappropriated within China. However, was it really impossible to manage international funds in a way that could have made a difference—for example, through

milestone plans with the prospect of continued support upon
successful completion of collaborative projects? Money talks,
after all, however unfortunate that may be. If direct financial
support really proved to be too much of a problem after all, why
would it have been so difficult to support active baiji conservation efforts through other means, such as providing much-needed
equipment or practical expertise from researchers versed in the
safe capture and handling of dolphins elsewhere in the world, to
minimize the risks that everyone was worried about in setting up a
breeding population? And what about campaigning, public pressure, and generally raising the profile of the baiji outside China?
Why was none of this ever done to any appreciable extent? Why
do most people I have spoken to, if they know anything about the
baiji at all, tell me that they have only ever heard about its plight
in *Last Chance to See* rather than through 'official' conservation
channels? The most prominent of these international conservation
organizations even has a large Chinese mammal as its logo. If it
wasn't their job to make sure that the baiji didn't become extinct,
either by providing financial support for conservation projects or
by campaigning and generating international pressure to try to
force the Chinese authorities to act, then whose was it? Could any
of these organizations really justify standing by as an entire species
died out?

In fact, the only significant international funding that was ever
provided for active baiji conservation efforts—not just 'safe' support for workshops or passive surveys that documented the dolphin's decline without stepping in to do anything—came from
Japan. The first Japanese money was donated in the early 1990s
by Enoshima Aquarium and the Japan International Cooper-
ation Society,[6] to support baiji capture efforts and to replace
the poorly equipped outdoor holding pools at the Institute of
Hydrobiology with a state-of-the-art US$2 million dolphinar-
ium,[7] where Qi Qi would be the prime attraction. But the head
of Enoshima Aquarium, Yukiko Hori, told the other international players involved with baiji conservation that she wanted the

River Dolphin Research Group (now renamed the Baiji Research Group) to send the first baiji that was captured to Japan, where it would become the Enoshima Aquarium's prime attraction. She was even bold enough to ask some of the Western scientists to help her out. Inevitably, the idea met with fierce resistance—this plan would deal a serious blow to the crucial attempts to establish a baiji breeding population. Then, a few years later, more Japanese funding—this time around US$100,000—was donated to the Chinese Ministry of Agriculture to support the *ex situ* recovery programme. But even though some international funds were now available specifically to carry out baiji captures, in the years that followed the money was never actually spent. The baiji recovery programme had got one step closer to becoming a reality, but it seemed that there were still some hurdles within China that needed to be overcome after all.

~

To the Westerners, the attitudes of the Chinese researchers, their seeming misunderstanding of the term 'conservation', and their preference for *ex situ* management above all else didn't bode inspire confidence for the use of captive breeding as a measure for saving the baiji. However, some of the Western researchers who had attended the baiji meetings didn't even seem to see any real difference between trying to set up a breeding programme at Tian'e-Zhou and keeping dolphins in concrete tanks in the Wuhan dolphinarium. I was told that if the natural habitat of the baiji had gone, and there was no clear plan to try to fix some part of the main Yangtze channel, then there was no point in keeping any dolphins alive in a reserve just so that people could come and see what a baiji looked like—it was the same as being extinct as far as they were concerned. It seems in retrospect that many of the Western cetacean specialists also had a disconcertingly limited appreciation of what conservation could actually entail. George Schaller's book *The Last Panda*, which details the misunderstandings, disagreements, and cultural barriers that hindered the

successful development of the collaborative giant panda conservation programme, was published just before the 1993 international
baiji meeting in Nanjing, and several of the Western attendees
later told me that they'd joked that if the word 'panda' was
replaced with the word 'baiji', the book could describe their experiences perfectly as well. But this off-hand panda analogy seems
to have been the only time that any of the participants really
considered any other endangered species recovery programmes.
Instead, they said, the situation facing the baiji was unique. It was
the first time that a species of cetacean had been pushed so close
to extinction as a result of the kinds of human factors operating
in the Yangtze; and it was a marine mammal problem that only
marine mammalogists could solve.

But while the baiji's plight was certainly unique for a cetacean,
some extremely valuable insights into possible strategies for saving the dolphin most certainly could have been gained through
a wider awareness of conservation measures applied successfully
with other kinds of species. Establishing closely managed breeding
populations of highly threatened species under semi-natural conditions was not something that had been dreamt up by the Chinese
for the first time, but had actually already been carried out for
almost a century in other parts of the world. Most famously, it had
been the key strategy used in New Zealand to save many of their
endemic bird species. New Zealand is the world's most isolated
major landmass, and has no native species of land mammals (only
a few seals and bats). As a result, many of its native birds nest
on the ground and have lost the ability to fly—because although
we may consider flight to be a defining characteristic of birds,
a tremendous amount of energy is required to grow and power
their flight muscles. If there is no need to maintain flight as a
means of escape from hungry ground-dwelling carnivores, then
this energy can be used instead to raise more offspring. But being
flightless, ground nesting, and generally innocent and naive in
the face of danger didn't help New Zealand's bird species very
much at all once a wide range of hungry predatory mammals

were introduced, either accidentally or deliberately, by Polynesian and early European settlers. By the nineteenth century, the North and South Islands of New Zealand were overrun by Pacific, black and brown rats, feral cats, and stoats, and there was no way to eradicate any of these predators or prevent them from eating the country's native birds. Around half of the bird species that were found on New Zealand before human arrival have become extinct in the past few hundred years, and the great majority of these have disappeared due to predation by these vicious exotic mammals.

As early as the late nineteenth century, concerned New Zealanders came up with the only solution that seemed to have any chance of success: they started moving as many of their threatened birds as possible to predator-free offshore islands and established carefully managed breeding populations under these semi-natural conditions, so that even if the birds died out on the mainland, then at least a few individuals would be able to survive elsewhere. This simple strategy has saved many unique New Zealand species—such as the little spotted kiwi, the stitchbird, the saddleback, and the kakapo, the world's largest parrot—from disappearing forever. Although the threats faced by these birds are very different to those faced by the baiji, in neither situation was it realistically going to be possible to remove the threats from the natural habitat. And whereas the international participants at the various baiji workshops felt that establishing an *ex situ* dolphin population in a semi-natural reserve could only be a cheap parody of conservation if there wasn't a long-term goal to clean up the Yangtze, the New Zealanders have still not come close to working out a way to get rid of the rats, cats, and stoats that infest their forests—which is, arguably, much less of an issue than expecting the Chinese to clean up their main industrial artery in a region of massive overpopulation and economic growth. The survival of the kakapo on a series of offshore islands that represent only a tiny fraction of its former range is rightly hailed as a conservation success story. No one feels that it is the ideal solution, but at the end of the day, if there is nothing else that can realistically be done to keep a remarkable species from becoming extinct, then what other choices are there? Just because you don't feel that maintaining a viable population of baiji in a large protected oxbow is the ideal conservation solution, can you *really* then walk away and condemn the species to extinction, knowing that there's no other option?

It's not unrealistic to think that, maybe one day in the not too distant future, it will prove possible to reverse the damage done to the Yangtze and return it to a semblance of its original natural environment. After all, we need look no further than London to see that river regeneration on this kind of scale can be carried out. As Conrad's Charlie Marlow said of the Thames in *Heart of Darkness*, 'And this also has been one of the dark places of the earth.' Until the past few decades, the river had become so fouled up by industrial pollutants and human effluent that in 1957 it was declared to be 'biologically dead'—incapable of supporting life— by the British Museum of Natural History. Parliament infamously had to be dissolved in the 1850s because of the so-called 'Great Stink' caused by raw sewage in the river, and a century later a 20-kilometre stretch had become completely anoxic, worse even than the current state of the Yangtze. However, by the start of the twenty-first century, thanks to effective waste treatment and pollution control, the Thames has been repopulated by a wide range of fish species that were once locally extirpated, and also by seals, dolphins, and porpoises in its lower reaches. It is a rousing conservation success story. The difference between the Thames and the Yangtze, though, is that the Thames was not home to any endemic species, whereas many of the Yangtze's inhabitants are found nowhere else on earth; they cannot simply recolonize the river from elsewhere, and if they disappear from the Yangtze they are gone forever. Surely, then, it is not irrational to consider that a crucial conservation concern for the Yangtze is to maintain viable populations of its unique species—ideally under conditions as close as possible to its pre-industrial ecosystem— which can be used to restock the river when the time comes, rather than demanding that without a definite reintroduction date the whole plan is futile. And let us not forget that protection of unique species is an international responsibility—if these species are found in a developing country with little conservation experience and very different economic priorities, it is surely incumbent on more experienced countries to provide this support.

And, despite everything that went wrong at the Tian'e-Zhou oxbow, it seemed that it *might* actually constitute a suitable venue for a baiji breeding programme, after all. Researchers from the Baiji Research Group who studied the finless porpoises that were still left alive in the reserve reported that every year, between May and June, they observed clear mating behaviour between the animals. Then, calves started appearing. At first there was some confusion among the Chinese researchers over whether these animals had been conceived in the oxbow, because several of the translocated porpoises had definitely been pregnant when they were first captured in the main Yangtze channel. However, by the spring of 1992, it was clear that one of these calves had been conceived in the reserve. The animal survived. Over the following years, the semi-natural porpoise population continued to reproduce successfully in the reserve, and between April 1997 and April 2000 seven calves were born to the group.

So maybe if the reserve had been properly prepared, and more international advice, funding, pressure, and expertise had been provided to confront the problems of accidental mortality during capture, illegal fishing, and potential escapes during the high-water season, then it could have been possible to make Tian'e-Zhou into the safe haven that the baiji needed to survive and breed. We'll never know for sure any more. Although the oxbow conservation plan was popularized outside China— ironically even by George Schaller in *The Last Panda*, which documented so many other problems with Chinese conservation— almost no practical support was ever provided by the international community to carry out the necessary preparations to realize Tian'e-Zhou's potential and make it suitable for the baiji recovery programme. Instead, as the years passed, the arrogant

Western empire continued to lock antlers with the arrogant Eastern empire—and the situation in the Yangtze continued to deteriorate.

~

Despite the near total lack of support from the wider world, though, the Baiji Research Group *did* actually make several attempts during the early 1990s to capture baiji in order to establish a breeding population at Tian'e-Zhou, financed entirely by money they had acquired from the Chinese authorities. The first five efforts all failed, leading some members of the international community to argue that the semi-natural reserve strategy was clearly impossible to achieve, and that it was already too late to do anything to save the baiji: it was time to walk away. But the Chinese themselves reported bluntly that their resources were insufficient: they had 'primitive equipment and not enough manpower'.[8] They saw baiji several times while on the river, but their boats were so slow that they could rarely keep pace with the animals. During the first capture attempt in May 1993, the researchers managed to get close to a small group of baiji, but the animals made holes in the capture nets and swam away.[9] In contrast, the team that caught Lian Lian and Zhen Zhen in 1985 had used double nets, so that although these two baiji had got through one layer of net, they were still caught successfully.

And then, amazingly, the Chinese managed it. On 19 December 1995, over a decade after the only previous wild capture of baiji, two dolphins were sighted in the main channel near Shishou. The capture team made eight attempts to encircle the animals over the course of nine hours; then, just before sunset, one of the baiji finally entered the nets. During the commotion, the other animal escaped, but the team was still triumphant—they had caught an adult female baiji. The breeding programme could begin at last.

Unlike all of the captive baiji held in Wuhan and Nanjing over the years, this animal was never formally given a name. She was immediately transported by car to the Tian'e-Zhou oxbow, and was placed straight into the reserve, as no temporary holding facilities where she could be closely monitored had been constructed at the site. The team were worried that the animal might be in shock after being moved, but after a few days she was observed feeding normally, making shallow dives, and scaring shoals of small carp. She also started swimming with the group of finless porpoise that had already been introduced to the reserve, and the Chinese observers who made regular visits to the oxbow did not report any unusual competitive or aggressive behaviour suggesting that there were any problems between the two species.

Even the international community felt hopeful that this early Christmas present would mean that the baiji at last had a chance of survival, however small that chance may be. But, as had already happened many times before in the baiji saga, events soon took a turn for the worse. The Western advisers had been assured repeatedly by the staff of the Institute of Hydrobiology that, in the event of a successful baiji translocation, Qi Qi would also be transferred from the Wuhan dolphinarium to Tian'e-Zhou. Certainly, now that a sexually mature female baiji was present in the oxbow, such a move appeared to be the only strategy that could possibly give the baiji recovery programme any hope of success. Sadly, though, the Baiji Research Group soon showed that they had quite different plans for Qi Qi. The old male baiji, which had now lived in captivity in Wuhan for sixteen years, was just too important a political pawn to give up. He was the jewel in the crown of the Institute of Hydrobiology; he had been the tool that gave them dominance over Zhou Kaiya and his team; he was a television star and a national icon. The Wuhan group weren't going to give Qi Qi up at any cost, it seemed, even if this move pushed the entire baiji species closer towards extinction.

It's very hard to say whether transferring Qi Qi to the Tian'e-Zhou oxbow would have done much good. The old dolphin had spent nearly all of his life alone in captivity, and although the Wuhan researchers had given him a beach ball and a few other toys to play with, foreign visitors familiar with behavioural problems in captive animals were quick to notice that he displayed classic stereotyped behavioural patterns, the dolphin equivalent of the way that big cats pace up and down in zoo enclosures. [10] Possibly he would never have been able to readjust to a more natural environment again after all of his years in a small concrete tank, or—in spite of all the electro-ejaculation—would have known what to do if he ever encountered a female baiji.

And after a few months the debate became academic anyway. During the high-water season in the summer of 1996, the oxbow flooded and overflowed into the Yangtze. At the same time as fourteen of the reserve's porpoises escaped back into the river, the female baiji was found dead, entangled in nets that had recently been put up near the mouth of the oxbow to try to keep the animals in during the floods. It was never properly established why she died, partly because she was already beginning to decompose when she was found. The currents were strong near the nets, and the animal showed no signs of having been affected by rolling hooks or other fishing gear, so that it is possible that she had become trapped in the nets and drowned. However, she had lost almost half of her body weight, and analysis of her stomach contents revealed no fish remains, but only fragments of snails, plant seeds, and one small rock. She seemed to have been starving at the time of her death, the critics said—maybe the reserve's porpoises had bullied her to death, after all? It's certainly possible, although aggressive interactions between the solitary baiji and the porpoises were never observed by any of the researchers who monitored the cetaceans in the reserve during the early months of 1996. The absence of any fish remains in the stomach of the dead female at Tian'e-Zhou may not have any bearing on the cause of her death. It's possible that she was ill—maybe that's why the Chinese researchers had been able to capture her in the first place—or, maybe even more likely, that she had been injured during her capture, and had slowly deteriorated over the next few months. Observations made by the Baiji

Research Group staff lend some support to these ideas, because they noted that her respiration rate was much slower than either that shown by Qi Qi or by any of the many baiji that they had studied in the wild, and this raised concerns even before she died about whether she might have had some pathological condition. In the absence of any proper veterinary examinations at the time of her capture, or effective monitoring of her health status during and after her transfer to the reserve—which could have been provided by trained foreign experts—we will never know.

No more attempts were made to try to capture any baiji to translocate to Tian'e-Zhou after the death of the female dolphin in the reserve in 1996. This may not necessarily reflect any change of attitude by the Baiji Research Group towards the project's chances of success, but rather the limit to their resources for actually carrying out any further conservation work without any support from the outside world—or even, given the Japanese funding that had been donated to the Chinese Ministry of Agriculture, without sufficient support from their own authorities.

The picture didn't look good for the baiji. Over the next few years, from 1997 to 1999, a series of further surveys were carried out by the Wuhan team along the entirety of the dolphin's range in the main Yangtze channel. The results showed that the rapid decrease in baiji numbers was still continuing, and that the surviving population was now desperately low. In 1997, seventeen animals were seen in the river. A year later, similar surveys found only seven. By 1999, the team saw only two pairs of animals. While they admitted that some baiji must have been missed, the Wuhan team were forced to conclude that the baiji was now almost gone. Based on an assessment of all three surveys, they suggested that there might be as few as thirteen animals left in the wild.

One might expect, or at least hope, that these appalling findings would have acted as a wake-up call to spur the wider world into action, and make the international conservation community finally step in and save the day. After all, when faced with the knowledge that one of the world's most distinctive species of large mammal is condemned to certain extinction within the next few years without intensive conservation action, what kind of possible excuses could any major conservation organization have to justify acting otherwise? And yet ... instead of generating any further action, these latest survey findings seemed to have the opposite effect. Baiji conservation efforts were actually stepped down in the late 1990s—even further down than they already were, if that's possible. No one even made any plans to carry out another survey, to passively document the baiji's continued decline and at least publish a nice scientific paper on the subject, let alone do anything practical to actually try to save the species from extinction.

And then, in 2002, after twenty-two and a half years in captivity, Qi Qi died, of diabetes, stomach problems, and old age. His death hit the Baiji Research Group hard; Wang Ding later said that 'it was like losing a family member'.[11] In keeping with his superstar status, Qi Qi even had a funeral that was broadcast on national Chinese television. Schoolgirls singing plaintive songs lined the procession and placed flowers in his open casket. Then he was stuffed.

The river dolphin conservation workshops still kept on coming, though. The last published workshop report, entitled 'Biology and Conservation of Freshwater Cetaceans in Asia', contained only one paper on the baiji, describing the respiration rates and swimming behaviour of groups of animals that had been observed in the wild in 1987 and 1989. The authors wrote that 'we do not wish to attribute too much significance to these brief observations of baiji. They would hardly be worth reporting if there were a reasonable chance to gather more data ... Alas, such data may not be easily gathered on this highly endangered species. We hope that the baiji will survive and increase in number, so that our data can serve as a baseline of information from snapshots of the species' bleakest times.'[12] Randy Reeves, the new Chairman of the

IUCN's Cetacean Specialist Group, wrote with his co-editors in the report's introduction that the extinction of the baiji would be 'a national tragedy and an international disgrace';[13] but even though the wider world now seemed to appreciate its responsibility to baiji conservation, it seems that, once again, no one at the meeting actually tried to push for any affirmative action to be taken to do anything for the species.

The cover of the workshop report shows a photograph of Qi Qi swimming away from the camera, but with his head turned to look back. With a little bit of imagination, it looks like he's saying goodbye.

Part Two

THE END

5

THE RAREST ANIMAL
IN THE WORLD

Professor Zhou watched the baiji swimming out of sight on the expansive river, and there surged in the depth of his heart the cry—'Save the Yangtze river dolphin!'

Zhou Kaiya and Zhang Xingduan
Baiji: The Yangtze River Dolphin and Other Endangered Animals of China

Give me a child until he is 7 and I will show you the man, the Jesuits said. I must have been about 7 when I saw my first aquatic mammal. Although I grew up in Bristol, the gateway to England's West Country, having parents of different nationalities meant that I ended up spending most of my holidays in Finland, staying at my uncle's farm close to the Russian border in the calm summer countryside south of Savonlinna. My childhood memories are full of bright sunlight and water, the smell of the pines, and the sanctity of the forest. The nearest farm was a mile away, and the vitality of nature could be felt peering in from around the corners of the fields and whispering in the hush of the dusk. New discoveries were made every day by the intrepid young explorer with his Wellington boots on the wrong feet—an adder stretched out and sunning itself on the jetty; a deep velvet Camberwell

Beauty drifting like a dream through an alder grove; the larder of a red-backed shrike in a dry thornbush in the old cow pasture; a nightjar flushed almost from underfoot near the decaying Russian threshing machine on the hill behind the farm.

Steve Jones once described Finland as 'a dilute solution of land in water'.[1] The entire southeastern portion of the country is covered with a vast web of lakes carved from the cold granite by the passing of the glaciers at the end of the last Ice Age 10,000 years ago. Finland has almost 190,000 lakes, and most of them are found in the Savo region close to my uncle's farm. The farm itself was on an island called Partalansaari, situated in the complex network of interlinked pine-lined waterways that make up Europe's fourth largest lake, Saimaa. Many thousands of years ago, when the Finnish landmass was weighed down by glacial ice sheets, this lake had opened onto the Baltic Sea, and now it was home to a relict of its marine past that had become trapped as the land rose again after the retreat of the ice. The animal was called *norppa* in Finnish, and was extremely rare; when I was a child it was estimated that there may only have been 100 *norppa* left in the huge lake, because although it was one of Finland's most-loved animals it had been heavily hunted for the past century. I had seen many old *norppa* pelts hung up on the walls of summer cottages, as we covered the rounds of the vast and obscure series of relatives who lived in the forests and islands around Saimaa.

And then, one day out on the lake, fishing with my uncle under a huge blue sky, there it was. I looked up from the red-and-white cork bobbing beside the boat to see a whiskered snout and inquisitive black eyes peering back at me out of the water, out near the skerries close to the shipping channel and far from shore. Then, maybe only a second later, the shiny wet seal disappeared again into the tea-black waters of Saimaa. I never saw it again.

~

Thanks to the environmentalist movements of the 1970s and early 1980s, my generation was the first to be brought up with a real awareness of endangered species. My enthusiasm was fired by children's books, documentaries, and World Wildlife Fund sticker albums, which all described in exhaustive detail the range of animals that were threatened with imminent extinction. Whales and dolphins always received a mention in the books of my childhood, but the focus was typically on anti-whaling campaigns instead of more obscure freshwater species. However, I learnt about a much wider range of cetaceans from Bernard Stonehouse's *Sea Mammals of the World*, which despite its title included information about river dolphins as well. Stonehouse described how the Ganges and Indus dolphins—lumped together in his book as a single species—were now endangered and declining fast. The section on the baiji, however, was far more equivocal: 'Some concern is felt for their future, and local scientists are seeing how they can best be protected.'[2]

But it was not until after I had first visited China for my doctoral research that I learnt anything different about the status of the baiji. In a lavishly illustrated coffee-table book on recently extinct species published in 2001 called *A Gap in Nature*, the author—the famous Australian zoologist Tim Flannery—set the scene by describing some species that still survived today but were on the absolute verge of dying out. Most of these accounts of endangered animals were retellings of sadly familiar stories, but Flannery's most shocking example was horribly new to me. 'China's bizarre Yangtze River dolphin, with its white skin, slender beak and reduced eyes, is down to a single individual, and when it passes away another name will be added to the death list.'[3]

I was stunned. Could this be true? If so, how could this horrendous situation have seemingly been ignored completely by the conservation community and the world's media? Surely the imminent extinction of a beautiful and distinctive dolphin, especially one that was held in such high esteem by the Chinese people, should have been an easy target for publicity and fund-raising. After all, everyone loved dolphins, didn't they—the capacity for popular support for their conservation was illustrated by the tremendous public outcry about accidental dolphin deaths in the marine fishing industry, which had led to the development of 'dolphin-friendly' (and hence consumer-friendly) fishing techniques for tuna and other species. So what could possibly have gone so wrong for the baiji?

Looking back from where I sit now, at the end of the story, I don't remember exactly how I went beyond being just another concerned bystander and first became actively involved with the baiji. I had just completed a postdoctoral research fellowship in New Zealand, and was starting a new position at the Zoological Society of London (ZSL). But the precarious status of the baiji kept nagging at me. I couldn't stop wondering about what was being done to try to save the species from extinction. Was the international community pulling together, galvanized to carry out a vital, concerted last-minute recovery strategy? I read everything that I could find about the beautiful, enigmatic, pearly-white dolphin that had captured my imagination and passion like nothing else. I was obsessed. Was there anything that I could do to help?

∼

I think that first of all I must have contacted Randy Reeves at the IUCN. Certainly it was Randy who told me all about the current state of the international conservation movement that was ostensibly working to save the baiji, almost two decades after the first river dolphin workshop in Wuhan: a wobbly coalition, as he phrased it, of researchers who were spending mostly volunteer time to try to manage a very complex and delicate situation. There was a lot of intellectual and moral support, I was told, but there didn't seem to be much actual progress. Apparently one of the major hold-ups had been their inability to form a committee. Even worse, although representatives from Conservation International—one of the world's most important conservation organizations—were apparently integral members of this baiji network, nobody seemed able to identify any major sources of funding to do anything active to save the species. It didn't sound very inspiring or positive. Is this all that the international community could muster for the world's most endangered mammal?

Undaunted, I corresponded with Randy, Wang Ding, and the other members of the 'wobbly coalition' about their plans for actually pushing forward beyond debate, and finally carrying out some conservation action for the baiji. I was restless and enthusiastic—what could I contribute to the project? Maybe ZSL could help to promote public awareness and raise some funds to support the baiji recovery programme, as well as channel whatever international expertise was needed to help make the project succeed.

But maybe I wasn't the only concerned, frustrated idealist out there after all. Randy suggested that other people had apparently also been thinking along the same lines. He informed me that an independent organization had recently been formed that was dedicated to baiji conservation, and more generally the restoration of the Yangtze ecosystem. It was called the baiji.org Foundation, and was run by a Swiss businessman called August Pfluger. This small organization had already made significant progress over the previous months in getting the baiji back onto the international conservation radar. It had recently convened a workshop in Wuhan that had addressed what was needed to try to save both the baiji and the Yangtze finless porpoise, and had done wonders in re-energizing the jaded Western conservationists who had been involved with the project. Now it was planning to take the next essential step: to carry out the first range-wide baiji survey for almost a decade. In fact, the foundation was now committed to this second project, having signed a legal survey contract with the Institute of Hydrobiology. It was planned that the survey would be carried out during the Yangtze's low-water season, from autumn to spring, when the river would be narrower and any surviving baiji would be easier to detect. The survey had to be rigorous, systematic, and intensive: nothing could be left to chance. This might be the world's last hope to do something to save the baiji from extinction.

And it did still seem that there might be some hope to do something. Although the last baiji surveys had been carried out between 1997 and 1999, there had been several more recent reports of baiji that suggested there must still be a remnant population left in the river, which could become the focus of an intensive conservation programme. In November 2001, the carcass of a pregnant female baiji was found washed up near the city of Zhenjiang, between Nanjing and Shanghai in the lower stretches of the river. Several months later, on 22 May 2002, a live baiji was photographed in the protected reserve section of the main river near Tongling. Although this was the last authenticated record of a baiji, several more recent unverified sightings had also been reported to the Baiji Research Group in Wuhan by fishermen employed by the Baiji Monitoring Network in the Honghu and Tongling reserves, with singletons, pairs, and occasionally even groups of three animals being seen in both river sections. The preponderance of reports from these two regions reflected a lack of concerted monitoring effort elsewhere along the river, rather then necessarily indicating an absence of baiji in other sections of the Yangtze into the start of the twenty-first century. What's more, several of these recent reports were of adults with calves, suggesting that the last few surviving baiji were still somehow managing to breed—so perhaps pollution hadn't played much of a part in their decline after all. The official party-line held by the Chinese researchers was that there were 'fewer than a hundred' baiji left,[4] and the species was officially listed as Critically Endangered, the highest category of threat, by the IUCN. But nobody thought that it was extinct.

The 2004 Wuhan workshop had concluded that, although the debate over whether any captured baiji would be sent by the Chinese to the Wuhan dolphinarium or to the Tian'e-Zhou oxbow had still not been resolved, the IHB's efforts to establish and maintain a breeding population of finless porpoises at the oxbow had eventually proved successful. At long last, the international participants at this latest meeting now accepted that the semi-natural reserve represented an 'adequate' *ex situ* environment for freshwater cetaceans, and they finally seemed to be prepared to support translocations of baiji to the reserve as an ultimately necessary 'emergency' conservation strategy—although only as a key short-term goal in a longer-term plan to release baiji back into the main river 'when the threats have decreased and the natural environment has improved'.[5] The baiji.org Foundation's survey plans were therefore aimed not only to establish how many baiji were left in the main Yangtze channel, but also to try to identify any geographical 'hotspots' along the river where small populations of baiji might still occur regularly, and where animals could be caught for the recovery programme with the greatest ease, safety, and efficiency. Based on the distribution of informal baiji reports since 2000, the Chinese participants suggested that the three river sections of Honghu, Balijiang, and Tongling might be the best bets for finding and capturing these last few surviving baiji.

However, August had repeatedly maintained that the baiji.org Foundation did not intend to be actively involved in these planned baiji capture attempts. Furthermore, before any captures could be carried out, the international participants at this latest workshop were adamant that a series of infrastructural and technical improvements had to be met at the reserve. The on-site research facility at Tian'e-Zhou still lacked any laboratory, veterinary, or support equipment, or even an internet connection. A water-quality monitoring programme had to be established, and a new analysis of the number of dolphins and porpoises that the reserve's resources could actually support also needed to be conducted urgently. In particular, a series of dolphin holding pens had to be constructed near the shore of the oxbow, in which any translocated baiji individuals could be kept for a period of up to a couple of weeks, in order to ensure that they were healthy and eating normally before their 'soft-release' into the reserve. And there was more. In addition to all of the pressing requirements at the oxbow, there was still worryingly little understanding among the international community about how to actually carry out a series of

well-coordinated and maximally effective baiji capture efforts—
although it was clearly imperative that captures to establish a baiji
population at Tian'e-Zhou had to be started straight away. It was
all very well finally giving the green light for the capture project,
but without a much better understanding of exactly how it could
be carried out, nothing was going to happen. Would the capture
efforts be conducted straight after the survey, or would there be
a delay? What kind of international training and expertise was
required? Did anyone have any idea what would be the best way of
actually catching a baiji? And—maybe most importantly of all—
how much would it all cost, and where was this funding going to
come from? The Japanese money that had been donated to China
a few years earlier to support the capture programme seemed to
have disappeared into the woodwork, and so we couldn't rely
on any funds becoming available from official Chinese sources:
it all had to be raised from scratch and to be tightly managed.
Pulling all of this information together wasn't exactly the most
glamorous job in the world, but it was integral to finally getting some action in the world of baiji conservation. At least it
was something that I could really get my teeth into. Juggling my
'official' work commitments, I established Yangtze River dolphin
conservation as a formal ZSL project, under the organization's
'Biodiversity and Macroecology' and 'Marine and Freshwater
conservation' themes. Then I started to work with Randy and his
colleagues to make some headway with all of the project's baffling
logistics.

~

When I first heard about the baiji.org Foundation, the survey was
planned for March 2005.[6] But when March arrived, there was no
survey. Instead, the foundation organized 'BaijiSwim '05': a team
of athletes carrying out relays for three hours in the Limmat River
in Zurich, apparently to 'show solidarity with endangered Asian
river dolphins' to the watching media.[7] Wang Ding was flown in
from China to attend and comment to the press. What was all this

about? Now the survey couldn't be carried out until the autumn of 2005 at the earliest, because the Yangtze was about to enter its high-water season. August was, apparently, a wealthy philanthropist, the heir to a trucking fortune.[8] He was, he said, investing his own money into an eleventh-hour project to pull the baiji back from the brink. Time was of the essence: so if August was really going to spend his personal fortune on saving the baiji, then why was he messing around like this, and jeopardizing the success of the recovery programme with unnecessary delays? All of a sudden, something about the baiji.org Foundation didn't quite make sense. It was time to get in touch and find out what was going on.

Randy told me that the international project manager of the foundation, a woman called Leigh Barrett, was also based in the UK. She seemed like the most obvious person to contact to begin with. I dropped her a line, letting her know about my interest in trying to help conserve the baiji and that it would be great to meet up to discuss project ideas and further opportunities. Leigh came down to London to meet me, and I was greeted by a very attractive young lady, a year younger than me, with a vibrant personality and an extremely efficient nature.

Like me, Leigh had learnt about the plight of the baiji by chance, when it was mentioned in an environmental lecture at university on the state of the Yangtze. Like me, she had rapidly become obsessed, as though a switch had been flicked inside her head. Straight after the lecture she had researched all that she could about the species, and became fired by disbelief that so little was known in the wider world about the baiji and the apparent lack of action to conserve it. She felt as though people were giving up without even trying. Over the following months, she contacted Randy and the various other personalities that I had also got to know. A year passed by with despondent responses about the potential success of a capture operation from the international community, no replies from messages sent to the Baiji Research Group, and a frightening lack of interest in the subject from members of the international media. Natural history

film-makers she contacted claimed that the subject was too difficult to film and that general commissioners disliked conservation
films—documentaries were there to entertain, not inform. In the
end, she took time out from her job with the RSPB Film Unit to
visit China in February 2003.

One of the first people Leigh met when she arrived at the
dolphinarium was Wei Zhuo, the research group's chief ecologist,
who had seen more than 110 baiji in the wild over the years during
the course of his research. She explained, using a mixture of pidgin
English, sign language, and diagrams, that she wanted to help
raise international awareness for the plight of the baiji, and was
greatly concerned by the apparent lack of conservation action. Wei
became very interested. He was surprisingly outspoken about his
frustration with the lack of concerted baiji conservation efforts;
however, it seemed clear that any efforts to save the baiji could
only happen with greater international support. Leigh spent the
following two weeks travelling up and down the Yangtze by ferry
conducting her own informal baiji survey, before returning empty-
handed to the UK. She continued to stay in regular contact with
Wei over the following year, and eventually took out a bank loan
and paid for him to come over and stay with her in the UK in
January 2004, to work around her day job on developing plans
to raise awareness and set up an international fund-raising organization for baiji. During his visit, Wei talked about the baiji
capture operation that the Baiji Research Group were planning in
conjunction with the Japanese government. Leigh suggested that
the IUCN Cetacean Specialist Group should offer some advice to
the Chinese on how to capture animals safely, but found that the
proposed Chinese-Japanese capture was news to them. In fact, the
latest international baiji workshop, which had been convened in
2003, hadn't even recommended conducting another survey.

And then Leigh met August. He first got in touch with her
to explain that he had heard about her work from Randy, and
thought that they shared the same vision. He explained that he
was also very interested in communicating the baiji issue to a

wider audience, and setting up some kind of baiji foundation. By the end of their first two-hour conversation, Leigh thought she had finally found a kindred spirit, somebody else who was also appalled by the lack of dynamism in the international community, and who grasped the concept that time was on the verge of running out for the baiji: action was needed, not words. August, it turned out, was a former journalist who had covered one of the baiji surveys of the late 1990s. He told her that he had stayed in Cabin Number One on Boat Number One during the survey. We would both hear this story many times more. He told Leigh about the highly successful goodwill social projects he had worked on in the past, his unfulfilled interest in baiji, and that he was finally in a position to do something for baiji conservation, by investing a large amount of his own funds into the issue. Although he was more hesitant about the potential success of a baiji capture operation, it was clear that he and Leigh were trying to achieve similar communication and fund-raising goals: he had the money and she had the energy to see it through. Leigh couldn't quite figure him out; he seemed genuine enough, but she had difficulty understanding why someone would invest such a large proportion of their estate into such a supposedly doomed conservation effort. However, she couldn't think of any possible gains that could be made out of the baiji issue, and so she decided not to look a gift horse in the mouth. It made sense to cooperate.

The purpose of the new foundation began to clarify: they could better coordinate future workshops, and encourage international experts to advise on and support safe capture techniques for the eventual establishment of the breeding programme that would ultimately be required to save the species. Wang Ding was keen to support their initiative, and Randy became a board director, lending credibility to the foundation. It received its legal status in August 2004, and the workshop on 'Conservation of the Baiji and Yangtze Finless Porpoise' took place in December. Although August talked about offices in London, and the foundation's offi-cial address was in Zurich, Leigh ended up running things from her home in Bedfordshire. However, at first it all looked like it really was going to be the brave new initiative that she had dreamt about, and the workshop was a success. First of all, the international participants visited the Tian'e-Zhou oxbow, and this visit drastically changed their opinions about the reserve's viability and suitability. This new generation of advisers, who had mostly not attended the workshops of the 1980s and 1990s, had made judgement calls about the oxbow based on information that had filtered down to them from other informants, without having seen the site for themselves. The participants had originally been persuaded to attend the workshop only to advise on the planned Chinese capture operations without willing to be more actively involved themselves, but now they began to realize that it might still be possible to do something to help the baiji after all. Although outstanding problems still remained apparent—for example, the participants were openly served fish that had been illegally caught in the oxbow when they visited Tian'e-Zhou—in general everyone became far more optimistic than they had been for years. It was decided that conducting a survey was, in fact, the critical next step, which would first require an initial pilot study to address the best survey techniques that were required in the Yangtze's specialized conditions. August stated that he would pay for the survey, members of the international community would manage the biological and scientific side of the study, while Leigh would be in charge of communications and logistics.

It had all seemed so positive to start off with; but soon cracks started to show. Funds did not become available to establish the international conservation committee that had been recommended at Wuhan, and the workshop participants met with mysterious delays when trying to have their travel expenses reimbursed, in some cases being left severely out of pocket. And although Leigh had by now given up her job at the RSPB to focus full time on the baiji, her new legally binding contractual employment agreements with the foundation kept being reneged; she would go for months without being paid, and her salary was often only half the agreed amount when it arrived at all. She became increasingly frustrated; questions about integrity and genuine interest were becoming harder and harder to ignore. What was going on? But she had invested far too much to simply walk away now—and at least the international community was working towards a proper baiji survey for the first time in almost a decade.

At the end of our first meeting, Leigh turned to me and smiled. 'Whatever you do, keep hold of your optimism. Please don't become bitter and cynical.' I thought that she was joking.

~

Would it have been cynical to wonder whether the recovery programme really had any chance of saving the baiji, though? The species had been cripplingly rare for decades, and although the official Chinese population estimate stated that there were 'fewer than a hundred', in reality there were probably only a handful of animals left at most, which would be incredibly difficult to find, let alone capture with safety. Was it in fact already too late to attempt an eleventh-hour rescue for the species—was the baiji actually 'doomed' to extinction?

When species experience severe declines, and are reduced to tiny remnant populations consisting of only a few surviving individuals, it is certainly true that they face a much higher risk of extinction even if the external pressures that have brought about the decline in the first place—in the baiji's case, rolling hooks, electrofishing, and boat collisions—remain the same. Such tiny populations can be wiped out almost accidentally by chance events— a local disaster, say, such as a particularly bad chemical spill in one section of the river where the last surviving baiji are hiding out—which would not be quite so catastrophic if the species still occurred in higher numbers and across a wider geographical area. If the species only occurs at an extremely low population density, then the last few survivors may not even be able to find any other individuals with which to breed. However, an insidious new factor also emerges to threaten tiny populations of endangered species if the survivors *are* lucky enough to find a mate: they are prone to inbreeding depression.

All animals inherit two sets of genetic alleles—forms of a gene, the coding blocks that provide the necessary information for generating a new organism—one from each of their parents. Under normal conditions, these two sets often comprise different pairs of alleles for the same gene. For example, if your mother has blue eyes and your father has green eyes, you may inherit one blue-eye allele and one green-eye allele at the genetic position (or locus) for eye colour. This condition of having two different alleles at a locus is termed being heterozygous. Some of these alleles have combinative effects, meaning that both alleles together will determine the appearance and structure of the offspring. Alternately, other alleles are either dominant or recessive, meaning that only the dominant allele will be expressed; the recessive allele instead remains a secret presence, lurking away in the genome but never making itself known. The key problem that leads to inbreeding depression is that many of the recessive alleles which we all carry about with us in our genomes will actually produce harmful effects if they are ever able to express themselves—but they have not been weeded out of the population, because their effects are rarely noticed for natural selection to work on if they are paired with dominant alleles under most normal circumstances.

However, if a population is reduced to only a few surviving individuals, the picture changes. These animals may already be more related to one another than would be expected by chance, and, more importantly, their offspring will all have to mate either with each other or with close relatives if they want to mate at all, simply because there is so little choice of available partners left. This means that far more genes will become homozygous instead of heterozygous: they will consist of two pairs of the same allele rather than two different alleles. And that's where the problems caused by recessive, deleterious alleles come in: they remain secret no longer, but instead finally get expressed.

So inbreeding can lead to serious problems for a population that has already become endangered due to other factors. Not only will the limited amount of remaining genetic variation make the tiny population less able to respond to environmental changes and variability, parasites, and diseases, and to recover from natural disasters, but inbreeding depression will also seriously affect its ability to recover at all. Problems caused by recessive alleles can impact all aspects of an organism's biology, but the most prominent problems are those associated with reproductive fitness. For example, inbred organisms will typically produce fewer offspring, which may have lower body weights and higher levels of infant mortality; they may lack the behavioural abilities to find mates and act as good parents; and they may have lower milk yields, slower growth trajectories, and shorter lifespans. These internal pressures will make small populations more and more non-viable, and the harmful effects of inbreeding depression are far more likely to be expressed in harsher, more stressful wild environments rather than in animals kept in captivity. At some point, scientists predict, an irreversible threshold will be reached. The population growth rate will switch from positive to negative, and the species will experience a so-called 'mutational meltdown'. It will slide, irreversibly, towards extinction.

Could we make any predictions about how rare the baiji had to become before inbreeding depression would take over, and negate the possibility of salvaging the species through an intensive recovery programme even despite our best efforts? Some scientists thought so. At the 1986 Wuhan workshop, a lot of consideration had gone into exploring these demographic and genetic questions surrounding the baiji's minimum viable population size. The official workshop report contained papers which specifically tried to estimate how many animals would be required for a breeding programme in order to retain the genetic health and evolutionary potential of the species. Based on the existing principles of conservation genetics, Katherine Ralls, a researcher based at the National Zoological Park in Washington, DC, suggested that the

semi-captive population should have a number of founder individuals equal to an effective population size (that is, the number
of animals able to contribute genetic information to the next
generation) of at least twenty to twenty-five baiji.[9]Subsequent
workshop reports also operated on the idea that around this
many baiji would be taken out of the wild to form the nucleus
of the breeding programme.[10]But now the likelihood of finding
and catching anything like this number of animals from the wild
seemed like a fantasy. There were probably even not that many
baiji left in the world. At best, we hoped to have a founder population of six, maybe eight animals; I couldn't imagine ever locating
any more baiji than that in the river even with months or years of
intensive searching. So did this mean that there was no hope after
all for the breeding programme to succeed?

It is possible that the remaining baiji population was in such
dire genetic straits that it was already too late to do anything
to save them. However, a wider look at a range of conservation
success stories that have brought other species back from the
brink shows that this viewpoint is actually more pessimistic and
limited than its adherence to the 'hard science' of genetics might
make it seem. Whereas population geneticists have variously suggested that a standard minimum viable population size might
have to consist of 50, 250, 1,000, or even as many as 5,000 individuals, many species have been miraculously salvaged through
intensive conservation efforts involving desperately fewer numbers
of founders. The most remarkable of these success stories, the
recovery of the Mauritius kestrel and the Chatham Island black
robin, have now passed into conservation legend.

By the 1970s, the Mauritius kestrel was regarded as the rarest
bird in the world, with a global population of only two breeding
pairs plus a couple of other non-breeding individuals. Its massive
population decline had been driven by deforestation and habitat
fragmentation, organochloride pesticide contamination, and the
effects of introduced species such as mongooses, monkeys, deer,
and pigs, which ate the bird's eggs and changed the island's forests

into inhospitable tangled scrub. A captive breeding programme initiated by the International Council for Bird Preservation was attempted but went nowhere. The kestrel's prospects looked bleak. Norman Myers, one of the most prominent conservationists of the day, wrote that 'we might abandon the Mauritius kestrel to its all-but-inevitable fate, and utilize the funds to proffer stronger support for any of the hundreds of threatened bird species that are more likely to survive.'[11] Then a young, bloody-minded Welshman named Carl Jones appeared on the scene. He had originally been sent out to Mauritius to close down the failed kestrel project, but instead, through years of hard work throughout the 1980s—involving clutch and brood manipulation, nest guarding, supplementary feeding and predator control for the few remaining wild birds, and much more intensive captive breeding—he managed to turn it around. Although recent studies have shown that genetic diversity, measured as both allelic diversity and heterozygosity, fell by over 50 per cent as a result of the massive population 'bottleneck' through which the kestrel went in the 1970s—a loss without precedent in the bird's earlier evolutionary history—the species managed to recover astoundingly well. By the early 1990s, a self-sustaining wild population of kestrels had been established, and today there are more than 800 wild birds on Mauritius, all of which are believed to be descended from a single wild breeding pair in 1974.

The story of the Chatham Island black robin is very similar. The global population of this tiny bird also experienced a precipitous crash during the twentieth century, again due largely to the introduction of exotic predators to its isolated island home. By 1980, there were only five birds left, three males and two females, restricted to the 1-square-kilometre island of Little Mangere. Only one of the females, 'Old Blue', laid fertile eggs, but she was about twice the age at which robins were thought to be reproductively viable. However, an intensive, hands-on management programme similar to that employed for the Mauritius kestrel once again led to success. Old Blue did what she had to, and almost single-handedly saved her species from extinction; all of the black robins alive today are descended from Old Blue and her mate, 'Old Yellow'. Ten years later, there were 116 Chatham Island black robins, and today there are almost 300. Old Blue, now the biggest celebrity that the Chathams have ever produced, is commemorated by a special plaque on display in the archipelago's airport.

Maybe island birds are not a good analogue for other kinds of species, some geneticists have suggested; maybe they share some fundamental biological differences related to their original colonization of remote islands and their subsequent isolated ecological histories, some purging of deleterious alleles that could have made them better able to withstand inbreeding and population bottlenecks? It's always possible. However, similar 'miraculous' population recoveries from far below the predicted minimum viable level have also been widely documented in a range of other species, many of which share far more in common with the baiji. If you're interested in vulnerable large mammals with slow reproductive cycles, look no further than Père David's deer, the Hainan subspecies of Eld's deer, or the European bison, all of which have been successfully brought back through intensive conservation management from only a handful of founder individuals. And for an even more obvious comparison, how about the northern elephant seal, which was reduced by massive overhunting to a population of only 20–30 individuals by the 1890s, but which has now recovered to over 100,000 animals?

If population geneticists think that inbreeding depression represents such a major problem to species recovery, how have all of these conservation success stories been possible? The answer is one of probability. It is certainly true that population declines will increase the likelihood of inbreeding depression, as a result of deleterious recessive alleles being inherited from two closely related parents. However, we still know so little about the genetics of endangered species that it is impossible to predict exactly which recessive alleles will lead to inbreeding depression, and whether any of these alleles will actually become homozygous in any given circumstance. To use the appropriate scientific terminology, inbreeding depression is a stochastic rather than deterministic process. So, our attempts to save the baiji may have already been overruled by the effects of inbreeding depression, or, alternatively, they may not. We simply have no way of telling. Inbreeding depression is a calculated risk, but one that can only be calculated very loosely at best. To me at least, this was not a reason to give up before conservation efforts for the baiji had even begun.

Indeed, the uncertainties surrounding the significance of inbreeding depression in conservation may go even deeper. In 1994, Graeme Caughley wrote an influential paper entitled 'Directions in conservation biology', in which he identified a fundamental dichotomy within conservation science.[12] This was, in many ways, a more applied equivalent of C. P. Snow's famous 'two cultures', or Isaiah Berlin's literary and philosophical metaphor about the hedgehog and the fox. Caughley suggested that conservation consists of two separate paradigms: in Caughley's words, these are the 'small-population' paradigm, which deals with the effect of smallness on the persistence of a population, and the 'declining-population' paradigm, which deals instead with the cause of the smallness and its cure. These two paradigms have attracted very different kinds of research attention. The small-population paradigm has become the focus for what some might consider to be a more 'scientific' research approach, because it allows conservation problems to be considered within a single theoretical framework, which permits the rigorous mathematical investigation of issues such as inbreeding. As a result, this paradigm dominated much of the science of conservation biology following its inception in the 1970s and 1980s. In contrast, the declining-population paradigm requires conservation problems to be considered on a more case-by-case basis, since the specific declines experienced by different populations, although frequently influenced by a range of more general factors, are ultimately all unique events. However, as Caughley and subsequent authors such as Alan Rabinowitz have noted, it is the declining-population paradigm that is ultimately relevant to most real conservation problems, which have to be overcome on the ground by those people interested in protecting species from extinction; in contrast, the small-population paradigm has only a tenuous relevance to such practical challenges—it is almost completely removed from the real world. In the critical words of Alan Rabinowitz, the proponents of the small-population paradigm 'do their field work in the laboratory, in captive-holding facilities, and at the computer'.[13] While this paradigm has its theoretical benefits, these authors argue, it has yet to actually contribute anything significant to the actual conservation of endangered species.

~

So, if saving the baiji from even a handful of surviving individuals was still an option, then there was no excuse not to try—and the extreme urgency of the situation left no excuse not to make it the top conservation priority. If this wasn't enough reason to pull out all the stops, consideration of the baiji's evolutionary history provided an even greater incentive to fight its imminent extinction. In the words of George Orwell, 'all animals are equal, but some animals are more equal than others.' The baiji was one of the world's few species of river dolphin, the survivor of an ancient group of mammals that had once lived in the world's oceans before the evolution of modern-day marine dolphins. Although Gerrit Miller originally placed the baiji in the same family of mammals as the Amazon River dolphin, he noted that the two species differed in a number of major respects—the curve of the beak, the shape of the fins, and the structure of the skull. Zhou Kaiya, who had access to complete baiji specimens rather than just a skull and a photograph, expanded this list of differences, citing other key divergences in the internal organs and teeth. Zhou suggested that the baiji was so distinct from any other river dolphins in its structure and appearance that in fact it should be classified in its own unique family, the Lipotidae.

In the past 500 years, since European explorers, missionaries, and colonists began spreading out around the world in earnest, humans have wreaked unspeakable amounts of damage on the natural world. This is the period of history which saw the disappearance of the dodo, the icon of extinction, together with literally hundreds of other unique mammals, birds, and other species. However, in all this time, only four other entire mammal families have also died out. The nesophontids or West Indian island-shrews, a group of tiny primitive insectivores isolated on the Caribbean islands of Cuba, Hispaniola, Puerto Rico, and the Caymans since the time of the dinosaurs, were probably wiped out by the arrival of black rats, accidental stowaways on the ships of Columbus and later explorers. The giant koala lemurs and sloth lemurs of Madagascar, which may have reached weights of over 75 kilos—far larger than any living lemurs— disappeared around four or five hundred years ago, as their forests were progressively invaded and destroyed by Malagasy settlers who had reached the island over a millennium earlier. It's possible that stories reported by a seventeenth-century French governor of Madagascar of a strange animal called the 'tretretre-tre', which had the face of a man and was around the size of a 2-year-old calf, and which would apparently flee into the forest upon seeing humans, might represent the last of the island's giant lemurs, although we can never know for sure. The only other entire mammal family to have been wiped out in the last few hundred years is the extraordinary thylacine or Tasmanian tiger, which superficially resembled a dog but which was actually the world's largest predatory marsupial, and which was heavily persecuted for allegedly killing sheep—although it now seems that the sheep losses resulted instead from feral dog attacks and bad farm management, with the thylacine used as a scapegoat for insurance purposes. The last known wild thylacine was shot in 1930, and the last captive animal (a female allegedly called Benjamin) died a lonely death in Hobart Zoo six years later.

The baiji's combination of unique evolutionary history and extreme threat therefore placed it in desperate need of conservation attention. Its ancestors had lived and evolved for 20 million years in the Yangtze Basin, independent from all other cetaceans. In contrast, the Yangtze population of finless porpoise probably had less than one million years of unique evolutionary heritage, and was closely related to finless porpoises in the seas all around Asia and also to a far greater number of other species of porpoises and dolphins. The disappearance of either animal would be a tragedy, but the disappearance of the baiji would represent a far greater loss to global biodiversity. Quite simply, if the baiji died out, there would be nothing like it left on earth.

～

Our preparations moved forward slowly. Qualified cetacean veterinarians came on board the baiji project from SeaWorld and the Ocean Park Corporation in Hong Kong, two organizations with great experience in handling, managing, and caring for captive dolphins. Some of our successes came from the most unexpected sources. Jim McBain at SeaWorld entered the world of high strangeness, obtaining Pentagon approval for the US Navy to donate their comprehensive construction plans for permanent floating dolphin holding pools, which they used in San Diego for training dolphins to conduct military exercises. These would be the perfect blueprint for the baiji holding pools required at the Tian'e-Zhou oxbow, with the specific pool dimensions able to be modified according to the project's needs. However, given the extreme rarity of the baiji and the previous experiences of Chinese researchers, each capture attempt was likely to take up to two months to aim for any chance of success—and we would need a series of attempts to build up a viable *ex situ* population of dolphins. All of the best dolphin behavioural, capture, and veterinary specialists led busy lives with many other commitments. Did anybody have that kind of time to donate?

More fundamental hurdles also soon became apparent. I learnt that the relationship between August and the rest of the international community had become worryingly strained. The survey was apparently now scheduled for November, but by the summer of 2005 nobody had received any confirmation from August as to whether anything was actually going to happen. Leigh was taking a break from the foundation out of sheer frustration, after several months of not having been paid any salary, and August seemed to be maintaining a complete silence with everybody. Who was actually going to be involved in the survey, if it ever even took place? Would it include anybody with prior experience in surveying freshwater cetaceans in a rigorous way? What would the results of this secretive project actually be able to tell us, if no one with any outside knowledge was seemingly going to be involved or even consulted? The situation was ridiculous, and because the survey was supposed to provide the rationale for any future capture and relocation work, it had become very difficult to have meaningful discussions and plan sensibly for the subsequent steps needed in the baiji recovery programme.

This was a major problem in itself, but it was made much worse: for some reason, very few people in the international community seemed to be prepared to even consider the long-term logistics of the baiji recovery programme before the results of the survey were in. It seemed obvious to me that we had to be ready to act immediately to initiate the recovery programme as soon as we knew how many baiji were left in the river—otherwise we would waste even more time trying to start from scratch with fund-raising and planning, delaying the desperately needed project even further. But there was a perverse resistance among the international community to thinking beyond the immediate next step. So we were in limbo: for some reason, nobody seemed prepared to do anything until the survey was completed, but it was looking increasingly as though there might never actually be a survey at all.

And even this was not the worst of it. As well as helping with the coordination of the recovery programme, I also started sounding

out all of the major conservation organizations and other funding bodies about their potential willingness to help support this
critical project. Surely it would be possible to persuade them to
get involved once we presented them with our plans: after all, how
could they not, in all good conscience? But an alarming pattern
soon became very clear. Oh yes, every organization I contacted
was so very supportive and so very concerned. We understand how
crucial it is that a solution be found as soon as possible, and we
admire the work you are doing, I was told. We strongly agree with
the severity of the situation with the baiji . . . we understand the
need for a breeding programme . . . we very much support the work
that you do . . . your work is obviously extremely urgent . . . oh, but.
We don't accept unsolicited applications. At the moment we don't
see any immediate funding possibilities but I am very thankful
for the introduction to this important work. I will remember it
when further investigating funding opportunities and also discuss
it further with my colleagues. I am afraid that it will not be
possible to give you any further feedback on your application.
One of the major conservation organizations, who shall remain
nameless, told me bluntly over the phone that 'dollar for dollar,
it's not worth trying to save the Yangtze River dolphin'.

Our only victory came from a most unlikely source, as I too
experienced a brush with the world of high strangeness. After a
hard day's work filling out yet another funding proposal, Leigh
and I needed a break in a nearby pub—where we found the
Radio 1 presenter Chris Moyles already enjoying a drink. With
thoughts of baiji fresh in her mind (and the help of a little Dutch
courage and a lot of chiding from me), Leigh went over and told
Chris all about our conservation efforts. The next morning the
nation woke up to several minutes of airplay about the need to
save the Yangtze River dolphin.

The international baiji group, Randy's 'wobbly coalition',
seemed to support my efforts. Congratulations on pulling all this
together, I was told; this is what has long been needed but for some

reason no one took the initiative. You turning up on the baiji scene was about the best thing that has happened for that poor species in a long while. I guess flattery is as good a way to get people to do things as any. But as time went on, I noticed that none of them seemed particularly keen to do that much to help, either. The problem with the baiji up to now is that no one really took ownership or had time to devote to fund-raising, they told me. It is a vicious circle: no one is paid to work on this, so they don't have time to write proposals which would ensure that they get paid in the future. And everybody is already so busy with too many projects to take on any extra. Funny; I managed to be holding down my research position and still finding the time to work on the baiji project. After all, what was actually the top priority here? 'Are you getting frustrated by people's lack of initiative to help you apply for funds?' one of the group sheepishly asked after several months.

I was exhausted by all of the paperwork, the funding deadlines, and the dismissive attitudes that I met from all sides. It was like banging my head against a brick wall. One potential donor just wrote: 'This looks like a good project. Good luck. Let me know how it goes.' And, yet, the harsh reality that nobody seemed prepared to fund our baiji recovery programme—the only strategy that seemed to have even a fighting chance of saving the baiji—contrasted sharply with the publicity provided by many of these same organizations, which suggested that active work to save the baiji was already being carried out. To take one example of many, WWF was publicly committed to conserving the world's endangered river dolphins,[14] and according to the WWF-China website, the Yangtze River dolphin was already one of the few 'popular' species which was the focus of almost all of the resources available for research, while lesser-known species and their habitats may decline or disappear with little fanfare.[15] Although I had now realized that research and action were two very different things, to the concerned outsider it must have seemed as though these organizations were already doing all that they could to fight the baiji's extinction.

~

It was now clear that the survey wasn't going to take place in 2005 at all, for reasons that remained unclear if August really was able to finance the project easily with his own money. Despite all of the hard work over the past few months, we had still made pitiful progress in achieving any of the goals required to provide the recovery programme with even a slim chance of success. There was a desperate need to give the project's flagging momentum a major boost, and to break the stalemate that had unwittingly been reached.

A year had now passed since the workshop in Wuhan, and it was beginning to look as though we had to try something new to re-energize the group. The obvious suggestion was to host another meeting, as soon as possible, but this time on a much smaller scale. This could provide a focus for finalizing a robust budget and timeframe for the recovery programme. Would it really be cripplingly, prohibitively expensive, as I had been led to believe? Given the deterioration of the relationship with August, the meeting could also constitute a politically expedient bridge-building exercise between the baiji.org Foundation and the other participants, as well as providing an opportunity to find out what was actually going on with the survey and offering the hand of international assistance. I was reluctant to be involved with organizing yet *another* baiji meeting, after all of the previous gatherings from the 1980s onwards that had ultimately generated no practical actions to conserve the species, but which had nevertheless been seen as successful accomplishments by the international community. Some of the other members of the baiji group felt the same way: enough talking had already been done, and we could not afford to simply revisit what had already been agreed and discussed in 2004 at Wuhan. However, some sort of action was now urgently required. If the meeting finally achieved this practical outcome—to get the Tian'e-Zhou oxbow up and running as a baiji reserve, and the capture operations under way before the Yangtze floods in 2006—then I was keen to support it.

Of course the meeting wasn't as simple to organize as I had naively assumed. First of all there were heated arguments about the most appropriate agenda for the meeting, and then further fractious exchanges over the most suitable venue. Trying to coordinate it all was like herding cats; Leigh suggested that I should get a job as a UN peacekeeper when it was all over. London and Hong Kong both had their benefits, but eventually San Diego was decided upon, because our meeting could be tagged onto the end of the 16th Biennial Conference on the Biology of Marine Mammals, which was being held in the city in December and which many of the key players would already be attending. Once again Jim McBain came up trumps, and provided a free venue complete with catering at SeaWorld. But it turned out that my troubles were far from over. As usual, I had ended up bearing the brunt of the fund-raising. With no warning and little explanation, a few days before the meeting was due to start our main financial backer decided to drop out, leaving everyone with non-refundable pre-booked tickets. In full damage-limitation mode and extremely aware of the fundamental setback that this latest mess could give to a unified baiji recovery programme, I attempted all that I could to persuade the funders to reverse their decision, while trying to publicly downplay the problem that I had no option but to resolve. Finally, the day before everyone was due to fly out to San Diego, I managed to persuade the backers to change their minds and provide the necessary funding after all.

The meeting itself went as well as we could have hoped; inevitably, though, the plans to actually carry out any baiji conservation met with yet another setback. We had hoped that the meeting would provide an opportunity for August to agree on a formal start date for the survey, and we were all under the impression that it would now be going ahead in March 2006. Instead though the survey was pushed back once more, to the following autumn, when apparently everything would finally be ready. I told August that it is time delays like this that kill endangered species, but it was to no avail. Then, after the workshop was over, I had to deal with reimbursing everybody's travel expenses. Among his expenses, one of the most senior members of the group sent me a receipt for US$1.

Frankly I was beginning to get a bit tired of all this.

6

THE POLITICS
OF EXTINCTION

*One searches in despair for signs that the lessons
learned in conservation efforts with one species might
commonly be applied to the conservation efforts for
any other species.*

Noel Snyder and Helen Snyder
The California Condor: A Saga of Natural History and Conservation

Why, exactly, was it seemingly proving to be impossible to
motivate anyone to try to do something—anything—to
help conserve the baiji? The reasons for this protracted delay are
inevitably complex, and, it seems, a series of different factors may
have all played a part.

To start off with, the planned baiji recovery programme
involved multiple interdependent organizations and participants,
from several different countries. The logistical minefield that
this situation presented certainly limited the possibility of quick
success, especially for something so delicately balanced, politically sensitive, and prone to misunderstanding as a large-scale
international conservation project. Developing a meaningful collaboration with China—given the substantial problems faced
by the international workshop participants during the 1980s

and 1990s over the best strategy for saving the baiji, potential misappropriation of funding, and what was even meant by the term 'conservation'—made the challenge even greater. 'Dealing with China then was almost like dealing with North Korea,' I was later told by one of the American participants. 'There were no good pressure points.'

However, suggesting that baiji conservation failed on purely practical grounds, because it was simply too difficult for Western- ers to work in China when there was still a realistic chance to save the species, is very far from the truth. Other international con- servation collaborations have proved far more successful at imple- menting active Chinese biodiversity projects, even during the same time period in which the baiji project failed to get off the ground. The most obvious example of this is the giant panda conservation programme, a collaboration between WWF and the Chinese Min- istry of Forestry that started in 1980 in Wolong Nature Reserve in the mountains of Sichuan. This collaboration aimed to estab- lish scientifically robust field studies that would permit a better understanding of the behaviour and ecology of pandas in the wild, together with increased protection of the panda's natural habitat, and the development of an *ex situ* breeding facility. Even though the early years of panda conservation in China faced serious chal- lenges and setbacks—as exhaustively described by George Schaller in *The Last Panda*—at least something actually happened on the ground in China, which is more than the baiji recovery programme ever really got. The panda was the flagship species of the WWF— they *had* to make the project succeed, despite all of the problems they were faced with. It feels like too much of an excuse to then suggest that it was impossible to work with the Chinese system to carry out any other conservation collaborations. Instead, the evidence speaks for itself. The international baiji recovery pro- gramme had never happened because the international players hadn't done enough to try to make it happen.

Instead, the persistent time delays that plagued baiji conser- vation efforts seem to have been driven by other factors. One certainty is that many of the international researchers involved with the baiji project over the years were extremely reluctant to make firm conservation decisions on the basis of the very incomplete biological and ecological data that have been available. Despite the series of surveys that recorded observations of wild dolphins in the Yangtze, and the intensive studies of Qi Qi and the other captive animals held at Wuhan over the past few decades, the baiji has always remained one of the most enigmatic and poorly understood of all the world's cetaceans. Because it was so distantly related to any other river dolphins, and the Yangtze ecosystem is so different from the Amazon, Ganges, or other river systems in which freshwater cetaceans are found, it was difficult to make meaningful inferences and fill in any of the numerous gaps in the scientific understanding of the species. This great uncertainty over even basic facts about the baiji greatly complicated all of the attempts to decide on appropriate conservation actions, which all advocated highly risky and intensive approaches that had never been tried before for any kind of dolphin.

However, it was also clear that the species was very rare even as early as the 1980s, and was continuing to decline precipitously. This meant that not only did nobody know very much about baiji, but, more importantly, it was obvious that no further new information on the species was likely to become available either, given its precarious status. Even by the time of the first baiji workshop, the problems created by lack of data for rare and threatened species—which by their very nature are hard to study— was apparent to the conservation community. Michael Soulé, one of the big names in conservation biology during the 1980s, had already written that uncertainty pervades the recovery process but should not impede it.[1] This maxim has since been consolidated into the 'precautionary principle' of conservation biology, which counters the presumption that activities should proceed until there is clear evidence that they are harmful, and which supports action to anticipate and avert environmental harm even without robust evidence to demonstrate that such action is necessary. In the words of Don Merton, who led the successful recovery programme for the Chatham Island black robin for over a decade, 'Do not wait until you have all the facts before you act—you will never have all you would like. Action is what brings change, and saves endangered animals, not words.'[2]

As such, when the problems of limited data became apparent to the experts involved in baiji conservation, a more pro-active approach should have been adopted. Rather than passively waiting for more information to become available that might help to inform the specifics of the recovery programme, the limited information that was already known about the baiji and its ecosystem should have been used to make 'best guesses' about the most appropriate conservation actions that needed to be taken, which should then have been acted on. But this never really happened. Our species has a demonstrably poor track record in decision making under uncertainty, and reacting to early warning signs of environmental threat. After all, what will future generations think of our continuing vacillations and denials in the face of increasing evidence for human-caused global climate change?

What was even worse, though, was that several researchers instead used the limited facts available on baiji biology to serve another purpose. Instead of trying to develop an optimal species recovery programme, they instead tried to use these patchy data to suggest that it would actually be impossible to save the baiji from extinction. The limitations of their conclusions are obvious, but when presented as scientific 'certainties' they only served to hinder baiji conservation efforts even further. For example, in a paper entitled 'Conservation options for the baiji: time for realism?', published in 2006 in the prestigious journal *Conservation Biology*, the authors—a team led by Professor Yang Guang from Nanjing, and consisting of researchers from China and the UK—reported that no baiji had ever bred in captivity.[3] This fact was used to support the argument that *ex situ* conservation, whether in a dolphinarium or an oxbow, was essentially doomed to failure. But this statement is extremely disingenuous, because reproductively mature male and female baiji had never been kept together either in captivity or in a semi-natural reserve. Zhen Zhen, the only female baiji kept in the same enclosure with Qi Qi in the Wuhan dolphinarium, died before reaching sexual maturity. Successful reproduction under such circumstances would represent a challenge to any species. The truth is that we just don't know anything about whether baiji could breed with any success in a dolphinarium; however, the reproduction of the translocated finless porpoise population in the Tian'e-Zhou oxbow, despite all of the management problems at the reserve, suggests strongly that baiji could also have established a viable breeding population there under the right conditions. Instead, though, such persistent negative attitudes seemed likely to bring about the failure of the baiji recovery programme before it had even properly begun.

The irresponsible behaviour of publicizing the supposed inevitability of the baiji's demise contrasts markedly with the extreme caution typically displayed by conservationists when ruling other species to be beyond help, and it can only serve to dissuade potential donors who might otherwise have been prepared to support baiji recovery. But this pessimistic attitude is more widespread among the conservation community than many people might realize. It has even been formalized in a specific conservation policy called triage. This approach was first developed on the battlefields of the First World War, when medical teams had to make quick decisions about their ability to save wounded soldiers under conditions of extremely limited time and resources. The term 'triage' refers to the three different groups of prospective patients on the battlefield. The first group, the superficially injured and walking wounded, could largely be left to fend for themselves. The second group, comprising individuals with serious but easily treatable injuries, was the main priority for medical attention. However, the third group, made up of soldiers who were extremely badly wounded but who might still be able to survive if given intensive treatment, had to be given up for dead on the battlefield. Put simply, the medical teams simply didn't have the capacity to try to save these heavily injured soldiers—with success a far from certain prospect even under more optimal conditions—without losing far more men who were less injured and who could be saved much more easily. As noted by Reed Noss in an editorial in *Conservation Biology*,[4] the triage policy has now been transferred from one battleground to another: it is now being employed in the unwitting war of humans against nature. The advocates of triage suggest that given our finite conservation resources, should we therefore only aim to focus conservation efforts on the middle group of species, those which are in trouble but which stand a good chance of surviving if we help them? In the case of the baiji, even if it really was theoretically possible to save the species, were there in fact too many practical hurdles of cost and logistics to allow the recovery programme ever to work? Even worse, would a dogmatic pursuit of the baiji project actually channel resources away from other conservation programmes that had a far greater chance of success?

The logic of triage is certainly compelling. However, as a conservation approach it is fundamentally flawed. It assumes that we know far more than we actually do about the survival prospects of a species, and the fixity of the resources that can be allocated to carrying out the necessary recovery programme. Could you ever actually rule out the possibility that if you hadn't tried just that little bit harder after all, you could have saved that endangered species that you had decided to turn your back on? In fact, dedicated conservation action has reversed the decline of species supposedly 'doomed to extinction' with surprising regularity—remember the examples of the black robin and the Mauritius kestrel. If defeatist attitudes had also been more widely adopted than they already were towards these once Critically Endangered species, then it is certain that they would also no longer be with us. Proclaiming the baiji to be 'doomed to extinction' is therefore a self-fulfilling prophecy—if it prevents essential conservation actions from being carried out, then of course the species is bound to disappear. Such an approach is anathema to true conservation. However, triage offers an easy way out from actually having to do anything, whether you believe that a species is truly too far gone to save or not. In the words of the conservationist Stuart Pimm, although nobody quibbles with the efficient allocation of resources, triage is seductive music to some managers' ears: it combines the semblance of a tough decision-making style with the substance of doing nothing.[5] Other conservationists have had other equally damning things to say about triage: it is both unworkable and misleading in its apparent common sense; it is ethically pernicious and politically defeatist when applied to biological conservation; it is a subterfuge; and it offers a convenient escape from our moral duties to other creatures.[6] I was far from alone, then, with my grave concerns about this conservation outlook.

~

Other factors also got in the way that seemed to make people feel uncomfortable with helping the baiji recovery programme, even if they did not necessarily advocate the triage approach. Because of the insurmountable problems involved with reversing the deterioration of the Yangtze ecosystem in the immediate future, it seemed that the only practical short-term solution to saving the baiji was to set up a breeding programme at Tian'e-Zhou, if the major on-site issues could be addressed in time. Because of the specific problems facing the baiji, an intensive species-specific management plan was the only option. However, such an approach constituted a fundamental problem for many environmentalists. Species-specific strategies, it seemed, were old-fashioned and too limited in scope. Instead, ecosystem-level conservation strategies represented a more appropriate solution. In the past, we'd had an overly simplistic view of the natural world, suggested many environmentalists. We could look at a species on its own, even away from its natural environment in a zoo, and think we could understand everything about how it had evolved, how it behaved, and how it lived. But we were wrong. Nowadays, we also understood the importance of ecology. We had to consider species as a part of larger ecosystems, filling vital roles in the web of life and in turn depending on their interactions with countless other organisms. The problems faced by a single species could not be considered in isolation. The only appropriate solution for saving the baiji, therefore, had to be the regeneration and restoration of the entire Yangtze. A species-specific approach just wasn't an appropriate way to think about baiji conservation any more.

That really seems to have been the way that a lot of people saw the problem. Indeed, it corresponds with the views of many of the American participants at the various baiji conservation workshops of the 1980s and 1990s, and apparently with the view of at least one of the major international conservation organizations. WWF, the international organization that had been heavily involved with the panda project at Wolong, had informed us that they were already working on baiji conservation through their HSBC Yangtze Programme, which was 'restoring the Web of Life in the central Yangtze'.[7] This programme would establish an 'integrated approach to solve river basin issues in the Yangtze',[8] primarily through restoring the natural connections between disconnected lakes and the main river channel. The HSBC website suggested that they were already doing everything that needed to be done to save the baiji. 'The Yangtze Programme recognises that the two main threats to the species are poor water quality and human interference. The Yangtze Programme has worked with the local government and citizens to increase the water quality, create reserves for the creatures, and relocate farmers so that they are no longer threatening the species' habitat.'[9] It sounded as though our work had been done for us.

Any attempts to restore the natural ecosystem of the Yangtze River and its associated waterways are, clearly, extremely important for conservation. However, this one-sided solution was not really a solution at all for the baiji. It should have been clear, to WWF and everybody else involved with conservation in China, that these sorts of measures simply would not be able to prevent the dolphin's extinction. Yangtze regeneration projects are certainly needed before any baiji could be reintroduced back into the river in the future, but adopting this approach at the expense of establishing an *ex situ* population in the first place is like trying to run before you can walk—it remains sadly insufficient for the continued survival of the species in the short term. That's what the many baiji workshop reports had been forced to conclude, and that's what we were trying desperately to tell everyone. Although intensive species-specific conservation programmes remain controversial—and even unfashionable—they are, unfortunately, crucial for conserving species with tiny population sizes and rapid rates of decline, and where the major causes of decline cannot be determined or quickly corrected. Ultimately, if you have a healthy river but no dolphins to live in it, can that really be considered a conservation success?

This wasn't the only reason that people seemed to shy away from intensive species-specific recovery programmes, though. These kinds of 'hands-on' projects, which involved intensive contact activity—the active capture and manipulation of extremely threatened animals—were inherently risky. The dangers had already been amply demonstrated during the implementation of the recovery programme for another species of extreme rarity, the California condor, which had dwindled to only a couple of dozen individuals by the late twentieth century. After a protracted legal struggle during the late 1970s and early 1980s, an intensive research and captive breeding programme, supported by the US Fish and Wildlife Service and the National Audubon Society, finally got under way. But disaster struck before attempts to catch all of the remaining wild birds and set up a captive breeding population could even begin. In 1980, at the very beginning of the project, a field team began taking measurements and running health checks on the nestlings of the last few wild condor pairs, in order to fill the huge gaps in scientific understanding about how condors reproduced and so give the planned breeding programme the best chance of success. However, when two researchers climbed into the first condor nest they planned to study and started handling one of the chicks in order to measure and weigh the bird, it put up a fight, making it difficult to handle gently and prolonging the time that the intruders had to stay in the nest. Suddenly, just as the researchers were finishing their work, the chick started to shake. Within minutes it was dead. An autopsy later determined that the bird had died of stress.

The condor project was already mired in controversy. It was being roundly attacked by environmentalists convinced that an *ex situ* breeding programme would mean the end of the condor as a real wild animal, even if captive birds could breed and eventually be reintroduced into their natural environment. 'If we cannot preserve condors wild through understanding their natural relations, we have already lost the battle,' wrote Carl Koford, the condor researcher who argued passionately that the only defensible conservation actions that could be carried out to save the species were 'hands-off' protection of the bird's environment rather than more intensive manipulations of wild or captive birds.[10] All nests should remain inviolate, Koford wrote; anything else represented 'mutilative biology'.[11] Many others took up Koford's cause, proclaiming that 'a condor is five percent feathers, flesh, blood and bone. All the rest is *place*. Condors are a soaring manifestation of the place that built them and coded their genes. That place requires space to meet in, to teach fledglings to roost unmolested, to bathe and drink in, to find other condors in (and not biologists), and to fly over wild and free.'[12]

So the death of the first California condor chick to be handled invasively by biologists was more than just a tragedy—it took place in a highly charged public arena, where a large and vociferous opposition were looking for any signs of weakness to attack the intensive species recovery programme. Even worse, the event had actually been filmed by the field team's cameraman. Activists instantly contacted reporters and television stations, and urged the Department of the Interior and the California state government to fire Noel Snyder and John Ogden, leaders of the condor field programme (who were not present at the death of the condor chick). The film of the chick's death was distributed around the country, and publicly analysed frame by frame by hostile environmentalists. Even though no more condors died during any of the intensive hands-on work, either in the field or later on when they had been brought into captivity, the damage was done to the condor recovery project, to the reputations of the scientists involved with the project, and to the organizations who supported this intensive conservation approach.

The baiji recovery programme faced similar risks. Indeed, the death of the translocated female baiji at Tian'e-Zhou in 1996 underlined the dangers of handling river dolphins and placing them into an alien environment, even though the exact circumstances of the animal's death remained unclear. Many of the past workshop participants from outside China whom I spoke to felt that this event had definitely been one of the key factors that made baiji conservation efforts wind down around ten years ago; certainly, there were no further concerted attempts even using internal Chinese funding to capture any baiji for the Tian'e-Zhou reserve after that. If capture efforts were to start up again, the death of one of the world's last Yangtze River dolphins in the hands of an international cetacean vet or capture specialist, as part of a high-profile and controversial conservation project under the close scrutiny of the world, would not only haunt that person for ever but would also not be forgotten by colleagues, funding agencies, or—especially—critics of the whole project. And in a wider context, too, fear of failure was a potent reason for conservation organizations to not want to get involved. On a pragmatic level, the costs of supporting an expensive, species-specific conservation project that had no guarantees of success, and which provided few benefits to any other surviving species, could easily influence the decision over whether an organization was prepared to get involved. Furthermore, even if no dolphins died in the media spotlight, if an organization threw its support into the project and came up with the necessary funding, its reputation was also put on the line. If it didn't manage to save the species from extinction despite all of its efforts, then how well would that reflect back on its wider abilities, irrespective of the tremendous—and possibly insurmountable—difficulties and challenges that would be faced? Were people just playing it safe? Were some species of extreme rarity simply too high risk to even try to save?

Of course it's self-evident that this attitude is supremely ironic. Whereas organizations may be wary of getting involved in a risky conservation exercise that has no guarantee of success, the baiji— and the California condor, as well as many other extremely threatened species with only a handful of surviving individuals—would be doomed to certain extinction in the absence of any concerted and intensive conservation action. The condor provides a perfect case in point. Although one individual was accidentally killed by field teams, an event that was seized upon and widely publicized by critics of the species' recovery programme, far greater numbers of the remaining free-ranging and reintroduced birds continued to be shot by hunters or killed by poison bait, putting paid to the idea that they were better off in the wild. Similarly, even though the baiji semi-natural reserve strategy was clearly risky, and one dolphin had already died in the attempt to set up a breeding population at Tian'e-Zhou, the species simply had no chance of survival whatsoever if it was left to fend for itself. Even conservationists now recognized and admitted this. In the words of Professor David Dudgeon, a Hong Kong-based freshwater ecologist who attended the 2004 Wuhan workshop, 'the baiji is certain to become extinct if left to languish in the Yangtze.'[13] The extinction of the baiji or the condor would be the ultimate conservation failure—the ultimate 'perverse outcome' of any plan to save a species. However, the difference here is that organizations which are officially involved with any eleventh-hour recovery efforts can be seen to actively fail if the target species dies out. On the other hand, organizations which are too timid to put themselves on the line instead only fail passively, and can cover their tracks and justify their inaction without even needing to apply too much spin. Paradoxically, if conservation organizations are run like businesses, then maybe not trying at all might even become the better option.

~

Ex situ conservation is certainly not a desirable recovery strategy for endangered species under most circumstances. Even support- ers of these last-ditch recovery attempts will freely admit that they are only a partial, short-term solution to a problem that has been allowed to go too far—they are risky and expensive; they carry the danger of allowing policy makers to neglect essential environmen- tal conservation efforts; and target species can be difficult to breed in captivity and even harder to reintroduce into the wild. Despite this, though, sometimes there are no other options left. Non- interventionist, ecosystem-level conservation solutions just don't work in these desperate cases. Time and again, experience has shown that this is the case: no other alternative solution will do.

However, it was already clear that the international experts who had offered their advice on the best way forward for the baiji recovery programme had not really considered the other situations when *ex situ* conservation had been required to try to save a highly threatened species; instead, they believed the situation they faced to be without precedent, and that the major problems posed by attempts to save the baiji were novel ones for the conservation community to address. If there had been some greater apprecia- tion of these other hands-on recovery programmes, though, then maybe the unfortunate necessity of such intensive efforts under many extreme circumstances wouldn't have been the only fact that became apparent. The other sad similarity shared by all of these conservation efforts is that the main obstacles in each project were not some innate biological barrier to saving a species that was already too rare to avoid extinction; and they were not even a lack of financial or infrastructural support. Instead, all of these projects—representing a wide range of species, and carried out in many different countries across a period of three centuries— share common patterns of having been hindered by scientific and

administrative conservatism. It is this key factor alone that constitutes the most significant cause of conservation failure in intensive
hands-on recovery programmes.

Far from representing a modern phenomenon, examples of
avoidable human mismanagement constraining intensive conservation with potentially fatal consequences go back as far as the
late nineteenth century. There is no need to look any further than
the famous conservation efforts for New Zealand's threatened
birds, which constitute maybe the best parallel to the planned
baiji recovery programme in terms of conservation management
involving the translocation of highly endangered species to semi-
natural reserves. In the last decades of the 1800s, the New Zealand
authorities established founder populations of many rare species
on a series of offshore islands, where—as we saw earlier—the
birds could prosper in the absence of the introduced predators that
were bringing about their disappearance on the mainland. It was
this early intensive conservation action that saved both the little
spotted kiwi and the stitchbird from extinction, as these species
had died out completely across their former mainland range by
the start of the twentieth century. However, even though it rapidly
became clear that this conservation approach held the key to saving what was left of New Zealand's avifauna, other species were
not so lucky.

From the 1890s to the 1920s, there were extensive official deliberations to transfer other threatened and declining native birds
to offshore islands. One of these was the huia, a glossy-black
member of New Zealand's endemic wattlebird family and one
of the world's most remarkable bird species. When it was first
described by Europeans, the early taxonomists thought that the
male and female birds were actually different species because their
bills were so different. The male huia had a short sharp bill, and
looked somewhat like a giant starling or a blunt-nosed wood-
pecker. The female instead was much more exotic in appearance;
her bill was over twice as long and delicately curved downward in
a long crescent, making her resemble a huge black hummingbird.

No one knows why this unique sexual dimorphism evolved, or what exactly the male and female birds used their different bills for. We are left with only a few tantalizing clues. Old Maori stories record that male and female huia always lived together in pairs, and if one bird died the other would also soon die of grief; this was borne out by limited observations made on wild and captive birds by European scientists during the nineteenth century. It seems that huias fed on insect grubs, and may have obtained this food through a unique partnership. The male bird would use his thick chisel-like bill to hammer grubs out of decaying wood, whereas the female would probe into deeper, narrower cracks and crevices in the bark with her long thin bill. It's possible that the birds actually worked together as a team, but maybe this is just an overly romantic misperception; instead, the drastically different bill shapes may have just allowed huia pairs to live together and avoid competition by finding grubs in different places from the same tree.

We'll never know any more, because despite the protracted plans to set up huia populations alongside those of the kiwis and stitchbirds, no one ever got round to trying to find any wild birds before it was too late. The last definite sighting of a living huia was made on 28 December 1907, but discussions about the need to try to catch the last remaining birds and transfer them to an offshore island continued for more than a decade. Eventually, an attempt was made to try to catch a few birds, but there were no longer any to be found.

The disappearance of the huia is the story of a forgotten human failure. Now the species is commemorated only by a few museum specimens, some Maori stories, and a suburb in Auckland that bears its name. All of the available scientific knowledge about the bird was gathered together in 1963 by W. J. Phillipps in *The Book of the Huia*. Phillipps expressed his scorn for the wasted opportunity to save the bird from extinction. On reviewing the decades of official deliberations to establish huia populations on predator-free islands, he wrote that 'one cannot avoid the feeling that had these efforts been pursued with a little more vigour at least some pairs of birds would have been available for liberation. As it was, no huia was ever placed on a sanctuary in spite of all the organising and proposing that apparently went on to that end.'

Little appears to have been learnt from this conservation failure, even within New Zealand. Only a few decades later, another avoidable tragedy struck the country's native bird fauna. Although the last individuals of many endemic bird species were by now restricted to tiny offshore islands, these islands didn't necessarily represent safe havens either. In the early 1960s, rats that had stowed away on fishing vessels managed to colonize Big South Cape Island, the last refuge of relict populations of four New Zealand endemics—the South Island saddleback, the bush wren, the Stewart Island snipe, and also one of New Zealand's three native bats, the greater short-tailed bat. But even though the dangers caused by exotic mammals had been clear to New Zealand conservation planners during the previous century, the tide of scientific opinion had now somehow changed. New ecological thinking, based on studies of simple predator-prey systems such as lynx and snowshoe hares in North America, suggested that in fact predators couldn't actually ever wipe out their prey, or they would die out themselves. Even though the disappearances of many bird species had been directly observed in New Zealand following the introduction of rats, cats, and stoats, many of the country's biologists now suggested that these extinctions must have been driven by subtle environmental shifts instead, or maybe because the native birds had been somehow at the end of their evolutionary lives, and were 'due to die out' anyway.

This was all completely erroneous reasoning. In fact, introduced predators can easily wipe out native species, because unlike the widely cited lynx-snowshoe hare example, they are not dependent upon just one type of prey—they can remain at high population densities by feeding on species that remain common (often other introduced species, such as rats) while systematically killing off every last one of the most vulnerable natives. But New Zealand's national conservation planners, influenced by the supposedly superior knowledge of their top scientists, refused to authorize any attempts to translocate any of the native species from Big South Cape Island, and practical conservation efforts to save these species were prevented for several years. By the time a rescue operation was finally permitted in the mid-1960s, on the first attempt it only proved possible to establish a population of thirty-six saddlebacks successfully on another island. All of the other species became extinct before further conservation work was carried out. Today, there are around 700 South Island saddlebacks on 11 different islands, and the populations are doing so well that the species is only considered vulnerable, not endangered. If it hadn't been for the completely unnecessary 'scientific' resistance to an obvious conservation solution, then it's very likely that we would also have healthy populations of bush wren, snipe, and maybe even greater short-tailed bats, too. As it is, they are gone forever.

Subsequent intensive recovery programmes have continued to fall foul of similar delays, based largely on scientific conservatism and subjective prejudice against ultimately essential *ex situ* conservation. The California condor recovery programme is a good case in point. Mainly because of unrelenting opposition from environmental groups with preconceived agendas who advocated non-interventionist conservation techniques, necessary intensive actions were delayed for years after they were first suggested, almost until the condor's complete extinction. Although *ex situ* breeding was eventually achieved for the species at both Los Angeles Zoo and the San Diego Wild Animal Park, Noel Snyder and others who were involved with condor conservation consider that earlier intensive action would have allowed the species recovery programme to have been much more successful, without the complete dependence on captive breeding that now exists and much of the great expense and difficulties that are now entailed in the conservation of the species.[14]

And this is far from the only example of such ultimately avoidable time delays leading to massive problems in a modern-day intensive species recovery programme. A scathing article by Robert May in the pages of *Nature*, the world's most prestigious scientific journal, described a depressingly similar story from the conservation efforts for the black-footed ferret,[15] which was later retold in considerably more detail by Tim Clark in the book *Averting Extinction*. Once widespread in grasslands and open plains from Canada to Mexico, and from the Rocky Mountains to the Great Plains, the ferret is a specialist predator of prairie dogs, a kind of burrowing squirrel which once occurred at astonishing densities—a single prairie dog 'town' in Texas once contained around 400 million animals. The ferret's population crashed as a result of extensive prairie-dog poisoning campaigns that accompanied agricultural development across its prairie habitat—ironically, unlike the situation with introduced predators in New Zealand, this really was an instance of a simple predator-prey system whereby decline of the single prey species led to a corresponding decline in the predator. After 1974, many researchers feared that the ferret might be extinct, but a remnant population was discovered in Wyoming in 1981, and over the next few years the numbers of ferrets grew steadily from 60 in 1982 to 128 in 1984. However, in 1985 this last population of ferrets suddenly began to disappear, and by October of that year only thirty-one survivors could be found. Veterinarians from the Wyoming Game and Fish Department soon found out that the cause of the catastrophe was an outbreak of canine distemper, a viral infection that was inevitably fatal.

Eventually, six ferrets were brought into captivity to establish a breeding programme to try to save the species. But two of these animals were already infected with distemper when they were captured, and because the animals were not isolated from each other, they all died. An emergency attempt to capture all of the remaining ferrets led to five more being caught in late 1985, twelve more in 1986, and what seemed to be the last surviving wild ferret in February 1987. After being isolated and vaccinated, all of these animals survived, and went on to form the basis of an amazingly successful intensive breeding programme. Active reintroductions started in 1991, and there are now over 600 wild ferrets at a series of reintroduction sites in the United States.

This sounds like a success story, and ultimately that's what it was. However, it very nearly ended in tragedy, and not because of the canine distemper outbreak but because of easily avoidable management decisions. After the last native Wyoming ferrets were found in 1981, various scientists and conservation organizations argued that a captive breeding programme had to be established in order to safeguard this single vulnerable wild population. These arguments became more insistent when the population was found to have increased above 100 individuals, because the removal of several animals into captivity would then have a minimal impact at most on the fate of the animals left in the wild. However, the head of the Wyoming Game and Fish Department's ferret programme, Harry Harju, remained completely opposed to the capture of any ferrets for a breeding programme. May stated publicly in his *Nature* article that Harju appeared to have been more concerned with bureaucratic issues than with biological ones, and reports that Harju thought that everyone who advocated captive breeding had selfish motives; however, Harju himself wanted to keep all of the ferrets in Wyoming because otherwise, in his own words, 'we'd have no control over them'. Other deconstructions of the history of ferret conservation have reported the consistent rejection of field data documenting the rapid decline of the wild ferret population during the summer of 1985; however, the field teams were met with government rhetoric which argued that there were no problems with the wild ferrets, only with survey methods.[16] May lamented that 'if such a mess can be made of efforts to save an attractive creature such as the black-footed ferret in a country as well organized and prosperous as the United States, prospects for conservation in other parts of the world are indeed bleak.' He ended his paper by stating that 'I do not doubt that Harju will in time attain mythical status in the conservationist's pantheon as a symbol of what can happen when the machinery and dignity of office come to overshadow the purposes the office was created to serve.'

And, unfortunately, there's still more. Other international, high-profile conservation projects in addition to the baiji recovery programme have also been plagued by perverse inaction. Conservation efforts for the Sumatran rhino—a species probably also once found along the Yangtze—provide a case in point. Alan Rabinowitz summed up the sorry state of the recovery programme for this species a decade ago in a pithy paper entitled 'Helping a species go extinct: the Sumatran rhino in Borneo'. After the international community established an Asian Rhino Specialist Group and stepped in to assist in the protection of the species, each successive management plan did little more than rephrase the initial conservation recommendations that had been made at earlier meetings; Rabinowitz noted dryly that the fact that there had been little progress on these issues ten years after they had first been discussed was not mentioned. However, once the causes of Sumatran rhino decline were recognized, the actions needed to remove or neutralize these causes were never carried out. Management activities such as anti-poaching patrols, education campaigns, and surveys were increasingly discussed but never actually implemented, because they were more difficult, time consuming, and sometimes controversial. Ironically, this meant that the greatest efforts were actually put into trying to establish a captive breeding population for the species, but these attempts still fell far short of expectations or actual conservation requirements. It was clear to Rabinowitz who was responsible for the failure of rhino conservation efforts:

> While some of the blame for the decline of the Sumatran rhino must be placed on the Indonesian and Malaysian governments, the rest of it falls squarely in the lap of international funding and conservation organizations. The international community, with its funding

and expertise, has played a major role in directing the course of rhino conservation over the last quarter century. Unfortunately, it has tried to avoid dirtying its hands with controversial and difficult issues . . . Foreign advisers and nongovernment conservation organizations have all too often avoided such issues because of the risk of becoming an unwelcomed guest.

While political, cultural, and socioeconomic issues in Indonesia and Malaysia continue to interfere with Sumatran rhino protection, these difficulties have never been insurmountable. The rhino has simply not been considered important enough for governments and large funding agencies to tackle these realities. Only when a firm commitment is made to save the Sumatran rhino will the species stand a chance of survival. Regrettably, our years of accumulated failures and avoidance of issues have not moved us closer to this kind of commitment.

After three decades of superficial international involvement with Sumatran rhino conservation, now only about twenty-five animals are thought to survive in Borneo. Does any of this sound familiar?

The final example I'm going to give is the most recent, and in many ways the saddest of all. It concerns the probable extinction of a Hawaiian bird called the po'ouli, an enigmatic honeycreeper with a distinctive black 'bandit mask' which was only discovered by scientists as recently as 1973, and which was not even known about by the native Hawaiians. Fossil remains show that it was once distributed across the dry lower elevations of the island of Maui, but by the time of its discovery it was already restricted to a remote 1,300-hectare area of wet montane forest on the northern and eastern slopes of the Haleakala volcano, and it declined rapidly from an estimated 76 birds/km^2 in 1975 to only 8/km^2 by 1985. Fieldwork in 1986 provided some information on nesting behaviour, but the species was already extremely rare; surveys in 1994–5 were only able to find six po'ouli, and by 1997 this number had fallen even further to only three surviving birds, which could still be located in 2000. Unlike the native birds of New Zealand on the other side of the Pacific, it seems that po'ouli may have been most vulnerable to vegetation disturbance by introduced pigs, which eliminates the endemic Hawaiian snails that form the basis of the birds' diet.

Obviously, something had to be done to try to remedy this dire conservation situation. Initial conservation attempts focused on non-invasive environmental-level protection, with the establishment of the Hanawi Natural Area Reserve and attempts to restrict feral pigs from the po'ouli core distribution area; but there were so few birds left that these efforts still didn't seem sufficient to guarantee the successful recovery of the species. Worst of all, the last three birds had widely distributed home ranges within Hanawi, and scientific monitoring carried out from 1995 onwards revealed that they stayed far apart from each other and never met—so they would never breed under natural conditions. A joint US State and Federal Environmental Assessment reviewed the remaining available conservation options in 1999, and recommended that intensive conservation manipulation was necessary to save the species. The assessment concluded that one or more birds should be translocated to the home range of a bird of the opposite sex, so that they might at least have a chance to mate in the wild.

However, it then took three years for anything to actually be carried out. It wasn't until 2002 that the first—and ultimately only—attempt was made to transfer one of the two remaining female birds into the home range of the only surviving male. And then it didn't even work. Although the female was successfully translocated, she simply flew straight back to her own home range the very next day. A new strategy was required, and so a plan was developed and approved in January 2003 to remove all three remaining po'ouli from the wild and transfer them to a specially designed breeding centre. Although capture efforts began in February 2003, it took until September 2004 for the first bird—the only living male—to be captured. He was found to have avian malaria and only one functioning eye. 'That the bird survived such physical challenges is testament to its toughness, and a reminder that it is the species that is endangered and not the individual', reported the project scientists.[17] He lasted only seventy-eight days in captivity before dying of old age, and before a potential mate could be found. Further surveys were unable to locate either of the two female birds. The species is now considered to be extinct.

The scientific field team that coordinated the ultimately unsuccessful recovery attempts for the po'ouli, led by Eric VanderWerf and Jim Groombridge, wrote that the substantial problems caused by the slow pace of the decision-making process cannot be ignored.[18] While careful attention to detail is paramount for successful and progressive conservation measures in extreme situations such as that faced by the po'ouli recovery team, it is also critical to translate these plans into recovery actions without delay, particularly for species of such extreme rarity. For the surviving individuals of a critically endangered species with only limited remaining productive years, they wrote, 'these delays could make the difference between extinction and recovery':[19]

> For the po'ouli, the decision to undertake captive propagation came too late, and it may be justifiably asked why this action was not undertaken earlier…The reluctance to undertake more invasive management actions may stem partly from a fear of risk and partly from fear of blame in case of failure. Lack of universal support for risky actions can increase the fear of blame, resulting in no action, which ultimately may incur the most risk of all. Perhaps the most important lesson from the case of the po'ouli is that action must be taken early, before a time when a species' future rests on a single risky endeavor.

It remains imperative for conservation planners to recognize that protracted decision-making not only increases the costs of eventual recovery efforts in terms of money, time, and stress, but also directly conflicts with the need for urgent conservation action when threatened species are reduced to very few surviving individuals. But despite this seemingly obvious truism, many of the players involved in the baiji project still appeared to have had a paradoxically limited sense of urgency. On the Chinese side, this might reflect some deeper cultural values that remain hazy to

Westerners, as exemplified by the former Chinese premier Zhou Enlai's famous comment about the historical effects of the French Revolution: 'It's too soon to tell.' But nobody in the international community seemed to appreciate that the baiji was in danger of extinction *right now*, either. The grave reality of the situation was even openly challenged by Professor Yang Guang and his team, who wrote in their 2006 paper that 'populations of larger vertebrates not under direct persecution have persisted for long periods of time at undetectable densities'. In their opinion, the remaining handful of baiji left in the Yangtze 'could conceivably survive for a longer period than currently anticipated by persisting at low densities and evading detection. Under this scenario it remains possible that any future remediation measures could arrive in time to reverse the decline of the species.' So the last few baiji, it seemed, would be fine—they were going to just hang around and wait patiently for us to scrape together the funding we needed to save them. We had all the time in the world to continue begging for funds from disinterested donors and oblivious conservation organizations. Extinction, it seemed, was something that only happened long ago in the distant prehistoric past to species such as dinosaurs and dodos, or alternatively would only take place because of human activity at some unspecified point in the future. Surely, though, the baiji wouldn't actually disappear for good in our own lifetimes. We were experiencing the disappearance of a species in real time, and the worst thing was that nobody even seemed to realize it.

7

END GAME

'Do you know about the Yangtze river dolphin?'
'No.'

Douglas Adams and Mark Carwardine
Last Chance to See

On New Year's Eve 2005, Leigh drove round to see me. We had yet another major baiji funding application with an imminent deadline to work on, after all, which would take us into the coffee-fuelled small hours as usual; but we both had a good feeling about the coming year. The emergency implementation meeting in San Diego had been a success: we finally had a robust working budget, methodology, and timeframe for the project, which would allow us to push forward in making sure that things got organized out in China at last. Finally, after all the powerplay, bickering, apathy, and seemingly interminable delays, it looked like something was actually going to happen.

I stood at the front door as Leigh walked up the drive. Then there was a loud crash. The bottle of New Year's champagne that she had been carrying had somehow slipped out through the bottom of her bag and shattered all over the driveway. We looked at each other. This was just a chance event, a moment of sheer bad luck. Why should we read any greater significance into it?

~

So how do you go about trying to catch a river dolphin? Each river system in which freshwater dolphins occurred was different, it seemed, and studying successful capture methods that had been used in other parts of the world could only take you so far. For example, Giorgio Pilleri had managed to capture several river dolphins in the Indus using techniques that had been used regularly by fishermen on the Indian subcontinent from at least as far back as the nineteenth century. Uniquely, Indus and Ganges dolphins will enter water as shallow as 30 cm deep when swimming on their sides chasing fish. A fisherman trying to catch a dolphin will stand motionless on a special platform (called *bhati* in Sind) that is mounted on a *trikhur* or wooden tripod driven into the mud in shallow water. With his arms stretched high above his head, he will hold a *kularee*, a special conical net braced with a bamboo ring and sticks. The *kularee* can be thrown quickly into the water if any river dolphin approaches within range, and other fishermen will then rush in from the bank to help subdue the panicking animal. Although Pilleri used this technique to capture dolphins safely for his research institute, under other circumstances any animals unlucky enough to be caught by local fishermen would be quickly dispatched for their meat and oil. Often they will meet an undignified end simply to provide bait for fishermen to use for catching catfish.

The behaviour of the baiji and the ecology of the Yangtze were extremely different from that of the river dolphins in the Indus and Ganges, though, so different methods had to be developed to try to capture baiji for the recovery programme that we hoped to set up in Tian'e-Zhou. We were working with a lot of unknowns, and it would be impossible to completely guarantee the safety of any dolphins during the recovery programme's capture-translocation operations. However, now at least we had been able to learn from the accumulated expertise of both the various Chinese researchers who had tried to catch baiji and finless porpoises in the past, and also from the world's top dolphin capture specialists who had extensive experience in many other freshwater and marine systems, and in the safe capture of species such as bottlenose dolphins, Amazon River dolphins, and franciscanas. Hopefully we would be able to give it our best shot.

The optimal baiji capture strategy that had been developed following extensive discussions at the San Diego meeting differed from previous capture attempts made along the Yangtze in the past. Earlier efforts had been forced to rely on small boats that the Chinese researchers themselves admitted were too slow to be of much use for the job. In order to compensate for this shortfall, fifteen or more boats and huge, 2-kilometre-long nets had been used in each capture attempt, with these complex efforts involving over fifty active participants. The potential for confusion and slow responses during the hectic captures, and the danger of accidental entanglement and drowning of dolphins in the long nets, was worryingly high. Instead, it was suggested that much smaller-scale operations should be carried out. The captures should be led by two fast, manoeuvrable boats with 200 hp engines, which would deploy two 500-metre long, 7–8-metre deep fine-mesh nets that could be fastened together to form a single longer net if necessary, and which could encircle baiji much more rapidly in the river. Once suitable safe capture sites in shallow water had been identified, the capture boats would be able to make a fast circle around the dolphins, then slowly drag the net circle close to shore and constrict it by pulling more and more netting on board. The whole tightly coordinated operation would be assisted by a small number of additional, unspecialized speedboats and fishing boats that would be able to scout along the river to look for baiji, quickly reach the nets in case of emergency, and control boat traffic. Once safely captured, the baiji would be transported immediately to the holding pens that still had to be constructed at the oxbow, preferably using fast helicopter transport as this would minimize the stressful translocation time for the captured animals. To further limit any potential for accidents during the captures, 'dry run' capture simulations involving all capture staff and any other participants should be conducted in the main Yangtze channel before each real capture attempt, and the main Chinese participants should also receive intensive training in capturing and handling wild bottlenose dolphins at the Sarasota Dolphin Research Program in Florida. We planned that five two-month capture operations should be carried out along the Yangtze before 2009 in order to establish a viable breeding population of baiji at Tian'e-Zhou, before the wild population underwent a further decline or became extinct.

How much was all of this going to cost? The budget for the first three years of the baiji recovery programme—involving the series of infrastructural improvements and ongoing maintenance costs at the oxbow, pre-capture training, the development of the baiji 'capture fleet', the running costs of the capture-translocation operations, and support for international participants—would come to around a million US dollars.[1] Saying that this was a lot of money is rather a case of stating the obvious. Where was it all going to come from? Would we have to break the budget up into lots of small manageable chunks that we would have to try to raise from a series of different funding sources, or would we be able to try for a few 'big hits' from major donors? It was fairly daunting.

But a look at some of the conservation initiatives that were already in place for many other endangered species showed that raising these kinds of funds should not be impossible. In fact, far more money had actually already been poured into some of the other intensive recovery programmes that had also met with similar unnecessary delays, caution, and inaction from the international community. Despite all of the blunders and ineptitude surrounding conservation efforts for the Sumatran rhino that were detailed by Alan Rabinowitz, over US$2.5 million had been spent over five years on the Sumatran Rhino Trust before it was dissolved in 1993. At the time when Rabinowitz wrote his critique of the subject, a new three-year cost for rhino conservation in Indonesia and Malaysia was estimated at approximately US$14 million, with a US$2 million Global Environment Facility sponsored project already underway.[2] Whereas single-species funding for the po'ouli recovery programme remained relatively low (less than US$500,000) in comparison with funds for ecosystem-level initiatives for Hawaiian bird species, over US$8 million has been spent so far on the development and maintenance of captive propagation and reintroduction programmes for the archipelago's highly endangered birds.[3]

Sometimes far more excessive amounts of funding are provided to support species that are not even particularly endangered at a global scale. One of the most controversial examples of extreme allocations of conservation funding concerns the research programme into the decline of the Steller sea lion, which has declined seriously off western Alaska in recent decades but which still has healthy populations along Alaska's southeast coast. Environmental groups believed that the decline of the western sea lion population was related to the commercial fishery for wall-eye pollock, and in 1998 the problem became further politicized when a legal complaint was filed alleging that the United States National Marine Fishery Service had failed to adequately assess the impacts of this commercial fishery on the sea lions. All of a sudden, US$40 million of national funding a year materialized for the newly formed Steller Sea Lion Research Initiative, which had to be spent quickly within particular budget years, and which also could not be spent on investigating some of the most key questions surrounding the relationship between fisheries and sea lion decline—notably assessing the relative survival of sea lions in different areas that were open and closed to pollock fishing. So far, US$190 million has been spent on this single species, but conservationists are still far from having even reached a consensus on the reasons for the sea lion's decline.[4]

In contrast, then, the baiji recovery programme would not have actually cost that much. How could we find this kind of funding, though? It would seemingly depend on whether any wealthy organizations or individuals could become successfully engaged with the project. But given the desperate urgency of the situation, did we actually have enough time?

~

In late January 2006, the world was gripped by news about the desperate plight of a cetacean in a river. A 17-foot-long juvenile female bottlenose whale had accidentally swum up the Thames as far as central London, and despite the best efforts of a closely coordinated team of rescuers, the animal died when attempts were made to transport it back to deeper water. The whole story was played out in a frenzy of international media attention. It seemed like a golden opportunity to tie in the baiji recovery programme. But, try as we might, it still seemed to be impossible to raise much interest in the more serious plight of an entire species of cetacean in another river. In our case, the river was on the other side of the world, and you couldn't get nice pictures or film clips to attract the news crews. So why should that be of any interest to the man in the street?

We continued churning out the funding requests and applications, but still to no avail. In fact, the snubs seemed to be getting worse. 'Overall, the Committee recognized the critically important nature of this work, but felt that there were too many risks for it to be successful. In addition, the Committee felt that it was more an "animal rescue" project rather than a biodiversity conservation project and was therefore not a priority for funding.' What was trying to save the baiji—preventing the disappearance of an entire mammal family, let alone a species—if not biodiversity conservation? How could they really think that the project was just about animal rescue? Surely they could tell that it was a bit different from saving donkeys on the pier at Weston-super-Mare. Other lines of enquiry also faltered; and the situation in China was not much better. Although it was confirmed that the Chinese authorities already had enough funding donated from Japan to establish the necessary infrastructure at Tian'e-Zhou and probably also to carry out an initial baiji capture operation, it seemed to be impossible to persuade them to actually release any of this money in time to do anything useful. International support would still be required after all.

But we continued to push forward. We prepared the formal report from the San Diego meeting and published a short note about the status of the baiji recovery programme in the conservation journal *Oryx*, and used these minor landmarks as the basis for issuing a press release about the desperate status of the baiji, and the need for urgent funds to allow the recovery programme to be finally carried out. We have to act now if we want to save the species, we cried out to the world. The story spread across the national and international news agencies. 'Last chance for China's dolphin,' proclaimed the BBC News website.[5] We all waited. Would this approach finally help us to find the support we so badly needed?

I'm not sure exactly what I was expecting from the press release, but we certainly didn't get what we hoped for. In addition to the trickle of excited emails from past friends and distant family members who had seen my name in the newspapers, we received precisely three memorable responses. The first response was from an eco-tour guide with an American client who was trying to see every mammal family in the world, and the baiji was one of the few that he hadn't yet seen. Any help or advice in this matter would be greatly appreciated. I couldn't bring myself to reply.

The second response was more amusing, if nothing else. I'm still not quite sure about who the person that emailed me actually was. Apparently he tried to contact me by phone, too: I'm glad that I was out when he called. He sent me a long, rambling message, following the somewhat unorthodox strategy of first telling me that he had a Swedish wife, four children ('29 to 16 mfmf'), and a little grandson as well. He had been taken by an 'enormous scientific situation', and had been working since to re-educate himself and others 'in the shadow (I thought so in start) of real science'. The words 'ezoterics' and 'paramedicine' were used, and I think (don't hold me to this) that he wanted 'to focus on water as the nano science of the amazing molecule'. He ended off his message by thanking me for my 'focus on the matter (as we call in atomist way . . . a dark one) that is a part of that genius solution for your river in China'. Once again, I thought it best not to reply. I think I even feared slightly for the four children (29 to 16 mfmf).

It was the final response, though, that was the most disconcerting. A few days after our press release, my boss received a letter from the Whale and Dolphin Conservation Society, the 'global voice for the protection of whales, dolphins and their environment'. Dear Director, it read,

> I am writing on behalf of WDCS, the Whale and Dolphin Conservation Society, to inform you that we are disappointed to learn yet again of proposed attempts to locate and capture highly endangered Yangtze River dolphins (baiji) in China for proposed relocation to an oxbow lake for breeding purposes. We are equally disappointed to learn of the Zoological Society of London's involvement in these plans and their proposed management; and that you are currently seeking funding to implement these plans. As far as we are aware, there are no capture experts at the Zoological Society of London to take responsibility for any capture procedures that take place. . . .
>
> Similar proposals for the recovery of the baiji have been planned in China over the last several years. The project would undoubtedly involve large numbers of boats surveying the vast and heavily polluted Yangtze River in search of a dolphin that has seen its habitat slowly destroyed by man, and as a result its numbers have dwindled to fewer than 50. WDCS believes it may well be impossible to find even one baiji. If caught, transportation and relocation could cause great stress for the dolphins and there is also a serious risk of them suffocating or becoming injured in the nets used to capture them. Scientific evidence has demonstrated that dolphin mortality rates increase six-fold immediately after capture from the wild and the baiji appears to be a particularly sensitive species.

A previously flawed plan was attempted in the mid-1990s and failed when those involved succeeded in capturing one solitary female who, after relocation to the so-called reserve, was found dead, entangled in a net and suffering from malnourishment. Many mistakes were made, including allowing finless porpoises to be present in the reserve (possibly bullying the solitary baiji and depriving her of food); fishing was also allowed to continue in the area. Additionally, despite promises that QiQi, a captive male baiji held at the Wuhan dolphinarium, China, would be released into the reserve once a female was caught and relocated there, he remained in captivity and has recently died. WDCS is not confident that further attempts at capture and maintenance in captivity of these animals would be successful.

It is devastating to know that the baiji faces certain extinction and, as they are endemic to the Yangtze River, they are unlikely to survive in any other habitat. It is not as simple as relocating them to another environment in the hope they will adapt and survive. At best the proposed reserve could only prolong the lives of specimens of a species (and family) that could not currently be returned to their natural habitat which unfortunately may be beyond help—at this moment man has gone too far in destroying the only home of the baiji. . . .

We respectfully ask you to reconsider your involvement in such a project.[6]

I don't know whether the letter left me more appalled or incensed. Much of the text was reproduced from the WDCS website, which also proclaimed that the 'last remaining river dolphins deserve dignity and respect'.[7] As though having your head staved in by a boat propeller is a dignified end. After all of my involvement and frustrations with baiji conservation efforts, I did not appreciate being patronized by a conservation group who seemed to be prepared to allow a species to die out just because they had a subjective distaste for a recovery strategy which recent international meetings had largely accepted was the only remaining short-term option. I was also surprised at the lack of knowledge shown in the letter; did they not remember that Western researchers had assumed for most of the twentieth century that baiji *only* lived in lakes, for example?

We organized a meeting with a representative from WDCS. It went well, I suppose; we discussed the sad necessity for the recovery programme and our exhaustive attempts to ensure that the best international expertise was involved, and that the safest, most ethically acceptable approaches were followed during all times when dolphins were to be handled and managed. After all, the last thing we wanted to do was to stress or injure any of the baiji we might be lucky enough to secure for the breeding population. The WDCS representative accepted our explanations and wished us luck. But by now I felt like Judith in *Life of Brian*, forever preaching that 'We've got to *do* something!' No matter what I did, nobody seemed prepared to listen.

~

At least things were finally beginning to move out on the Yangtze. In March 2006, a nine-day pilot survey was organized by the baiji.org Foundation in the Honghu section, a stretch of river between Dongting Lake and Wuhan, in preparation for the forthcoming full range-wide baiji survey. It provided an invaluable opportunity for a group of international cetacean specialists to develop the optimal survey methods to be used in the shipping lane of one of the world's busiest rivers, representing extremely unfamiliar survey conditions to most of the participants. Nobody saw any baiji. Leigh called me from China; for the first time since I had met her, she sounded disheartened. I tried to console her. If it was so easy to find baiji in a short section of the river over a period of only a few days, then we wouldn't all have to be working so hard to try to save the species. Bill Perrin never saw any dolphins when he spent a similar length of time on the river back in the early 1980s, when there were probably still more than 300 animals left. Even in the 1920s, it took the fishermen working for Clifford Pope a month to catch a single animal in Dongting Lake.

However, the lack of any baiji sightings during the pilot survey was picked up on by the wider scientific community. It was reported in the 'News' section of *Nature*,[8] and, more worryingly, it was also cited by Professor Yang Guang and his team in their paper on why the baiji should be allowed to die out. If a field survey carried out by a team from China, the USA, the UK, and Switzerland, as they described it, failed to locate any baiji in the wild, then the prospects of capturing a viable population of baiji for conservation seemed extremely improbable. The fact that the survey team were only out on the river for a little over a week was not mentioned. But the murmurings were getting louder. The hopes of the researchers are now focused on the full-scale survey in November, reported *Nature*. 'If none are found then, the burden of proof will change,' said Jay Barlow, one of the American researchers who had been integral to developing appropriate baiji survey methods in the Yangtze channel. 'The species will be considered extinct unless proven otherwise.'[9]

The months slipped by. I worked on more funding applications, while Leigh became more and more involved with the tortuous logistics of planning the forthcoming range-wide survey. But Leigh retained her mood of concern and despondence long after the pilot was over. Was there some other, deeper problem here? I discussed the latest application I was working on to support the baiji recovery programme: since the baiji.org Foundation were going to be covering the costs of the survey, then we only needed external money to support the subsequent dolphin captures. That was right, wasn't it? But Leigh put things in a different perspective. For a long time, she had been requested to write funding applications from the foundation to independent donors as well, on the premise that this was just a top-up for August's generous personal donation to baiji conservation. She had never understood quite why this was necessary; the various projects that the foundation had carried out had never warranted more funds than August had proposed to cover from his own resources. However, as time passed, it became increasingly difficult to avoid the conclusion that the foundation was only able to carry out its initiatives whenever it received external funding. So what would happen with the survey—would it be delayed again or, even worse, unravel and fall apart if the money ran out? But would any good be achieved by bringing her inside knowledge and grave concerns to the public forum? This could only jeopardize the sponsorship that she increasingly realized was essential to making things happen, both for the survey and for the subsequent planned baiji capture operations. The ideal survey team was being assembled, and the plans were almost ready for everything to go ahead and make the survey a success. It was imperative that things must not be postponed any longer. She could only hope that all of the necessary sponsorship money would be transferred before the start of the survey—or some very unpleasant financial problems indeed would come to a head when everyone was already in China.

~

A few weeks before the survey started, the London papers announced the sixtieth anniversary of the death of the last known thylacine in Hobart Zoo. I shared a bottle of champagne on Primrose Hill with some colleagues to mark the occasion. Funding for the recovery programme still remained intangible and unforthcoming, and the recent revelations about the survey's funding were still a shock. Despite all this, though, I felt a surge of optimism. Very soon now, I will finally be out on the Yangtze. Very soon, I will have seen my first baiji. And very soon, the recovery programme will finally be able to begin. Surely, I thought, the publicity and findings of the survey will finally mobilize the conservation community to act, before it becomes too late to save the species?

Hadn't I learnt anything by now? Very soon, I would be proved very, very wrong.

8

THE HUNTING
OF THE SNARK

...and no one has the right to say that no water-babies exist till they have seen no water-babies existing; which is quite a different thing, mind, from not seeing water-babies.

Charles Kingsley
The Water Babies

The two stags, their heads down, paced warily around each other. Grey steam stood frozen for a moment around their wet muzzles. Behind them, a herd of female deer stood motionless, long faces watching from the safety of the yellow reeds. Suddenly the males pushed into each other, their hooves slipping on the mud as they tried to maintain their grip. The clash of antlers drifted towards us over the marsh.

In addition to the surreal sensation of actually seeing any kind of wildlife at all in China, I felt supremely privileged to be able to witness the autumn rut of Père David's deer or milu at Shishou. If not for the concerted actions of a handful of dedicated individuals, this sight would already have disappeared forever. For almost a century after the last animals in the Imperial Hunting Lodge died, the milu was gone from China, with the sole survivors of the species kept in a closely managed herd on the other side of the world at Woburn Abbey in Bedfordshire. Following the success of the Duke of Bedford's intensive breeding programme, other populations were later distributed to zoos and parks across Europe as part of a coordinated conservation effort. After the Cultural Revolution, around the time that the first baiji surveys were being carried out along the Yangtze, a campaign was started for the return of the deer to China. Eventually, after considerable negotiation and bureaucracy, twenty deer were transported to Beijing in 1985, followed a few years later by another eighteen animals. These individuals were used to establish semi-wild milu herds in four Chinese nature reserves. The animals thrived. Here at Shishou, the herd living in the marshes and reed beds that line the banks of the Tian'e-Zhou oxbow now contains over 600 animals and is the largest in the world. A breakaway herd, which formed when a stag and his harem swam across the main river channel, has even become established on the south bank of the Yangtze opposite the reserve—representing the first truly 'wild' Père David's deer in centuries.

If the deer at the edge of the reed beds in front of us represented the end point of a long, difficult, but eventually successful conservation story, then maybe there was also hope for the rare and beautiful freshwater dolphin that the reserve had originally been established to protect. Earlier that day we had taken a boat trip out onto the oxbow. Oriental skylarks sang their proud, fluid songs as they disappeared high above us in the dry air. At the end of the track leading from the new, unfurnished research building to the boat launch, in front of fields full of dusty cotton bushes, I halted in complete surprise: a set of four dolphin holding pens, linked to the shore by a metal causeway, was floating in front of me on the surface of the lake. The set-up was not perfect: the pens looked much smaller than those specified in the American plans we had sent to the Baiji Research Group, and they still consisted only of the above-water structural framework, lacking the nets that would prevent any captured baiji from swimming off into the oxbow, but this at least would be an easy final step to complete. After all the going round in circles and the exhaustive correspondence, I felt almost caught off-guard. Maybe the Chinese authorities *were* committed to conserving the baiji, after all?

The oxbow was beautiful; it was hard to imagine a better place for baiji conservation. It stretched away for miles in either direction, and among waters that reflected the autumn sun, several finless porpoises broke the surface as they played and hunted close to the bank. At long last I had now seen one of the Yangtze's endemic cetaceans. However, it was immediately clear that they would be difficult animals to survey and study. Unlike their marine relatives, these freshwater animals almost never performed dramatic jumps—a behaviour known as breaching—but instead gently rolled their bodies in the water when they came up for air, exposing only a part of their head and back and submerging again extremely quickly. Lacking a dorsal fin, they were very hard to spot. What was much more worrying, though, was the fact that fishing was still clearly being carried out in the reserve, and not only opportunistically but on a massive scale. There were nets in the water everywhere, and on the bank beside the holding pens sat a complicated piece of wooden apparatus resembling a huge folded umbrella studded with light bulbs, which must be used to attract fish at night. The ambiguity of the Chinese attitude towards baiji conservation once again left me baffled. Why go to the effort of constructing an expensive series of holding pens—albeit using their own blueprints rather than those which the international community had recommended as best for the job—when the same deadly nets that had probably killed the only baiji ever introduced into the reserve were still not being policed in the slightest? Did they really not believe that the nets had any effect? Was it all just too much effort for them to try to change the status quo? Or did it all come down to money?

On the trees, the leaves were turning dry and brown. Shrikes sat in the cotton bushes, and a tawny-coloured hoopoe foraged for insects on the dusty track. Towards the oxbow, a flock of brown winter ducks rose up above the water. As we walked back to our minibus, ready to set off on the long drive back to Wuhan, I flushed a pair of short-eared owls that had been sitting in the tall grass. Two majestic dappled ghosts, immensely beautiful, they started up silently from close under my feet, landing only metres away and stopping to watch us with sublime scorn. This was a land of signs and wonders. I hoped that this sign was an auspicious one.

~

I had arrived in China a couple of days earlier, greeted by a clutter of bamboo scaffolding, neon, bricks, and concrete. Open shop-fronts pressed against each other behind the noisy river of traffic on the cracked streets of Wuhan. Liquid gold writing splashed out in plastic characters above rows of blackened trees. Everywhere there was the familiar mix of rapid development and gradual decay, and a kind of dusty vibrancy in the air. The future was spreading upstream from Shanghai all along the Yangtze.

All of the usual suspects were already here. Wei was to be the Chinese project manager—Leigh's counterpart—for the survey, and many of the other dolphin researchers from the Institute of Hydrobiology were also going to be on board, together with a group of cheerful young Chinese graduate students and several of the managers of the various baiji reserves on the main Yangtze channel. A team of international cetacean experts had also assembled, all eager to try their luck at spotting baiji. Bob Pitman, an easy-going salty old sea dog with an expressive droopy moustache, and Todd Pusser, a more youthful American with a broad North Carolina drawl, had between them already seen almost all of the world's other whales and dolphins; a survey to find the baiji, one of the few species that neither cetacean twitcher had on their list, was the ultimate draw to guarantee the involvement of their expertise. The other international participants were also mostly from other American research facilities—the National Oceanographic and Atmospheric Administration, the Hubbs-SeaWorld Research Institute, and universities in Seattle and Hawaii—together with Tom Akamatsu and Kotoe Sasamori, two Japanese experts in cetacean acoustics who would be listening for baiji whistles using underwater hydrophones while everyone else was up on deck scanning the water.

Qi Qi was there to see us off, or at least what was left of him. He was mounted pride of place in the tiny museum behind the dolphinarium where he had lived for over two decades, but these days he didn't look quite as lifelike as he did in the photos. It was hard to tell exactly what the museum staff had done to him, but they had certainly tried to pimp him up. It didn't look much like a standard museum procedure. He seemed to have been embalmed in a shiny fibreglass shell, so that he looked like a giant children's toy or a glazed confection which still had an original set of dolphin teeth stuck into the front end—a bastardized replica of the last baiji rather than the real thing. I hadn't seen anything like it before. I was told that he had died during one of the heatwaves for which Wuhan is notorious, and his skin had started to blister and peel very quickly after death; enamelling his body had apparently been the only option for salvaging anything at all of his remains. At least he looked better than the dusty, crumpled porpoises and sturgeons that made up the rest of the display, stitched together badly after their fins had snapped off or they had been broken in two, and slowly falling apart like old sofas.

But the final build-up to the survey was still overshadowed by the threat of financial and sponsorship problems that Leigh had dreaded. It seemed that the main project costs were now being covered by a host of external funders, but other major issues remained outstanding. In addition to his original vow to provide personal funding to support the survey, August was also to organize the essential optical equipment: several pairs of standard binoculars, together with two sets of much higher-power, telescopic binoculars or 'big eyes', one of which would be mounted on each of the survey vessels. After extensive discussions with the Americans involved in developing the optimal survey methods for the Yangtze, the precise optical equipment that would be needed for a rigorous river survey had been specified months earlier in the pilot survey design report. But despite repeated assurances that everything was already taken care of through sponsorship connections, in the days immediately before the survey was due to commence the optical equipment had still not arrived in China. By the time that the international participants had begun to arrive, the big eyes were stuck in the unpredictable process of Chinese customs because they had been shipped so late. Whether they would make it in time for the survey was anyone's guess, and at the last minute the start date was pushed back by a week. When the big eyes finally arrived, there was no time to have them cleaned before the boats had to set off, and they were full of dust and dirt. As for the binoculars, the day we were actually leaving, we were finally given five pairs of binoculars that looked like they'd come from a bargain bin. Two of them even had labels saying 'Sample 1' and 'Sample 2' stuck on with tape. A few days after we started the survey, the eyepieces fell off. The only thing that salvaged the situation was the late arrival of John Brandon, one of the American observers, who was only able to get out to China a few days after we had left Wuhan and who met us downstream. After a few hectic phone calls from Leigh, John was able to pick up eight pairs of high-quality Fujinon binoculars in the USA—paid for by his father and only later reimbursed—and bring them along with him, saving the day.

But never mind the problems with essential equipment—the marketing side of the survey proved slick and effective. Everyone was kitted out in jackets and caps covered with sponsor logos; we felt like racing car drivers rather than scientists. The lavish opening ceremony was attended by journalists and TV crews from all over the world, with Budweiser beer—one of the expedition's main sponsors—being poured down pyramids of cheap champagne glasses. It was obscene. August was filmed on deck pretending to survey for baiji, for some reason scanning the river for the cameras using a laser range-finder instead of binoculars. A couple of days later, once the media circus had died down, he headed back to Switzerland.

~

We had arrived in Wuhan at the end of October, when the weather was still deceptively warm and the mood was still naively optimistic. Finally—almost a decade after the last Yangtze surveys had been conducted, and eighteen months after the original supposed start date for the baiji.org survey—something was actually going to *happen* for baiji conservation. Our excitement increased when we were told about recent possible baiji sightings from the Honghu river section upstream of Wuhan. Amazingly, it seemed that a mother and calf might have been seen in the spring, along with a second possible sighting of a solitary animal a few weeks later in the same area. Surely we would find some baiji still alive in the river, and finally be able to persuade the conservation community to act in time to save them?

We set off in two survey boats, a vessel owned by the Honghu Baiji Reserve and the *Kekao No. 1*, the Institute of Hydrobiology's own research vessel. They were low-slung sixty-foot boats that sat heavily in the water, resembling nothing more than floating shoeboxes lined with railings, and with a pile of cabins at the front topped with a flying bridge observation post. Our team was made up of about forty researchers, crew, and associated hangers-on of indeterminate status. Between them, the two boats required a grand total of five captains, because it was apparently much too tiring for any one captain to have to navigate for more than a couple of hours at a time. I was most intrigued by the ancient man who was always to be found sitting on a stool at the stern of the *Kekao*, wearing a beret and shades and with the dog-end of a cigarette perpetually hanging from his lips. I never found out what he did, but I had a suspicion that he actually lived on board the boat when it was docked and it had been impossible to evict him.

Leigh and I shared a dingy ground-floor cabin aboard the *Kekao* right above the engine room, where the beds and floor were constantly vibrating. We had definitely been given the short straw as far as accommodation was concerned. The cabins on the upper deck that were home to the other international and Chinese researchers had been freshly cleaned and had new 'Hello Kitty' bedsheets. In contrast, the floor and beds of our new home were caked with an unidentifiable sticky black residue, the bedding was damp, and there was a distinct acrid smell of animal urine which we vainly tried to mask by burning incense all day. There was no storage space at all in the cramped cabin, so we ended up sleeping buried beneath piles of dirty clothing. We covered the prominent stains on the walls with pictures of Chairman Mao and the most provocative poster of Britney Spears that we could find in the local market.

I was part of the observation team based up on the exposed flying bridge at the top of the boat, where there were unobstructed 360° views over the waters of the Yangtze. While Tom, Kotoe, and three of the Chinese graduate students took turns below deck to listen for dolphin whistles using the acoustic equipment being dragged behind the boat, we took ninety-minute shifts slowly and patiently scanning the river to the front and sides of the *Kekao*. Our binoculars were mounted on wooden poles, which could be held at waist level to reduce arm strain during the long observer shifts. There were three primary observers on effort at all times, slowly rotating their position from left observer, data recorder, and right observer every half-hour. While the left and right observers spent all of their time looking for dolphins and porpoises, the data recorder also took down a set of standard information about weather conditions, distance to the nearest river bank and Global Positioning System location every ten minutes, and recorded all of the information about any cetacean sightings that were made. Behind us, Bob and Todd took turns as independent observers, scanning up to a mile ahead of the boat with the mounted high-power big eyes. It took a while to persuade the reserve managers, who had been invited on board out of face-saving courtesy rather than because of their field experience, to stop talking on their mobile phones and actually pay attention to the river when they were supposed to be surveying. We had an even greater effort trying to make Wei look for baiji and porpoises in the water, their natural home, rather than aimlessly pointing his binoculars into the sky for entire shifts at a time as though he might somehow chance upon a cetacean somewhere up in the haze. Between shifts I read novels in our filthy cabin, or sat in the boat's large meeting room drinking green tea that tasted of ash and practising my Chinese with the students, rolling the unfamiliar new words around in my mouth.

We started off heading upstream towards Honghu and Yichang, the western limit of the historical distribution of both baiji and finless porpoise in the Yangtze, travelling at a speed of about 15 kilometres an hour. These middle stretches are about a kilometre wide, and under optimal viewing conditions an observer in the middle of the channel would be able to spot animals breaking the surface across the whole river. However, the haze of pollution hanging in the air typically reduced our effective visibility down to only a few hundred metres, and so the two survey boats covered the north and south sides of the river separately, travelling no more than 300 metres from each bank.

As our boats puttered slowly upstream away from the grime of Wuhan, followed by blue clouds of engine smoke, sunlight played on the waves rolling inexorably past us down to the sea far away to the east. Tall smokestacks striped red and white, their fumes trailing in the air, stretched up to the sky from the banks on either side, replacing the lonely pagodas with trees sprouting from their crowns; ancient sentinels of a time now long gone, silent and crumbling on hilltops overlooking the river.

The Americans, in China for the first time, fretted about sanitation and possible health risks, and insisted on avoiding anything that might not have been boiled or cooked thoroughly. I treated them with condescension as I started my first watch of the survey on the flying bridge. I was blasé, a seasoned traveller in China; I knew what you could eat and drink safely by now. Or so I thought. As I began slowly scanning the river ahead of me, I felt my stomach give its first tell-tale lurch. I gripped the binoculars more tightly.

'Erm...what happens if someone starts feeling ill on their watch, and can't finish the entire shift?' I called out nonchalantly to Bob, who was manning the big eyes first as we left port. I tried to mask the sheepishness in my voice.

There was a pause. Bob's moustache drooped with suspicion. 'Why do you ask?'

Another pause. 'Erm...Could you give me a minute?'

Dropping the binoculars, I scrambled quickly down the ladder from the flying bridge to the upper deck. I nearly made it to the toilets on the lower deck before my stomach gave another kick, and my breakfast burst out of my mouth into the Yangtze. My retching was drowned out by the din of the ship's engines, which shook the railings as I spat and sobbed over the side.

Hauling myself back up onto the flying bridge, I wiped the tears from my eyes and managed a few more perfunctory scans with my binoculars before being forced to stagger back down to the railings once more. This time the retching wouldn't stop. Soon I was curled up in my cabin, dozing feverishly and vomiting every hour or so. Inevitably, within a few hours my bowels had also decided to join in the party. I spent much of the next three days hunched over the boat's squat toilet, a porcelain hole that emptied directly into the rushing waters of the Yangtze below me, which would back-flush whatever had just dropped into it all over the occupant's feet and legs whenever we hit a large wake from a passing ship. To add to the fun of it all, someone had decided to wedge a Yamaha boat engine up against the front of the squat, so that trying to ease my knotted bowels necessitated pushing my face into a propeller. A single slip was likely to have highly unpleasant repercussions at both ends. The delicate balancing act that was required sent my thighs into excruciating spasms.

My embarrassment at being the first member of the survey team to come down with full-blown intestinal shut-down soon faded when illness began to pick everyone else off one by one as well. Constant revisions had to be made to the survey schedule in the light of each day's new casualties, and the few healthy observers that were left had to work double shifts to maintain efficient coverage of the river. Our suspicions lay with the ship's cook, an unsavoury-looking character who had been caught washing the food bowls in the Yangtze during the pilot survey. We were all sure that he was up to the same tricks again. Certainly, the waves of lurgy died away once we began looking after our bowls and cutlery ourselves. Later on, Bob Brownell suggested to me, only half in jest, that maybe a hundred million people shitting in the river was all that was needed to kill off the baiji. If only a few drops of the water were enough to wipe me out for several days, maybe he had a point.

As our beleaguered team slowly pulled themselves back together, the boats reached Yichang, the westernmost point of the survey, and turned back again downstream. The water here was clear and cold, all of the muddy sediments that once poured down from the Tibetan Plateau now trapped behind the huge Three Gorges Dam only a short distance to the north. Although we were now over 1,500 kilometres from the sea, the Yangtze was still vast even here, as wide as the estuary of a respectable European or American river. Fast currents curled around gravel bars in the middle of the stately channel; we scanned them all diligently for baiji, but to no avail. They were home only to peregrines that sat in wait for the waders that flew low over the grey water, looking for a place to land. Herons hunched frozen on the low brown banks; behind them, huge flocks of bean geese grazed on the muddy grass. As we docked at Yichang, a mountain bulbul, the only one I saw on the entire trip, landed on the railing so close to me that I could have touched it. Once we saw a group of elegant black storks, a 'rare and declining seasonal migrant' according to the bird guide in my cabin, their glossy red legs knee-deep in the water.

Every evening we would dock at one of the dead-end towns that poured their waste into the Yangtze. At Shishou, the small town close to the semi-natural reserve that now held only wasted dreams, we were thrown a banquet by the reserve managers and regional fisheries authorities staff. They had arranged for a special film to be played on a screen in front of our dining table. As we ate, footage of Qi Qi swimming round and round his concrete pool played to the soundtrack of a Chinese rendition of 'Que Sera Sera'. It was too unintentionally and horribly poignant for words. Then the film of Qi Qi was replaced with footage of effluent flowing from a concrete pipe into the river, no doubt to help us with our digestion.

The impacts of China's vast population on the river ecosystem could not be missed. The main channel was busy with every possible kind of shipping: heavy-laden coal barges, car ferries travelling downstream from the metropolis of Chongqing, passenger ferries, small boats buried under immense piles of reeds with a lone old man in faded blue Communist slacks sitting on the top, and even the occasional cruise liner. Even worse, it was immediately clear that there was no enforcement whatsoever of any of the illegal fishing practices that had doomed the baiji. Before we even left the dock in Wuhan, two fishing boats circled the *Kekao* and set their rolling hook long-lines out into the water around the research vessel, as symbolic a gesture as any with which to start the survey. We saw people fishing illegally every day in the river, and these fishermen would frequently stop to sell us the prizes from their day's catch. The Chinese researchers on board our boats didn't see the irony in this, and so we often ended up stopping to buy our dinner from the very people who had probably driven the animal we were desperately searching for to extinction. Bob commented wryly that even if we didn't see any baiji on the survey, we would probably see the fisherman who had killed the last baiji. The stern of the lower deck became piled with the slimy bodies of striped loaches, carp, and huge wels catfish, notorious back in Europe for their supposed penchant for eating small children. The old man with the beret watched impassively from his small wooden stool while the cook cleavered the living, gasping fish into oozing chunks of flesh. Dark red clots of fish blood slithered across the deck and mixed with black grime.

And then, after we passed by the foul-smelling pulp-and-paper mill at the mouth of Dongting Lake, where Charles Hoy had caught his baiji almost a century before, the weather took a turn for the worse. I was used to the English autumn's gradual, stately sigh of decay; here in China, summer instead seemingly turned to winter overnight. We were stopped by fog as we reached Honghu, where the alleged baiji sightings had been made a few months earlier. There was nothing to mark this supposedly protected section—a National Baiji Reserve, no less—as being any different from anywhere else in the river; it was as clogged with boat traffic and illegal fishermen as everywhere else that we had seen so far. Its only distinguishing feature was the giant white baiji statue, a memorial in concrete, which marked its downstream boundary. By the time we reached Wuhan again, the rains had started. We spent a day moored at the dock, waiting for the sky to clear.

We had now covered the entire middle section of the Yangtze, twice, in two independent survey boats. On most days we had sighted finless porpoises, either lone individuals or small groups feeding close to the banks or swimming rapidly in the main channel, and the cry of *Wo kan yi tou jiangtun!* ('I see a porpoise!') became a familiar sound. But we had found no evidence of baiji. Paradoxically, after so many months and years of trying desperately to muster support for its conservation, now that we were actually out on the Yangtze the animal's reality seemed to be receding further and further away. As we slowly accumulated data each day on numbers and distribution of finless porpoises, I wondered whether any of the other observers were even really considering baiji any more. For the first time in my life, I caught myself thinking about it in the past tense. I lay in my cabin all day, overcome with lethargy. I ate dry crackers and read *The Idiot*. It felt like an appropriate choice.

~

Almost as soon as we left Wuhan again, the weather became truly foul. Fog hugged the river and the biting cold snapped at our fingers and toes, making us run to clutch at paper cups of green tea as soon as our survey shifts were over. For the first few days as we travelled down the right-hand branch of the Yangtze's 'W' towards Jiangxi Province, flocks of spot-billed duck and ruddy shelduck sat on the water and ribbons of migrating swans passed by overhead, rippling gently in the wind, headed for the vast expanse of Poyang Lake immediately to the south. Their voices drifted down to us before they were swallowed up by the fog. Then the cold tightened its grip and the wind hit us with full force. Even though we all wrapped ourselves up in Chinese green military greatcoats, surveying from the flying bridge, unable to move for ninety minutes beyond scanning with slow sweeps back and forth across the water, turned into an endurance test that was physically painful. Looking out over the choppy slate-grey waves, our cheeks red and raw and with puffs of steam rising from our mouths, Bob told me that this was what the Bering Sea looked like. The cold snap drove the migrant birds further south, and they disappeared from the river.

I had been shocked by the state of the Yangtze between Wuhan and Yichang, but the lower stretches of the river were like nothing I had ever seen before. It was a motorway for thousands of freight vessels, lined with oil refineries, factories, and chemical plants pouring pollutants into its waters, and full of sand dredgers ripping up the river bed to make concrete for China's booming economy. The observers up on the flying bridge were regularly distracted by yells from the acoustic team desperately trying to alert passing ship traffic not to run over the hydrophone being towed behind the boat. The river was choked with trash floating downstream—broken furniture, dead dogs and pigs, and black bin bags that looked deceptively like porpoises until you realized that they were bobbing up and down too regularly to be alive. The riverside towns could be smelt on the wind before they came into view, and before the black-eared kites that swarmed on the rubbish dumps could be seen dusting their talons over the surface of the water to scoop up fish which they ate on the wing.

During our regular stops we explored these grimy towns, made up of identical stores selling cheap electronic goods and plastic tat, where China's functional society was spawning a lowest-common-denominator consumer culture that grew hungrier and hungrier each day. In Wuxue, a town of black mud and coal heaps where crumbling Soviet-style tower blocks overlooked the water, we saw dogs being skinned and nailed up to dry, next to piles of greasy-grey mitten crabs crawling over each other in perspex boxes. Our visit to Anqing, a riverside town in Anhui Province, provided some of the deepest memories of the trip. When we arrived, teenagers were break-dancing to Tom Jones on a huge sound stage, and we were followed by a fat-faced young man who was either a party official trying to keeping tabs on us or was just after a pick-up. Eventually Leigh asked him for directions and he sheepishly sidled away, realizing he'd been busted. Suddenly we were surrounded by hundreds of young children, just released from school, who pressed us to sign autographs for them—we were Westerners, so we must be famous film stars. Trapped in the middle of a huge clamouring crowd that only reached up to my waist, I scribbled my name and some badly written Chinese characters onto whatever the children had to hand: notebooks, shopping receipts, ping pong racquets, even a picture of Chairman Mao. And in the midst of all this madness, at the city's octagonal Zhenfeng Pagoda temple, was a procession of old women threading their way slowly in an endless loop between round red cushions laid on the stone floor, crying and wiping their faces with handkerchiefs in their sleeves as they shuffled forwards. Their bags of shopping left at the entrance, they chanted the chant of *Ah mi tong ba* for ever.

~

The survey had become a dreary existence. The days stuck together like mud. The American team argued over whether *ex situ* conservation was the answer, and proclaimed that the international community had been caught unawares by the disappearance of the baiji. If there were any baiji left, they assured me, it would be easy to raise funds to get a recovery programme going for the species. Had I ever been that naive?

It's hard to say quite when hope had started to fade on the downstream journey. For each of us the dawning realization had arrived at a different moment, but I knew that now we were just going through the motions. 'Baiji' had become an empty word to me, a term that manipulative individuals used for raising money to advance their own careers; it wasn't a real animal any more. Alternating waves of acceptance and disbelief were accompanied by a creeping sense of something approaching dread.

Morale was lowered even further by August's latest antics. After he initially agreed to cover the salaries and reimburse travel costs for many of the international participants, once the survey had started and he had returned to Switzerland, he began to backtrack on some of these agreements. His sentiment of 'team spirit', quoted so often to an eager international press, seemed to disappear quite readily. The prospect of mutiny began to simmer. After the farce of the optical equipment, if August might not now even honour his financial arrangements, then they were under no obligation to complete the expedition, decided the Americans. A plan developed to leave the ship at Nanjing, leaving a large stretch of the lower Yangtze unsurveyed. That would spite August's vision. It took all of Leigh's persuasion to make the team agree to stay on board. No matter what she or anyone else thought of August, the amount of effort—almost all her own—that had gone into getting the survey together would all have been in vain if everything fell apart now, at the final hour. Who knows how long we would have to wait until another survey was eventually organized; in the meantime, the baiji population estimate would still officially remain at 'fewer than a hundred'. Nothing would change if we didn't see this godawful, soul-destroying experience through to the bitter end. I wouldn't have been anywhere else in the world.

When we passed through the Tongling river section, the last of the supposed baiji 'hotspots' left for us to survey, the weather was fouler than ever. To paraphrase a famous Chinese poem, *Chang Jiang shui lang de lang*: the waves of the Yangtze rolled on and on. Squalls of rain lashed hard at the boats. Scanning the whitecaps on the choppy brown water, I had to keep wiping the binoculars after every single sweep of the river, but managed only to smear water around the lenses rather than making them any clearer. We found nothing. A few days later, after we passed Nanjing, a city now at the centre of a pollution belt that stretched all the way to the estuary, the river became tidal. It was now several kilometres wide, but enormous suspension bridges still stretched away in either direction into the haze.

The evening before we reached Shanghai, Leigh and I drank Snow beer and whisky, and I climbed up onto the flying bridge when everyone else was asleep. The night was as sharp as a pin, and we were so close to the coast that the smog had been cleared briefly by the winds blowing in from the sea. For the first time on the trip I could see stars reflected in the cold water. The Yangtze looked beautiful, with gentle waves lapping against the hull of the *Kekao* lit softly by distant vessels. It felt like the ship was mine, and that no one else existed in the entire world. This must be what the Yangtze had looked like long, long ago, I reflected, before people came along and ruined everything. This must be what it had looked like when there were still baiji in it.

9

THE GOLDEN CHANNEL

Whales and dolphins have not really benefited from sharing a planet with humans for the past few millennia. It seems that almost as soon as prehistoric people were able to construct craft that allowed them to take to the water, they made a point of persecuting aquatic mammals, after learning of the desirable properties of whale oil and meat from salvaged carcasses that washed up from time to time along the coast. Even before recent centuries, aboriginal hunters in many different parts of the world had become adept at killing whales that came close to land, using harpoons and hand lances deployed from kayaks, dugouts, or skin boats. The oldest known evidence for such aboriginal whaling is a recently discovered piece of walrus ivory from northeastern Siberia dating from 3,000 years ago, which is inscribed with artwork depicting teams of hunters in skin boats pursuing whales.[1] Sometimes more innovative techniques were employed; hunters around the northern rim of the Pacific made use of harpoons dipped in aconite, a potent poison derived from the monkshood plant, whereas hunters in Norway and Iceland instead infected their weapons with lethal bacteria. From around a thousand years ago, Basque whalers from northern France and Spain began to venture further and further afield across the North Atlantic and Arctic to hunt whales from small boats, reaching Ireland, the English Channel, Iceland, and eventually even Newfoundland and Labrador, and setting up semi-permanent shore stations at these increasingly remote outposts to process the animals they killed. The coat of arms of Lequeitio, one of the most important Basque whaling towns, bears the legend *Horrenda cette subjecit*: 'Dominate the horrible whale'. Basque-style whaling—sighting whales from lookouts on shore and pursuing them in open boats—spread across Europe and to the new colonies in North America, but whaling methods continued to diversify and improve, allowing the slaughter to become more and more exhaustive. By the middle of the eighteenth century, whaling fleets capable of making long-distance voyages upon the high seas had spread around the globe, and a hundred years ago fleets of factory ships from Europe, Russia, Japan, and many other countries had started harvesting huge numbers of whales as far away as the Antarctic Ocean.

The impact of all the cumulative centuries of increasingly intensive whaling sadly comes as no surprise. Whales that passed close to shore on their migration routes—right whales, bowheads, and grey whales—were the first species to be hit hard. Right whales were so-called because they were the 'right whales' to hunt: not only did they swim slowly near to land, but, unlike other whales, so much of their body consisted of blubber that they floated when killed, making them perfect targets for the early Basque whalers. Once abundant along the coasts of western Europe, where in centuries gone by huge groups migrated every year through the North Sea, English Channel, and Bay of Biscay, the North Atlantic species now numbers only a few hundred animals restricted to the northeast American seaboard that escaped the attention of Yankee whalers. However, like the baiji, the species now has to survive in one of the world's busiest shipping lanes, where animals are not only regularly killed by collisions with huge cargo vessels but are also increasingly threatened by entanglement in fishing gear. The North Pacific right whale is even more endangered, with maybe only 200 animals still surviving. Both of these species may well become extinct within the next century or so.

The grey whale has fared slightly better, but although the eastern Pacific population has recovered to around 22,000 individuals, recent genetic studies[2] suggest that the North Pacific probably supported almost 100,000 grey whales before historical human hunting began, and only about 100 animals are left in the critically endangered western Pacific population. The species was probably wiped out in the Atlantic by the end of the seventeenth century. All that is left of this extinct population are a few old bones washed up on beaches or excavated from drained fields that were once below the sea, together with some enigmatic centuries-old descriptions by early American and Icelandic whalers of an animal called the 'scrag whale' or 'sand-lier' that doesn't match any of the known whale species found in the Atlantic today. I recently visited Torquay Museum to examine some of the only known remains of the extinct Atlantic grey whale. The museum holds three grey whale vertebrae, found on the beach at Babbacombe Bay in the 1860s by the local collector William Pengelly, and carbon-dated to the early 1600s. As old as the plays of Shakespeare, these water-worn relics, washed by the waves for one and a half centuries before they were found, are as smooth as pebbles. Afterwards I sat on the beach looking out over the English Channel under the summer sun, next to mums and dads having fish and chips on the beach with their children. Only a few centuries ago, the waters in front of me would have been witness to a great annual whale migration, as these mighty animals travelled back and forth every year between their seasonal feeding grounds and calving grounds. Now the whales are gone. The sea felt empty.

After the slaughter of the right whales and grey whales, the other great whales were then sequentially hunted down and depleted as well. With the advent of the factory ships, the whalers sought out first blue whales, the largest animals ever to evolve on our planet, and then, once the blue whales started to disappear, they targeted smaller and smaller baleen whales—fin whales, sei whales, humpbacks, and minke whales. Modern populations for all of these species are still a small fraction of their former numbers. For example, several decades after the ban on commercial whaling, there are now around 10,000 humpbacks and 56,000 fin whales in the North Atlantic, but recent research into patterns of genetic variation in these species suggests that there may have been as many as 240,000 humpbacks and 360,000 fin whales before widespread commercial exploitation began in the nineteenth century.[3] It is unclear how long it will take for whale populations to fully recover, if indeed this will ever happen.

However, despite the centuries of aggressive persecution, very few marine mammals have ever been completely wiped out by humans, and none of these have been whales or dolphins. In contrast to the giant ocean-going baleen whales that were the target of so much whaling, the only species to have been eradicated completely were a handful of animals with much more restricted ranges, a quirk of geography which made their populations much more vulnerable to hunting. The first and most famous of these was a strange animal that had one of the quickest turnarounds between first discovery and final extinction of any species. It was first encountered in 1741 by the German naturalist Georg Wilhelm Steller, the physician with Captain-Commander Vitus Bering's expedition aboard the *St Peter* to investigate the distance between Kamchatka and America. After becoming the first Europeans to set foot on the northwest coast of America—where Steller discovered the distinct sea lions that are now named after him, along with many other new species—the expedition was struck down on the return voyage by bad weather and illness, and the ship was smashed upon the reef surrounding a strange island. Flinging several dead soldiers and a dead trumpeter overboard in case the corpses of their dead comrades were the cause of the rising seas, the superstitious crew managed to set up camp on the island which they soon realized was nowhere near Kamchatka. They were trapped there for almost a year, with disease gripping at the wasted men. Bering himself died of a gangrenous anal fistula shortly before Christmas 1741. 'Everywhere we looked,' wrote Steller, there were 'nothing but depressing and terrifying sights.'[4]

The crew spent most of their time playing cards, killing hundreds of sea otters simply in order to gamble with their pelts. Steller reported that 'even before they could be buried, the dead were mutilated by foxes that sniffed at and even dared to attack the sick'; in return, 'we tortured them most cruelly before the eyes of others, letting them run off half-skinned, without eyes, without tails, and with feet half-roasted.'[5] But in addition to these species already familiar to the Russian sailors, Steller also found that the waters around the strange island were home to a much more unusual beast. It was some kind of manatee, thought Steller, but it grew to almost 8-metres long. Vast herds of these giants, maybe as many as 2,000 animals in all, could be found feeding on kelp in the shallows and bays around the tiny island. This remarkable animal, which may have been even heavier than an elephant, is now known to have been more closely (albeit still distantly) related to dugongs rather than manatees, and bears its discoverer's name—Steller's sea cow.

As well as being the only scientist ever to observe living sea cows, Steller—inevitably—also quickly realized how easy they were to hunt, and found that they made extremely good eating. The boiled fat, he reported, 'excels olive oil, in taste like sweet almond oil, and of exceptionally good smell and nourishment. We drank it by the cupful without feeling the slightest nausea.' The fat of the calves was similar to the meat of young pigs, whereas 'the meat of the old animals is indistinguishable from beef and differs from the meat of all land and sea animals in the remarkable characteristic that even in the hottest summer months it keeps in the open air without becoming rancid for two whole weeks and even longer, despite its being so defiled by blowflies that it is covered with worms everywhere.' Steller also noted that 'it was evident that all who ate it felt that they increased notably in vigour and health.'[6]

The culinary opportunities that the sea cows presented to starving Russian sailors, together with the ease with which these placid animals could be caught in the shallow offshore waters, rapidly condemned the species to its fate. After they repaired their ship and prepared to leave the island, later named Bering Island in honour of their late captain, the crew had no doubts that sea cows would provide all of the provisions they needed to go to sea with, and they set off with five barrels of salted sea cow meat, butter made from sea cow fat, and dried sea cow biscuit. Steller reasoned that 'the entire coast of Kamchatka could continually supply itself plentifully from them with both fat and meat',[7]but the idea that sea cows represented an infinite resource was sadly misplaced.

Once the *St Peter* made it back successfully to the Russian mainland, news about the remote island and its strange fauna spread rapidly, and only a year later Bering Island had already become a regular stopping-off point for Russian fur-hunting expeditions to stock up on provisions for their long voyages across the North Pacific. Hardly a winter passed over the next two decades without one or more groups of thirty to fifty hunters spending eight or nine months hunting foxes and sea otters on the island, during which time they lived almost exclusively on sea cow meat. Efficient hunting of sea cows, whereby all animals that were killed were exploited for food, would have been bad enough for a huge, slow-growing species which probably gave birth to only one young every few years, but what made the slaughter even worse was the tremendous wastefulness of the Russians. Although provisions for ongoing voyages were obtained by harpooning animals from boats, daily supplies were obtained simply by wading out into the shallows and wounding sea cows by spearing their backs with a sharpened iron pole. If the dying animal was cast up onto the shore the same day then it could be eaten, but typically it would panic and swim out to deeper water, where its body would either drift out to sea or only be washed up when it was already rotten. It is estimated that five times as many sea cows were killed by the fur hunters using this technique than were actually needed for food. Even at the time, the slaughter seemed horrendous. The mining engineer Petr Yakovlev, who wintered on Bering Island from 1754 to 1755, was so appalled that he even petitioned the Bol'sheretsk Chancellery in Kamchatka to issue a decree prohibiting the destructive hunting of sea cows.[8] But it was no use. The hunting continued, and the last known sea cow was killed in 1768, only twenty-seven years after the species was first discovered by Steller.

Unwilling to accept that small bands of hunters lacking guns and with only primitive weapons could have completely wiped out such a large animal, several marine biologists have suggested instead that the extinction of the sea cow could have come about for another reason. Because the Russian hunters were also killing huge numbers of sea otters, these researchers reasoned, maybe the removal of this second species from the Bering Island ecosystem could have led to ecological changes that brought about the sea cow's demise in a more indirect manner. This certainly seemed like a possibility. Sea otters are a classic example of a 'keystone species'—a species which, if it goes extinct, can precipitate a fundamental change in the state of an ecosystem. The analogy here is with the keystone in a stone arch, which locks all of the other stones together; if the keystone is removed, the arch will collapse. Sea otters feed mainly on sea urchins, and in doing so help to keep urchin numbers low. However, in many parts of the Pacific Northwest, sea otters were locally wiped out by the fur trade, and sea urchin numbers exploded as a result. Because sea urchins are voracious kelp-eaters, the removal of sea otters led to massive local depletion of kelp. And because sea cows depended entirely upon kelp for food, then the disappearance of sea otters could have led to the disappearance of sea cows as well.

This seems like a very neat argument, a clever scientific revision of the simplistic hunting theory. Unfortunately, though, it is very unlikely to be true. Together with my colleague Dr Claire Risley, one of my oldest and closest friends and who has the kind of mathematical abilities that intimidate mere mortals, I went back through the historical records that were known about the various eighteenth-century hunting expeditions to Bering Island. We developed a mathematical model using known records of sea cow hunting, and using biological data derived from dugongs, the sea cow's closest living relative, to estimate key parameters such as its lifespan and number of offspring.[9] Our findings revealed that direct persecution by Russian fur hunters was, sadly, more than sufficient to have wiped out the species without needing to invoke any other factors. The eighteenth-century visitors to Bering Island hunted sea cows at more than seven times the sustainable limit, and in fact our model predicted that, if the estimated hunting levels and sea cow population numbers were accurate, the species should have gone extinct even sooner than 1768—any additional effects caused by sea otter removal would therefore have been minimal. Hunting was, after all, the sole reason for the disappearance of the sea cow.

This shouldn't come as a surprise. The recent fossil record shows that sea cows were once found in shallow seas all around the North Pacific Rim from Russia to California, but they seem to have been hunted to extinction by prehistoric hunters as soon as modern humans spread across northeast Asia and into the Americas, leaving only remnant sea cow populations around isolated Pacific islands far away from the mainland. Recently discovered historical records[10] suggest that sea cows may also have survived until the eighteenth century on Attu, an island in the Aleutians, where a huge marine animal called the *kukh su'kh tukh* that matches the sea cow's description was so easy to kill that it was apparently left up to the local women to hunt them. This population also seems to have disappeared upon the arrival of the Russians. Less than a hundred years later, the fur hunters had also succeeded in eradicating Bering Island's only other unique species, a semi-flightless cormorant with a smart white eye-ring, which has been almost forgotten about today.

Even more recently, during the twentieth century, two other marine mammal species with limited geographical ranges were also completely wiped out by hunting. The first of these, the Caribbean monk seal, was once found in the Gulf of Mexico and around the islands of the Caribbean Sea. It was first recorded by Christopher Columbus, who reported that his men killed 'eight sea wolves, which were sleeping on the sands'[11] on a small island near Hispaniola during his second voyage to the Caribbean in 1494. The persecution of the monk seals by Europeans continued as it had begun, as the animals constituted one of the few readily available sources of oil in the tropical Atlantic. Sir Hans Sloane reported in 1707 that fishermen 'try or melt them, and bring off their oil for lamps to the islands',[12] and by the eighteenth century the species had become the basis for a profitable seal fishery. However, it was slaughtered so persistently that the seal populations on the many small islands across the Caribbean were progressively eliminated. By the close of the nineteenth century, there were almost no seals left, and the tiny remnant populations of survivors were restricted to remote cays far from the mainland. But still the slaughter continued—and not only for oil, but increasingly also through additional persecution by fishermen who blamed the rare seals for depleting their fish catches, and by scientists trying to obtain precious museum specimens. Edward Nelson, who visited the Yucatán Peninsula under the employment of the United States Bureau of Biological Survey in June 1900, described one of the last known monk seal populations on the Triangle Keys:[13]

> We found these seals much less numerous than they were reported to be by men at Campeche who have visited the Triangles to kill them for oil during the past few years. The man from whom we hired

our schooner has made two sealing expeditions to the Triangles and under his directions hundreds of the seals have been killed with clubs. The blubber was removed and tried out [i.e. melted] on the spot and taken back to the mainland in 5 gal. oil tins and sold to the R. R. Co. for $3 per tin for lubricating purposes. In this way the great majority of the existing seals of this species have been destroyed within the last ten years. At the time of our visit we landed on two of the 3 islets making up the group called the Triangles and the total number of seals observed during our week's stay did not exceed 75 of which we obtained a good series [i.e. of museum specimens] about one half the number. Should the sealers again visit the islands it is possible that all of the survivors will be killed.

Nelson's prophecy soon came true; in January 1911, fishermen returned to the Triangle Keys and killed about 200 more seals. The species only survived for a few more decades. The last reliable records are from 1952, when a small colony of seals was observed on the Serranilla Bank, a group of tiny coral islands between Jamaica and Honduras.

Another species of seal, the Japanese sea lion, also disappeared around the same time. Much less is known about this animal, even down to whether it was really distinct from the surviving California sea lion. It was formerly found around the islands of Japan and the Korean Archipelago, but like the Caribbean monk seal it was again massively overexploited for its oil; Japanese trawlers may have harvested 16,500 sea lions in the early twentieth century, and only a few dozen were known to survive by the 1930s. The last Japanese sea lions were apparently reported by Korean coast guards in the 1950s.

But the baiji's story was different. Unlike these other marine mammal extinctions, and unlike all of the historical extinctions of other large, charismatic mammal and bird species such as the blue-buck, Falkland Island wolf, thylacine, passenger pigeon, and great auk, the disappearance of the baiji had not come about because of active persecution. Instead, it was merely the result of incidental mortality caused by huge-scale fishing efforts and development projects that were not actively trying to target the dolphin at all, and combined with a general inertia and feeble-mindedness on the part of the conservation organizations that were supposed to be trying to save the species. The fact that the baiji now seemed to be gone was simply the latest stage in the progressive ecological deterioration of the Yangtze region, which didn't look set to stop any time soon.

~

As December arrived and the survey finally drew closer and closer towards its end, everywhere we looked there were nothing but depressing and terrifying sights on the Yangtze as well. Travelling back upstream from Shanghai, along a river lined with petro-chemical plants and rusting dockyards and with its banks totally consolidated with concrete, we were passed by a never-ending procession of huge cargo boats pulling in timber from Russia, southeast Asia, and other developing countries from Brazil to the Congo to the Solomon Islands. Half of all traded timber in the world is now destined for China, and the rampant Chinese trade in illegal timber is one of the main drivers of large-scale forest destruction across the globe.[14]In the 1,669 kilometres between Yichang to Shanghai, we counted a minimum of 19,830 large shipping vessels on the river—more than one every 100 metres. China was reaching its tendrils out from the Yangtze to devour the world.

We had already surveyed the entire historical range of the baiji in the main Yangtze channel and found nothing left, and now we were just retreading the same grey, dead river, already knowing that it was empty. The mood onboard was quiet and sombre, interrupted only when tensions occasionally flared. Our feelings were soured even further when we learned that August was still acting as spokesperson to the international media. Hope dies last, he proclaimed.[15]What would he know? He wasn't even there; and anyway, everything was gone now, hope and all. We would soon find out that he had also taken the responsibility to tell the world that the baiji recovery programme had been shelved.[16]

New challenges of daily life in the field still continued to arise, even in the last few days of the survey. One lunchtime when we were somewhere in Anhui Province, a skinned and beheaded young dog, still readily identifiable by its large puppy paws, lay in a basket next to the rice in the kitchen. Later on that day, a nauseating smell of decay started to spread across the boat from the stern, and that night the rats arrived. They were suddenly everywhere in our cabin: in the walls, under the beds, and gnawing through any possessions left out in the open. Worst of all, they seemed to single me out, making nests in my clothes and fouling them all with their pungent urine. I very quickly grew tired of being kept awake by the sound of gnawing through plastic, and feeling rats running across my arms as soon as I turned out the light. I took to sleeping with my walking boots in my hands, ready to throw them in the direction of the persistent scamperings and scrabblings.

A few days later, at dawn, Wei suddenly burst into my cabin, brimming with excitement. 'Dr Sam! Dr Sam!' he cried. 'There is a baiji beside the boat!' Wiping the sleep from my bleary morning eyes, I stumbled to the railings and looked out over the water. There right in front of me, less than ten metres away from the ship, was a pair of finless porpoises, rolling and breathing noisily in the still morning air. It was the best view I had had of the animals during the whole expedition, and it was immediately obvious that they were black, with no fin and no beak. It was absolutely impossible to mistake them for baiji. I stood for a long time watching the beautiful spectacle and saying nothing. 'Ah,' said Wei eventually. 'Maybe...they are porpoises?' I was too tired to reply. Later that day, Leigh reminded me that this was the man who had reported over 110 official baiji sightings on previous surveys, including some of the last verified reports from the surveys in 1997 to 1999. How many of these sightings had been imaginary too? Did that last estimate of thirteen surviving individuals have any real meaning? Had the baiji actually disappeared even earlier than we had thought?

The final false hope was exhausted on 11 December. We had once again reached Balijiang, the short section of river at the border between Jiangxi and Anhui provinces where the channel leading from Poyang Lake and a major 20-kilometre side-channel both empty into the main Yangtze. The section had historically been known as a baiji 'hotspot', and one of the final two official baiji sightings from the 1999 survey (albeit one reported by Wei) had been made at the mouth of the side-channel, a region known as Balijiangkou. Baiji had also been known to occur in the large side-channel, which until sixty years earlier had actually been the main channel of the river. Wang Ding described to us how this was in fact the only place along the whole river that he had spotted a pair of baiji during a survey in 1995. Although we had already surveyed the entirety of the baiji's range in the main Yangtze channel, we also had to investigate the remote possibility that some dolphins might have clung onto survival here away from the busy shipping in the main river.

We passed slowly between soggy mud banks heavy with wet grass and the skeletons of trees. The still waters of the side-channel were broken only by eddies that blossomed like flowers on its smooth surface. Both water and sky were made up of the same soft damp greyness; fishing boats appeared to be suspended in air heavy with mist and drizzle, and in front of the ship everything faded into a grey void. It was completely silent. We stood vigilantly on deck, peering out into the blankness. Everything felt poised and expectant ...

... and then, ahead of us, the end of the side-channel condensed out from the grey air. We had seen nothing.

I thought that I had already become resigned to the loss of the baiji over the past few weeks, but as this one last chance came to an end, I found that I still had the capacity to surprise myself. Lifting my hand to my face, I felt that my cheeks were damp. I suddenly realized that I was crying.

~

Everything else went by quickly after that. On the last day of the survey, we moored next to a lumber boat, loaded with pines that smelt of Christmas. We arrived in Wuhan on a cold, clear day. There was, inevitably, yet another press conference, held at the dock as we were still disembarking from the *Kekao*. August was there, of course, reiterating his catchphrase of 'team spirit'. August and Wang Ding sat next to each other answering questions in front of the cameras, but while August confessed that 'we had lost the race' to save the baiji, Wang Ding was giving subtly different responses in Chinese for the national press: just because we didn't see any baiji, he said, we can't say that there aren't any left.

That night a big party was thrown by the Institute of Hydrobiology in an upmarket restaurant in Wuhan, to celebrate the 'success' of the survey. The next day, we all went home.

10

SO LONG, AND THANKS FOR ALL THE FISHING

This is the way the world ends
Not with a bang but a whimper.

T. S. Eliot
The Hollow Men

Over the next few weeks, the survey slipped quietly into the past and became consigned to memory, the daily grind of life on the river ossifying around the story told by a handful of photographs. I had no desire to relive the experience and tried to avoid my work colleagues, who wanted to hear all the details. They were sympathetic, but asked whether maybe I was being too pessimistic, unable to separate the cumulative failures I had experienced throughout the whole sorry baiji saga from the ecological reality out there in the Yangtze. Surely, as Wang Ding had told the Chinese press at the end of the survey, there must still be a chance that a few animals might survive?

The question of whether a species has really become extinct is a perennial problem in conservation science, because it can never be answered with absolute certainty. The reason why this is the case is outlined by a pair of scientific idioms: absence of evidence does not indicate evidence of absence, and it is impossible to prove a negative. Quite simply, before a species dies out it becomes very rare, which by definition means that it becomes extremely difficult to find. So just because a survey does not find any indication that a rare species is still around, that doesn't necessarily mean that the species has become extinct. It may be persisting undetected at an extremely low population density, making it highly unlikely to be detected. While progressive surveys that also find no evidence for its survival can strengthen the likelihood that the species really is extinct, none of these surveys singly or together constitutes conclusive proof.

Only in a very few instances do we think we can pinpoint the exact time of a species' demise. The best-known example is the passenger pigeon. Until only a couple of centuries ago, this single bird species occurred in North America in flocks of a size unimaginable today. The famous ornithologist John James Audubon reported that one day in autumn 1813, the sky was darkened from horizon to horizon for fifty-five miles by a cloud of passenger pigeons that he estimated to consist of more than a billion birds. Other documented flocks stretched for 300 miles and probably contained over 3.5 billion birds, and there may have been as many as 6 billion pigeons alive on the continent into the nineteenth century. Up to 40 per cent of all the birds in North America a few hundred years ago were passenger pigeons. Who could have ever thought that a species of such gross abundance could ever become extinct? Certainly not the swathes of hunters, who used the new railroads to search out the pigeon's great nesting grounds, and kill not only adult birds but also all of the nestlings, sealing the bird's fate. The same railroads were then used to send countless barrels of pigeons across the continent to the ravenous markets of New York. All of a sudden, the huge flocks were gone. The species only just saw in the new century before it met a pathetic end in March 1900, when the last known wild bird was shot by a 14-year-old boy in Sargents, Ohio. As Audubon himself wrote in what would later become an unwitting epitaph for the pigeon, 'it passes like a thought, and on trying to see it again, the eye searches in vain; the bird is gone.'

The passenger pigeon was a species that seems to have required vast flocks in order to survive. Huge masses of birds roosted, migrated, and nested together, and—maybe most importantly— seem to have needed the company of countless other pigeons all around them to encourage them to breed successfully. Although it is difficult to reconstruct the behaviour and ecology of a species that disappeared in the wild over a century ago, it is widely considered that the pigeon would simply have been unable to persist if its population fell too low to allow large flocks to form. This phenomenon is termed the Allee Effect, after the eco- logist Warder C. Allee, whose laboratory studies on lowly flour beetles in the 1930s and 1940s demonstrated that low popula- tion densities could have negative effects on population growth. The survival of the passenger pigeon would therefore have been immediately betrayed by huge flocks of the birds; if there were no remaining flocks, there were probably no birds left at all.

We can be fairly confident, then, that the bird shot in Sargents could well have been the very last wild passenger pigeon of all. Even if some other birds survived for a few more months, or maybe even for a couple of years, the species was certainly extinct in the wild by the beginning of the twentieth century. But this was not the final end. Before the passenger pigeon finally disappeared from North America, a handful of birds were taken from the wild to form a small captive flock. By 1900, some of these birds were still alive. The last of the captive birds, an old female called Martha (named after George Washington's wife), lived on until 1914, long after any remaining wild birds would certainly have died. At around 1 p.m. on 1 September 1914, Martha was found dead at the bottom of her cage in Cincinnati Zoo. Her death brought the story of the passenger pigeon, the 'blue meteor' of the American woods, to a close. Without a doubt, the last of the pigeons was gone.

But Martha's story is the exception rather than the rule. In nearly every other instance, we have to infer whether extinction events have actually taken place, using indirect evidence such as sightings records, oral histories, or data associated with museum specimens. However, this approach obviously leads to fundamental difficulties and ambiguities of interpretation. Until recently, an arbitrary cut-off of fifty years after the last confirmed sighting was used to determine whether a species should be formally considered extinct. While this may have some bearing on reality in geographical regions that are intensively studied, though, much of the world remains very poorly understood by Western scientists even today. Just because a species from a remote corner of the world has not been officially recorded for fifty years, this may actually reflect a lack of concerted scientific research in that region rather than the genuine disappearance of the species.

This is ably illustrated by the case of the New Caledonian owlet-nightjar, an obscure and enigmatic bird that, as its name suggests, resembles a cross between a small owl and a nightjar—and combines the cryptic properties of both. Owlet-nightjars are found across Australia, New Guinea, and some of the larger Melanesian islands in the tropical Pacific, but they are extremely hard to survey. Although the Australian species is apparently one of the commonest nocturnal birds on the continent, it is very rarely seen, because unlike other night-flying species, for some unknown evolutionary reason its eyes lack the tapetum lucidum layer, which means that they don't reflect light back if you shine it at them. They are, therefore, effectively invisible to anyone trying to find them. And in Australia, at least, people do sometimes try to find the birds. On New Caledonia, in contrast, relatively little ornithological research has been carried out, especially in the more remote regions of the island. As a result of all of these factors, the New Caledonian owlet-nightjar is one of the most poorly known birds on the planet. The first known specimen was collected in 1880, when the unsuspecting bird accidentally flew into someone's house. It was not until more than a century later, in 1998, that another owlet-nightjar was definitely reported on the island, by a team of English students who had travelled to New Caledonia specifically to conduct intensive surveys for possibly extinct birds. A few years later another owlet-nightjar specimen, which had apparently been shot on New Caledonia in the early years of the twentieth century and then forgotten about, was found in the collections of a museum in Rome. We still know next to nothing about the bird's ecology, behaviour, or distribution across the island. Given this pitiful track record of scientific encounters with the species, before 1998 one could have been forgiven for thinking that it was certainly already extinct—as, indeed, was the opinion of many scientists who specialized in Pacific birds—because the time since it had last been seen was over double the 'official' waiting period of fifty years.

In the case of the owlet-nightjar, the main problem until 1998 was trying to find any information at all that could inform scientists about the possible survival of the species. Similar problems have also presented major obstacles to understanding the extinctions of other species which we've already considered. For instance, we now know that Steller's sea cow, the giant relative of the dugong that was hunted to extinction in the middle of the eighteenth century, was restricted by historical times to an extremely narrow relictual distribution around Bering Island, a smaller neighbouring island called Copper Island, and possibly also some of the western Aleutian Islands. But this was not readily apparent to researchers in the nineteenth century, when extinction first began to be widely recognized as a real ecological process. The possibility of the sea cow's continued survival in other remote parts of the North Pacific, a region well away from familiar western European trading or whaling routes, was suggested by several notable scientists during this period. Indeed, Leonhard Stejneger, a researcher from the Smithsonian Institution, carried out an eighteen-month stay on Bering Island during the nineteenth century which partly served to assess the veracity of a supposed report of a living sea cow seen in the waters around the island in 1854. Stejneger concluded that the animal had in fact been a stray female narwhal. However, although Stejneger also collated all of the known historical records of sea cows and concluded that the species had last been reported in 1768, a question mark still remained hanging over whether the animal was really extinct for another century. In the *First Report of the President and Trustees of the World Wildlife Fund*, published in 1965, the sea cow's status was listed as 'inadequately known—survey required or data sought'. It was not until the 1980s that the IUCN formally recognized the species as being extinct.

As suggested by Stejneger's investigation of what turned out to be a misidentified narwhal from Bering Island, a lack of data from poorly studied parts of the world isn't the only obstacle facing researchers trying to understand whether a species has really died out. In many situations, scientists also have to contend with reports which suggest that a possibly extinct species might still survive, but which unfortunately consist only of rumours from the backwoods, second-hand stories, or, at best, sighting claims that are unverified and ultimately unverifiable. The problem in these instances therefore concerns not only data quantity, but also data quality. This is exemplified by the case of the thylacine, the marsupial 'tiger' that is known to have survived on Tasmania at least until the 1930s. Out of all the world's 'officially' extinct species, the thylacine has probably generated the largest number of unsubstantiated post-extinction reports—constituting both direct supposed sightings and also associated field evidence—that have been used to suggest to a huge community of 'believers' that this beautiful and mysterious animal still survives in the remote forests of Tasmania.

The huge volume of reports that have been gathered over the years is certainly tantalizing. Although the last captive animal died in September 1936, a series of surveys conducted in 1938 collected large numbers of recent eye-witness sighting records, and obtained several plaster casts of fresh thylacine prints from the Jane River and other regions of Tasmania. The leaders of the survey felt that this evidence provided uncontroversial proof that healthy populations of thylacines still survived in several parts of the island.

Hundreds of subsequent supposed sightings, almost all of solitary animals seen at dusk or in the early hours of the night, were reported throughout the later decades of the twentieth century and continue to be reported today, together with footprints, sheep kills, and droppings that have also all been suggested to be the work of thylacines. A scientific review of 84 sightings from 1960 to 1969 and 104 sightings from 1970 to 1979 provided 'a basis for cautious optimism' for the paper's authors, D. E. Rounsevell and S. J. Smith.[1] Interestingly, the distribution of recent thylacine sightings in Tasmania corresponds with the distribution of government bounty payments made by the thylacine bounty scheme that operated during the nineteenth and early twentieth centuries, and statistically matches the predicted distribution of optimal thylacine habitat based on historical occurrence records, but is not closely related to the distribution of roads or to the island's human population. A recent bio-economic model which re-evaluated the historical thylacine bounty records also suggested that the species could not have been driven to extinction by the bounty scheme, with a 100 per cent probability that a viable population of 50 or more individuals (and probably more than 500 individuals) survived well into the twentieth century.[2] Even more curiously, there have also been a number of notable eye-witness reports of thylacines from both mainland Australia and New Guinea, where fossil finds indicate that the species definitely survived until only a few thousand years ago. Most notably, a series of five photographs purporting to show a live thylacine photographed in Western Australia in 1985 were published a year later in *New Scientist*,[3] and other thylacine sightings continue to be reported both in this state and in Victoria, primarily the Gippsland region.

But none of these reports, not even the photographs, has been conclusively confirmed by scientists. Instead, intensive official searches, often lasting for several months, have never revealed any firm evidence for the survival of the species past the 1930s. In all of the thousands of nights spent surveying the remote wilds of Tasmania using camera traps, or identifying animal remains from the countless miles of road-kill knocked down by cars across the island, no thylacines have ever been found. While it is certainly possible, maybe even likely, that thylacines survived into the middle decades of the twentieth century, it is also increasingly likely that today they are no more. When I was younger I used to be a thylacine believer myself, caught up in the romance and affronted by the attitudes of Western armchair critics who had never been to Tasmania to actually assess the situation for themselves. Now I'm not so sure.

The fifty-year rule on extinction has now been replaced by more flexible IUCN guidelines which state that a species should only be considered extinct when 'there is no reasonable doubt that the last individual has died', and that this is reliant on exhaustive surveys in known and/or expected habitat, at appropriate times throughout its historic range. This is being increasingly complemented today by a range of statistical methods with names such as optimal linear estimation, which can be used to try to determine an extinction date based on the mathematical properties surrounding the relative timing of the last historical records of a questionably extinct species. However, these approaches still have their limits. The various statistical methods all rely on a number of assumptions, such as constancy of search efforts over time by researchers trying to find enigmatic species, which certainly do not hold true for the highly sporadic field research into the status of the New Caledonian owlet-nightjar or in many other instances. The inevitable uncertainty surrounding the survival or extinction of poorly studied species in poorly known regions seems destined to remain a perennial problem for conservationists.

The fact that we found no surviving baiji during our exhaustive Yangtze survey does not, therefore, constitute solid proof that the dolphin is definitely extinct. However, there are a number of significant differences between our baiji survey and the search efforts for species such as the New Caledonian owlet-nightjar and the thylacine that compel us to reach this inevitable but unwanted conclusion. Whereas New Caledonia and Tasmania are wild places full of possibility, rich with forests, mountains, and valleys where researchers have still to tread and where there is always the possibility that hidden populations of unknown species may yet remain concealed, nowhere along the Yangtze is 'remote' any more. The main Yangtze channel, which constitutes almost all of the baiji's historical range, represents what is effectively a huge line transect that can be surveyed in its entirety with relative ease. Furthermore, our survey was conducted with two survey vessels, both of which travelled twice across all of the baiji's range—from Wuhan to Yichang, then downstream to Shanghai, then back up to Wuhan—effectively representing not one but four independent surveys. Whereas we found no evidence that any baiji still survived in the river, the two survey vessels counted extremely similar numbers of finless porpoises during this extended survey period, both on a daily basis and over the entire course of the survey—the observers aboard the *Kekao* saw 460 animals, while those aboard the Honghu reserve vessel saw 428—which constitutes further persuasive evidence that no baiji were missed in the main channel by the survey teams.

The question remains: if there are any baiji left, then where were they hiding? We didn't survey either Dongting or Poyang Lake, both of which once supported populations of baiji, but both lakes are already surveyed every three months by staff from the Baiji Research Group who are studying the resident finless porpoises. However, it's true that we didn't go down all of the side-channels, even the major ones, or into the various tributaries that empty into the main Yangtze channel. But the side-channel which we surveyed at Balijiangkou, one of the largest along the entire river, was in no way large enough to support anything like a viable population of dolphins that might have remained undetected, especially since the countercurrent eddies where the side-channel meets the river, which represent the region of most suitable baiji habitat in all of these channels, lie within the area covered by our survey efforts. Similarly, all of the main tributaries are now dammed within a few miles of the main channel, and so could contain at most one or two baiji that would only be transient visitors rather than permanent residents.

It is conceivable that we missed a few, maybe a handful, of baiji individuals during our survey. But at the end of the day, what does it actually matter? This may sound like heresy at first, especially from a conservationist who has spent much of the past few years trying desperately to save the species, but wait—hear me out. Over the past few decades, we have increasingly realized that the baiji faced certain extinction if it was left to fend for itself in the Yangtze without the support of an *ex situ* recovery programme. Our survey represented by far the most intensive and exhaustive attempt to find baiji that has ever been carried out in the river, and yet, if there were any animals left, we were simply unable to find them. So what does it matter if a couple of dolphins are still struggling to survive out there, eking out a lonely existence among the long-lines and the boat traffic, and waiting for that inevitable moment when they are eventually snagged by hooks and nets, electrocuted, choked by pollution, or cut in two by propellers? Even if we tried to launch an all-out conservation effort now, if we can't actually find the animals in order to translocate them, then what would be the point? And if it proved impossible in the end to raise any funding to capture them when at least everyone still thought that the species was just about hanging on, then what hope on earth do we have to muster up any support to put together a six- or seven-figure recovery programme when the likelihood is that the animals are not even there? So, even if there are still a few baiji left, the species is in reality already extinct. This may be the hardest thing of all to bear. For my own sake, and maybe also the sake of those last few imaginary baiji, part of me hopes that they're already gone.

~

Over the months that followed, I worked together with the other researchers involved with the survey to put together a scientific paper documenting the project and its grim conclusions. A huge amount of time was spent deliberating over the exact wording with which to describe the status of the baiji. I favoured using the term 'probably extinct', but some of the other participants, notably the Chinese, felt that this was too strong. Eventually we settled for writing that 'the species is now likely to be extinct. While it is conceivable that a couple of surviving individuals were missed by the survey teams, our inability to detect any baiji in the main channel of the river despite this intensive search effort indicates that the prospect of finding and translocating them to an *ex situ* reserve has all but vanished.' However, this wording was still not regarded as ideal by the Baiji Research Group, who feared that such a statement would prevent the Chinese government from offering further support for baiji conservation if any animals still survived. I ended up as the lead author on the paper that documented the baiji's possible extinction. This was not the legacy I had hoped to achieve when I had first started out, younger, enthusiastic and still unjaded, along the path of baiji conservation.

Even deeper disagreements over the survey's conclusions soon emerged. As we were finishing off the paper, one of the researchers from the Baiji Research Group wrote to inform us that, in fact, we couldn't suggest that the baiji was extinct after all: there had been a recent sighting within the past few months. A retired schoolteacher called Jian Bingzhang was doing his morning exercises with a colleague two or three metres from the shore of the Yangtze in Huangshi Beach Park, Hubei Province, when he saw two cetaceans swimming downstream. The animals were 60–70 metres from the shore and about 20 metres apart, and disappeared after surfacing three times. There was no glare on the water, and the teacher and his colleague reported that the two animals both appeared to have dorsal fins.

Could they have been baiji? Maybe . . . who can say? It's impossible to evaluate an opportunistic sighting of this kind, but it's also important not to rule it out without careful consideration. One thing that is noticeable about this report, though, is that neither the baiji's beak nor its distinctive white colouring were mentioned; the only diagnostic feature used to identify the animals are their apparent dorsal fins. During our survey, we frequently observed finless porpoises rolling sideways or diving steeply and exposing their pectoral fins or tail flukes, which superficially appeared to be dorsal fins on a dark-bodied, beakless animal. For a tantalizing millisecond, the porpoises would resemble baiji on initial viewing, even to the survey team's most experienced observers.

What is more disconcerting, though, is the timing of this possible sighting. It took place on 2 December, and the Baiji Research Group confirmed that it had been reported to them while we were all *still in China*—and yet they seem to have decided not to mention it to us at the time. What on earth could be the reason behind this? Did they not realize that the sole purpose of our time and efforts while we were in the country was to try to find any evidence at all of the possible survival of the species? Or was the real answer even worse? I could not help but think that if we had been told immediately about the report, we would have returned upstream to Hubei and resurveyed this section of the river one more time; and, maybe, this is what the Baiji Research Group didn't actually want to happen. Maybe an unverified possibility, a white flag of hope still fluttering in the river, was what the Chinese wanted to end the survey with, not the rigid, quantified absence that we had provided for them. So if the international team wasn't told about the sighting until it was too late, then it couldn't be disproved— and, by a marvellous coincidence, the door was also left open for further funding for the Baiji Research Group's institute. Am I being too cynical? I don't know; but, after everything that had already happened, something about this report didn't quite add up.

The survey paper was published in the Royal Society of London's journal *Biology Letters* in the summer of 2007. The news response was incredible and overwhelming. The story went round the world; I ended up giving over forty live television and radio interviews on the day that the paper came out, fuelled by a single bar of chocolate (all that I could stomach eating because of my nerves). Somewhat amusingly and completely coincidentally, the story was also released on the same day that the Chinese authorities launched their official publicity for the 2008 Beijing Olympics, and obviously the two stories were run together by most of the main stations. They can't have been very happy about being unexpectedly upstaged by news of their own ecological neglect.

When I could catch my breath from all of the rushing to and fro, though, I felt a crushing sadness, even a sense of failure. It turned out that it was possible to galvanize the world's media on behalf of the baiji, after all; but, it seemed, people were only really interested when it was already too late. That's what would sell. That's what constituted a *story*. If there had been this response ten, maybe five, maybe even two years ago, to drum up desperately needed support for the recovery project, then who knows what might have happened? As it was, now it didn't matter any more for the baiji. Although most of the reporters seemed to have already decided that the Three Gorges Dam was responsible for the baiji's extinction, I tried to use the opportunity to get the message across that the Yangtze still needed urgent conservation efforts for its other massively endangered species, and that many other species of small cetaceans were also today on the brink of extinction. Who knows if it did any good. I hope so.

As I was waiting to give one of the first interviews of the day, fate decided to play the latest of its many tricks on me. The other guest on the radio programme, a senior biologist involved with judging grant applications, came up to me and introduced himself, then seemed to recognize me. 'Oh yes—didn't you send us a funding application for your Yangtze project?' he said cheerily. 'I reviewed that one.'

I felt myself instantly tense up. So, on this of all possible days, I had finally met the man who had rejected one of our best, last chances to muster up any meaningful support to save the baiji. 'I sent in two applications, actually,' I replied. 'And you rejected both of them.'

The other guest seemed only momentarily put out by my response. 'Oh well,' he commented airily, 'there's no point in throwing money away on lost causes.'

I did all that I could to stay calm, but I could feel my cheeks burning. 'Causes only become lost if no one gives them any support,' I replied tersely. There was nothing more to say after that.

Later on during the day, I was handed a press release that had just been issued hastily by WWF in response to our story. It stated that the organization did not think that the baiji could be declared extinct or even 'effectively extinct' because our survey had, apparently, been 'conducted with a short period of time over a limited area of the river'. The press release contained several inaccuracies, reporting that fishermen had allegedly seen two baiji in Lake Hong in 2007, and that the official definition of extinction was still the outdated fifty-year rule. But although the chance to recover the baiji was small, 'this does not mean that conservationists should give up efforts to save the species now . . . it is expected that small surveys will be conducted in some hot-spot areas in the future. WWF will support such efforts accordingly.' Leigh and I wanted to return to China, to interview fishermen about freshwater dolphin and porpoise declines. Since a range-wide boat survey had been unable to throw any light on the baiji other than its apparent extinction, maybe talking to local people who spent their lives along the river could generate new information on when and why the species had disappeared, as well as providing an invaluable opportunity to gather and assess recent alleged sightings such as the report from Huangshi. Encouraged by their statement, we contacted the organization immediately to enquire about funding for further survey work along the Yangtze. For some reason, though, no support was forthcoming.

~

The baiji had just been publicly declared to be in all likelihood extinct, but the story was still not as clear-cut and black-and-white as the wider world seemed to want. We had to concede that there could maybe—just *possibly*—still be a few animals left in the river, even if they were doomed to extinction if we couldn't find them. After all, extinction can never be conclusively proved, only disproved. Was there any evidence, then, which could indicate that the baiji might not actually be quite extinct after all? However, something robust and irrefutable would now be required to convince people that there might still be a few baiji somewhere out there—something more than just an unsubstantiated report from an unqualified witness who may have misidentified a finless porpoise. New photographs, or even film footage, showing a live baiji would be the only kind of thing that would now be adequate to the task. But the last time that a baiji had been photographed in the river—a sighting which constituted the last confirmed report of a wild baiji, in fact—had been over five years earlier, in May 2002. After the grim conclusions of our exhaustive survey, what would be the odds of that kind of evidence ever coming to light now?

And yet . . . who would have guessed it? Just a couple of weeks after our survey paper was published to its international media fanfare, all of the international researchers and participants who had been involved in the Yangtze expedition were contacted by Wang Ding. Amazing news!, he told us. A baiji may have just been seen—and filmed!—in a side-channel of the Yangtze near the baiji hotspot at Tongling! The story went as follows. A local man called Zeng Yujiang who worked for a decoration company had spotted a 'big white animal' in the river at Xuba ferry between 3.10 and 3.20 p.m. on 19 August, and filmed it from the bank with his digital camera for several minutes. 'I never saw such a big thing in the water before, so I filmed it,' he later told China's Xinhua News agency. 'It was about 1,000 metres away and jumped out of the water several times. I suspect it was a baiji dolphin. It jumped in a beautiful arc out of the water. So I set up my camera by the river, hoping it would appear for the second time.'[4]

It turns out that the footage had apparently been sent first of all to the staff of the Tongling Yangtze Cetacean Reserve. By a complete coincidence, some staff from the Baiji Research Group had been visiting the reserve on unrelated business, and learnt about what had happened.[5] Wang Ding told us that he had gathered together with his team in Wuhan to scrutinize the film footage. Unfortunately, because the mystery animal—whatever it was—had been filmed at long range on a non-specialized digital camera, the picture quality was extremely poor. Although Wang told us that it was certainly possible—maybe even likely—that the animal might be a baiji, because it looked pale in colour and also because of the way it seemed to move in the water, he couldn't rule out the alternative possibility that it was just a porpoise after all.

We were all certainly excited by the news of the film, but—after everything that had happened in the merry-go-round world of false expectations and dashed hopes that constituted baiji conservation, and especially because of the undeniably suspicious coincidence between the timing of publication of the negative survey paper and then the emergence of this supposed positive new evidence—Leigh and I were also wary. As we feared, alarm bells soon started to ring. The first priority, obviously, was for everyone to see the footage, and make their own judgement. However, it seemed that this one crucial step would not, in fact, be possible. Apparently, so we were told, it would infringe the copyright of the footage for the Baiji Research Group to send it to us. So, after all that had happened, we just had to take it on faith that the animal on the film was a baiji.

Copyright issues didn't seem to be much of a problem a few days later, though, when the footage was released to the international media. All of a sudden, it seemed that there was little question that the film showed anything other than a baiji.[6] As reported by *National Geographic News* on 31 August, for example:

A team of marine-life scholars led by Wang Ding, a scientist at China's Institute of Hydrobiology, examined digital video footage recently taken along the eastern section of the Yangtze River. The video provides evidence of the survival of the baiji, or whitefin dolphin, the team confirmed.

Wang said he and others at the hydrobiology institute are now convinced that the last survivors of the dolphin might be found along small tributaries of the Yangtze in eastern China's Anhui Province.

A confirmed sighting of a baiji dolphin just months after it was declared 'extinct' has prompted scientists to launch an against-all-odds plan to save the last of the rare Chinese river dwellers.

Now experts at the institute are studying the feasibility of transporting the survivors to a natural preserve in a Noah's Ark-like operation, said Wang, one of China's leading authorities on the nearly decimated species.... Wang, with the help of the baiji.org group, might even attempt to engineer the recovery of the dolphins through a captive breeding program.

Once again we heard from many of our old friends. A spokesperson for WWF announced that 'other species have been brought back from the brink of extinction, like the southern right whale and white rhinos, but only through the most intensive conservation efforts'; however, apparently this meant that 'the keys to the survival of the baiji are conserving oxbow lakes in the central Yangtze, creating a network of nature reserves along the river, and managing the river's entire ecosystem from a holistic perspective'.[7] At least August mentioned the *ex situ* recovery programme, although somehow it had now turned into something a bit different when he talked about it. 'Should the baiji sighting be confirmed,' he announced, 'it will be crucial to organise an unbureaucratic, well-coordinated capture and transfer the baiji as soon as possible into the dolphinarium of the Institute of Hydrobiology in Wuhan.'[8]

At least this new media circus meant that we actually got to see the supposed new baiji footage. It wasn't quite what I expected. From what we had heard from the Baiji Research Group, I had assumed that you might actually be able to see something on the film. All that it seemed to consist of was a pale dot that broke the surface to the far left of the frame a couple of times—that was it. To my mind, it could have been almost anything. You couldn't really make much of the footage at all, far less be confident enough to use it as the basis for an international press release. What was also noticeable was that whatever the object on the film was, it certainly wasn't behaving as Zeng Yujiang, the man who filmed it, had described. There was no animal jumping in a beautiful arc out of the water. A charitable reading was that something had been lost in translation. Bob Pitman voiced the concerns that we all shared in an interview about the footage for the *New York Times* on 1 September. He pointed out that 'there's a natural motive for some people to seize on a baiji-sighting report now that goes beyond any sentimental attachment to the animal: "Not to be too cynical here, but those same people have gotten a lot of their institutional funding for nominally protecting baiji over the last couple of decades—no baiji, no funding." '

And then everything fizzled out again after that. The Yangtze River dolphin soon became yesterday's news, and everyone went back to whatever they were doing beforehand. It looks like the final word on the whole baiji story is: everything's OK again. It didn't really die out. They found one. We've got nothing to feel guilty about any more. Nobody's worrying about which conservation organization is actually going to cover the costs of the wonderful recovery programme that's going to save the species, or why the results of the Baiji Research Group's follow-up survey to the Tongling region,[9] which failed to find any evidence that there were actually any baiji anywhere in the river section, for some reason didn't get reported by the international media.

So as the curtain finally falls on our story, maybe the baiji really is still out there somewhere, but it's swimming further and further away, into waters so murky that we can't make anything out any more. All that's left on stage are the commemorative baiji statues, standing alone in a hundred towns and reserves along the river. As for the baiji itself ... it looks like that's the only thing not made in China any more.

Poor old baiji. You deserved better.

11

WHAT HAVE WE LEARNT?
COLLECTED FICTIONS

The baiji, indeed the vaquita of Mexico, or the bhulan of Pakistan, or other dolphins not yet so endangered, may well disappear despite our best efforts, so great are the challenges they face. But let it not be because we have failed to do our best to save these little dolphins as vital parts of healthy aquatic ecosystems on which we humans also depend.

Steven Leatherwood
Closing statement in the opening address
of the Nanjing baiji workshop, 1 June 1993

So everything's over. The baiji is gone, and with it we have lost 20 million years of unique evolution, an entire mammal family, the top predator of the Yangtze ecosystem, the reincarnation of a drowned princess—and one of the most enigmatic and beautiful creatures on earth. This is a tragedy, but it is also more than that: it is a travesty. It is simply not true that this extinction happened so quickly that it caught us unawares. For almost thirty years, scientists and conservationists have repeated time and again what needed to be done in order to save the baiji: at workshops, conferences, and meetings, in popular literature, in official reports, and in formal papers in international scientific journals. And yet, for all of this superficial concern, almost nobody ever really *tried*. The baiji was allowed to slip unchecked towards extinction despite many international conservation organizations expressing their alleged commitment to try to save the species. The recovery programme was clearly far from being a straightforward enterprise, but ultimately it represented no more impossible a venture than many other intensive conservation efforts, which have eventually proved successful in restoring viable populations of other critically endangered animals. The project would have cost more to implement than any of us could personally have afforded, but in the grand scheme of things it was also relatively inexpensive. Although now I will never be able to know for sure, I firmly believe that our recovery programme could have saved the baiji from extinction, or at least would have had a damn good go at doing so, if it had been carried out in time. But, it seems, who could really be bothered to put themselves out for the baiji, and who stepped forward to take on any responsibility for actually trying to do anything? Almost none of the essential conservation measures that had been recommended were ever carried out. Only the easiest, most palatable, and ultimately most ineffectual steps were taken, and the path of least resistance does little to assist endangered species. Talking is easy; sadly, nobody ever really attempted to do anything more.

As the sorry story finally played itself out, some conservationists have even admitted this themselves. In the words of Randy Reeves and Nick Gales,[1]

There has been a lot of hand-wringing, yes. Many of us have given lip service to the need for greater efforts (actually, any effort) to improve the baiji's survival prospects. But there is precious little evidence of this vanishing creature's supposed celebrity. No large nongovernmental organization has campaigned forcefully or invested more than a pittance to its cause; most have simply looked the other way. For its part, the Chinese government seems to have weathered the squall of occasional international outrage over the baiji's imminent demise without making any serious investment . . . Finally, those of us who should have been hounding the bureaucrats and refusing to be stonewalled over the last 15 years have been doing a lousy job. Even now, we dither and keep looking for an elusive magic bullet. If the baiji truly had been a cause célèbre before now, surely we would be a good deal farther along than we are in saving it from extinction.

Such contrition is, on one level, refreshing. However, it seems that recognizing the failings of the conservation community still wasn't sufficient to actually motivate anybody to try harder to finally make something happen. Contrast this with the opinion of Don Merton, who led the successful Chatham Island black robin recovery programme for over a decade. He wrote that although little was published during its implementation, 'We do have lots of robins!'[2]

While open discussion and debate will always be an invaluable stage in refining strategies for successfully carrying out recovery programmes, a more dynamic response to baiji conservation was also what was ultimately required to save the species from extinction. So what would have been needed to actually make something happen? Other conservationists who have been involved with other desperate eleventh-hour recovery programmes have also stressed the need for establishing active, goal-oriented recovery teams that are primed for decisive and timely intervention on behalf of species of extreme rarity.[3] But in a conservation world where funding hurdles and bureaucratic inertia constitute the sad reality, how can we ever hope to achieve any more success in the future? Is it really likely that some kind of centralized dynamic task force that could champion the speedy conservation of critically endangered species will ever be created, without having its momentum lost in financial mires and its energy sapped away by officialdom and higher management? Who will co-ordinate it, fund it, police it? Are we fated to lose more and more species that could actually still be saved if only people could get it right?

Maybe, at the end of the day, success or failure in these cases just comes down to the involvement of charismatic leaders, people who burn with a fierce inner passion and a refusal to take no for an answer, figures such as Noel Snyder or Carl Jones. The baiji recovery programme certainly didn't have any senior figures even remotely matching this description when I became involved. Instead, the gaping cracks in baiji conservation had allowed all sorts of unscrupulous characters to come creeping through, ready to exploit the species for their own ends when it needed them most: petty warlords who emerge at the fall of an empire. And yet, maybe worst of all, only a few years ago—during the critical period in the 1990s when maybe there had still been a real chance to save the species—the baiji *did* have its very own special saviour, too. His name was Steve Leatherwood, and he took over from Bill Perrin as chairman of the IUCN's Cetacean Specialist Group, as well as working for Hong Kong's Ocean Park Conservation Foundation, one of the few non-governmental organizations that did actually try to provide some form of ongoing support for baiji conservation. Steve had a special interest in river dolphins, recognizing that they were among the world's most endangered mammals but that their conservation was being sorely neglected. He was later described by colleagues as 'a shining example of the contribution that one individual can make to science and conservation', travelling this world 'in a sparkling whirl of enthusiasm and goodwill'.[4]Everyone I have spoken to over the past few years has stressed just what a remarkable person Steve was, and how, if anyone had the drive, the enthusiasm, the interpersonal skills and the fund-raising prowess to have saved the baiji, it would have been Steve. But, tragically, Steve never quite had the chance to get everyone mobilized for the great cause. In January 1997, he died of lymphatic cancer. Until only a few weeks before his death, he was still advising Chinese members of the Asian River Dolphin Committee (which he had been largely responsible for establishing) on baiji conservation efforts. And nobody else ever really came along after that.

~

So what are we left with? The disappearance of the baiji must serve as a potent reminder to conservationists that even large charismatic and nominally protected animals are still in grave danger of being lost. Species cannot be expected to save themselves, and intervention may need to be swift and decisive. But instead of positive intervention on behalf of critically endangered species, I found to my disgust that the world of international conservation seemed at times to consist only of press releases and empty promises; worst of all, it was a world without accountability. I realize now that by the time I became involved, it was probably already too late to do anything for the baiji. Maybe there were still a few left; maybe, though, the species had already gone for good. But none of us knew this at the time. In fact, none of us really had any inkling of how bad the situation actually was until we were finally able to carry out the survey at the end of 2006— and neither did the many conservation organizations we applied to in vain for funding throughout 2005 and 2006. The reasons they gave for rejecting our requests and pleas were spurious, ignorant, and false. However, it wasn't my job to try to save the baiji. It was theirs.

The last thing I want would be to dissuade anybody from supporting conservation—that would be the worst outcome of all. But if this story were allowed to go untold, then the same mistakes and the same tragedies will be fated to play themselves out again and again. If the baiji has to have an epitaph, then let us hope that, at least, it may help other species to be saved from the manifold mistakes that were made time and again in this pathetic tale.

But maybe we can't even hope for that. As I write, the mantle of 'most endangered cetacean in the world' has passed onto the vaquita, a tiny porpoise that is found only in the northern tip of the Gulf of California, and which has the smallest geographic range of any dolphin, porpoise, or whale. The vaquita has been almost entirely obliterated by accidental by-catch in gill nets, which are used heavily by fishermen across the entirety of its meagre range. The latest official vaquita population estimate is about 150 individuals, and as I write this it has just been predicted that only two years remain before it will be too late to do anything for this species. The only solution is to establish a total fishing moratorium on all entangling nets throughout the vaquita's range, a plan which requires close collaboration between scientists, socioeconomists, and the Mexican authorities. However, scientists and conservationists have been expressing their deep concerns about the vaquita's survival for as long as they were about the baiji, and many of the same people have been involved with the conservation deliberations surrounding both species. 'To say that time is running out is, if anything, an understatement,' the latest paper on the plight of the vaquita tells us.[5] But the race against time is once again in grave danger of being lost. I can only hope that, as you read these words, it hasn't proved to be too late for the vaquita as well.

And the situation is no better elsewhere in the world. Before we finish for good, let's return one last time to the Yangtze. Even before the baiji had disappeared, Reeves' shad—once one of the region's most commercially important fish species—had vanished completely from the river. Today many other species are now also on the very brink of extinction. However, whereas the need to save the baiji at least became the subject of thirty years of ineffectual debate and hot air, these unique and remarkable animals have been almost completely ignored by the conservation community.

At around the same time as the last few baiji individuals were fading away, it seems that almost nobody even noticed that the Yangtze paddlefish, probably the largest freshwater fish in the world, had also quietly vanished. Until 1980, the annual paddlefish harvest on the Yangtze was 75 tons. Then the Gezhou dam was built just upstream of Yichang, preventing the paddlefish from migrating upstream to their spawning grounds. The paddlefish harvest crashed almost overnight. By the late 1980s, fewer than ten paddlefish were being caught each year, and this number continued to decline. It was hoped that a few paddlefish that had been trapped upstream of the dam might still be able to spawn in the river section around Yibin, but soon the evidence for even this remnant population dwindled away. A government-sponsored scientific expedition failed to find any paddlefish anywhere along the river in 2002, and by the time of our range-wide baiji survey, the last known paddlefish anywhere in the Yangtze had been caught near Nanjing in 2003, three years earlier. Then, in January 2007, a 3.6-metre, 250-kilo paddlefish was caught by two illegal fishing boats in Jiayu County, Hubei Province. The fish had six hooks in it, and although a team from the local reserve tried to get the fish back into deep water, it died from its injuries. 'The case is rare because the fishermen continued trying to pull the fish from the water even after villagers warned them that the species was under top state protection,' an official from the reserve blithely reported. 'Most fishermen would report to the reserve if they accidentally caught rare fish.'[6]

The populations of Chinese and Yangtze sturgeons—called 'patriotic fish' because they swim out to sea but return to their homeland to breed—have not fared much better. Both species have also experienced dramatic declines following the construction of the Gezhou and Three Gorges Dams, with the natural breeding grounds of the Chinese sturgeon having contracted from 600 km to only 7 km.[7] However, Chinese conservationists have been successful in propagating sturgeon in artificial breeding facilities along the Yangtze, with thousands of young sturgeon being bred in captivity and released into the river each year. It seems that conservation in China can be successful if endangered species are prepared to breed in concrete tanks completely removed from their natural ecosystem; anything else seems to be too much of a challenge. But despite the precarious status of the Chinese sturgeon, huge efforts that could be spent on protecting the species are instead exhausted on trying to subvert the existing conservation legislation. It is illegal to eat the sturgeon, which is a State One Protected Animal in China. To get round this, large numbers of Chinese sturgeons are hybridized with Russian sturgeons to produce half-Chinese offspring, which would probably still be somewhat patriotic if given the chance—and which are eaten in great numbers.

The list goes on. Only eight individuals of Baer's pochard, a diving duck unique to eastern Asia, were found across the entirety of the Yangtze during a recent survey.[8] Wild Chinese alligators are now only known from a tiny region of Anhui Province which has been specifically designated as a reserve for the species, but which contains only a handful of remnant alligator populations in tiny ponds at the edges of farms or rice paddies, or even in the middle of villages. Each alligator population is made up of a maximum of only ten or eleven individuals, and only a single adult female. Nesting has only been reported from four sites in recent years.[9] At least the alligator, like the sturgeon, has been successfully reared in captivity in China. However, also like the sturgeon, many of the captive alligators are now being bred specifically for food.

And soon, perhaps, there will be no cetaceans left in the Yangtze at all. The river's finless porpoise population is also declining rapidly, and is officially recognized as being Endangered by the IUCN. Our baiji survey detected only about half as many porpoises in the main Yangtze channel as there had been only ten years earlier, but unlike the baiji, nobody even seems to have much of an idea about what is actually causing this decline—although the usual suspects of boat collisions, pollution, and mortality in electro-fishing and other kinds of legal and illegal fishing gear may again all be to blame. The warning is sounding right now for this animal, which is already being widely referred to as the 'second baiji'. How many more decades will it take before the world's only freshwater porpoise has gone, too? I suspect not many, unless action is taken right now to fight for its conservation. But the same sad story of inertia and inactivity seems to be playing out again right in front of our eyes. Who is really doing anything to try to save this animal? Is anyone going to step in to try to stem the tide of extinction on the Yangtze? In just a few years' time, will somebody else be writing their own story of how they failed to save the charismatic, beautiful little Yangtze river pig?

The mighty Yangtze is dying more and more each day. Boat traffic, industry, and construction all continue unstoppably, spreading across the waters which once upon a time used to be home to dolphins, paddlefish, and shad. The river which supports almost 200 cities and provides over a third of the country's freshwater resources was previously thought to be 'immune' to pollution, because the 900 billion tons of water that flow through into the estuary every year were assumed to be sufficient to flush out toxins. However, official Chinese estimates now predict that 70 per cent of Yangtze water will be unusable within five years, mainly because of the 25 billion tons of waste water dumped in the river every year, 80 per cent of which is untreated.[10] Levels of stomach cancer and cancer of the oesophagus, thought to be caused by drinking polluted Yangtze water and eating polluted Yangtze fish, are on the increase in communities along the river.[11] The first comprehensive study into the health of the Yangtze has recently reported that 600 kilometres of water are in a critical condition, and suggests that the impacts of human activities on the river's ecology are largely irreversible.[12] The toxic Yangtze has become the largest open sewer in the world.

The last remnants of what was once the most magnificent river system in Asia are being washed away for ever. And how many people are really doing anything to fight it?

Somebody out there, please, prove me wrong.

Epilogue

AND THEN THERE WAS ONE

Yangtse and Han have wasted my clear autumn.
My shadow sticks to the trees where gibbons scream,
But my spirit whirls by the towers sea-serpents breathe.
Let me go down next year with the spring waters
And search for you to the end of the white clouds in the East.

Tu Fu
To My Younger Brother
(trans. A. C. Graham)

'You can't love the dead, can you? They don't exist, do
they? It would be like loving the dodo, wouldn't it?'

Graham Greene
The Heart of the Matter

The winter had been a bad one; the worst in fifty years, they said. But now spring was finally here. The flurries of snow that had twisted in the air when we first arrived had melted away in the sun, and now the hazy pastel shades of the river lay below a sky that was almost blue.

Leigh and I had come back, to where everything had started. Maybe, after everything that had happened, we just couldn't stay away. But this time there were no grand and desperate plans to catch any dolphins, construct holding pens or a capture fleet, or manage a large-scale survey. Instead, everything felt much calmer. We were here to carry out a final post-mortem on the whole sorry baiji story, as well as to try to gather the first useful information on what was driving the decline of the Yangtze's population of finless porpoises. Travelling from town to town down the river, we were interviewing all the fishermen we met along the way, asking them not only about their livelihoods and experiences, but also if they had ever heard of dolphins or porpoises getting killed by boats or fishing gear, and when they or anyone they knew had last seen a baiji. The fishermen spent their entire lives on the water. If there were any baiji left, they were the people who would know.

One day we rented a fishing skiff and journeyed down the long, winding side-channel that led eventually to the small town of Xuba, where six months earlier a baiji had allegedly been filmed by someone waiting for the ferry. We talked to the crowd of curious locals who had gathered round when the foreigners arrived. They had lived by the water all of their lives, these people, and they often saw porpoises in the channel, but no one had ever seen a live baiji around here. The ferry driver told us that a long time ago, maybe twenty years earlier, he had seen a dead baiji floating along the channel. He knew what it was because it had a long beak. Another old man said that he had once eaten a baiji he had found dead in the main river sometime during the Cultural Revolution, but it hadn't tasted good. The crowd laughed when we asked them about the film footage that had been taken here. That wasn't a baiji, several people said. We all saw it on the news. But it was so far away, you couldn't tell what it was. It could have been anything. It was just a porpoise, that's all. There aren't any baiji around here.

A few miles upstream, we had spent the day talking to fishermen in the town of Datong. A lot of them had seen baiji many years ago, and it was disconcerting to learn how many of them also admitted to having eaten baiji during the 1960s. The town centre had a statue of a pair of dolphins in its main square. They must have been meant to be baiji, but someone had accidentally carved a pair of bottlenose dolphins instead. Here on the river, nobody seemed to remember what baiji even looked like any more. That made me sad.

But then one of the fishermen told us something. My wife, he said. My wife saw something in the water last September, when we were out fishing for river crab near Heyue Island. It came up near the boat. It wasn't a porpoise. We showed his wife some photos. It was big, she said. Big and white. With a long beak. That's what it was! she said as she flicked through the pictures. She pointed to a picture of a baiji. The fisherman took us out for the day on his boat, to visit the location of his wife's sighting, but the trail was cold. Whatever it was, the animal had gone.

What are my thoughts? I think that, just maybe, there might be a couple of baiji left, somewhere out there. Or, maybe, there's one left. Maybe just one. We couldn't find it in 2006 when we surveyed the river, and I doubt we'll find it now. It's already been six months since the fisherman's wife saw it, so maybe it's already dead. But maybe it's not. Maybe it's still out there, somewhere. So here I am, a new Captain Ahab for the conservation generation, hunting along a dying river for the Great White Dolphin. No doubt it will all be in vain. What good would it do if we even found it, anyway? What would it actually matter? But, just maybe . . . who knows. Who knows what we might find tomorrow.

~

On our day off we took a trip to Suzhou, the ancient moated city by Lake Tai. Only a stone's throw inland from Shanghai, it plays host to hordes of foreign tourists eager for a taste of 'real China': day-trippers buying silk and taking photographs of the famous canals and classical gardens before returning to their luxury accommodation near the Bund. That wasn't what we had come to do. Instead, we went to the zoo.

I never did get to see Qi Qi; I never managed to make it to Wuhan in time to have any contact with the lonely old dolphin before he died in 2002. I have often wondered, would it have made any difference to me if I had ever seen him—if I had actually seen a real live baiji before I got myself involved with all of this? In the end, I don't think it would. I would still have worked passionately for the conservation of the species, and, it seems, I would still have arrived too late to make a difference. But, I think, I will always be haunted by the fact that I just missed him; that I just missed the species by a heartbeat.

So here we were, beside a sunken water garden that was tucked in between the emus and a soul-destroying collection of badly kept big cats that I couldn't bear to see. This was what we had come for. Leaning over the low stone wall, beside children throwing bread at the brightly coloured carp, something moved in the thick green water. There it was: a huge, shiny black back that looked like a piece of burnt plastic, almost a metre long, with a piggy snout and two beady eyes at the end of a stretched snaky neck. There it was: one of the last two Yangtze soft-shelled turtles in the world.

Very little was known about how he had first arrived at the zoo, but he had been here for a very long time. It was thought that he was about 100 years old. When he hatched, there may still have been thousands of baiji in the Yangtze. Until a few years ago, there had also been a handful of other Yangtze soft-shells in other collections across China—one in Beijing Zoo, one in Shanghai Zoo, and two in an ornamental pool at Suzhou's West Garden Buddhist temple. But they were all old, so very old, and one by one they all died. Nobody has seen a wild Yangtze soft-shell in China in decades. A single mysterious giant turtle glimpsed from time to time in Hoan Kiem Lake in the centre of Hanoi, and another animal recently spotted in the wild in Vietnam, may also be Yangtze soft-shells, but local scientists believe that these animals may represent a different (and equally endangered) species. The only other known living individual is a female kept in a tiled concrete tank in Changsha Zoo, a spring chicken at only 80 years old. She was donated to the zoo in lieu of payment by a travelling circus in 1951, and was only actually identified as being a Yangtze soft-shell in 2006. Now she lives in a bulletproof enclosure under 24-hour surveillance.

Next month they are planning to move the female from Chang-sha to keep the old male company here in his pool at Suzhou. Maybe they will breed; everybody hopes so. But they are both so old. Maybe it's already too late.

So, with one final long look at the lonely old turtle in his pool, we turned and walked away, past the dusty lake swarming with holidaying couples out on pedalos, past the candy-floss machines and the magnolias ripe with creamy white petals. You can't stay forever. In the end, you have to leave.

Someday soon, it really will all be over.

March 2008
London—Wuhan

Suggested Reading

~

Accounts of early Chinese and Western encounters with baiji are given in:

Hoy, C. (1923). The 'white-flag' dolphin of the Tung Ting Lake. *The China Journal of Science & Arts* 1: 154–7.

Miller, G. S. Jr. (1918). A new river-dolphin from China. *Smithsonian Miscellaneous Collections* 68: 1–12.

Pilleri, G. (1979). The Chinese river dolphin (*Lipotes vexillifer*) in poetry, literature and legend. *Investigations on Cetacea* 10: 335–49.

Pope, C. (1940). *China's animal frontier*. New York: The Viking Press.

Swinhoe, R. (1870). Catalogue of the mammals of China (south of the River Yangtze) and of the island of Formosa. *Proceedings of the Zoological Society of London* 38: 615–53.

More information on the recent conservation efforts for the baiji can be found in:

Adams, D. & Carwardine, M. (1990). *Last chance to see*. New York: Ballentine Books.

Barrett, L. A., Pfluger, A. & Wang, D. (2006). Successful pilot Yangtze freshwater dolphin expedition. *Oryx* 40: 259–60.

Braulik, G. T., Reeves, R. R., Wang, D., Ellis, S., Wells, R. S. & Dudgeon, D. (2005). *Report of the workshop on conservation of the baiji and Yangtze finless porpoise*. Gland: World Conservation Union.

Lin, K., Chen, P. & Hua, Y. (1985). Population size and conservation of *Lipotes vexillifer*. *Acta Zoologica Sinica* 5: 77–85.

Liu, R., Yang, J., Wang, D., Zhao, Q., Wei, Z. & Wang, X. (1998). Analysis on the capture, behavior monitoring and death of the baiji (*Lipotes vexillifer*) in the Shishou semi-nature reserve at the Yangtze River, China. *IBI Reports* 8: 11–21.

Ministry of Agriculture (2001). *Conservation action plan for Chinese river dolphins*. Beijing: Ministry of Agriculture.

Perrin, W. F., Brownell, R. L., Zhou, K. & Liu, J. (eds.) (1989). Biology and conservation of the river dolphins. *Occasional Papers of the IUCN Species Survival Commission* 3: 1–173.

Reeves, R. R., Smith, B. D. & Kasuya, T. (eds.) (2000). Biology and conservation of freshwater cetaceans in Asia. *Occasional Papers of the IUCN Species Survival Commission* 23: 1–152.

Reeves, R. R., Smith, B. D., Crespo, E. A. & Notarbartalo di Sciara, G. (2003). *Dolphins, whales and porpoises. 2002–2010 Conservation Action Plan for the world's cetaceans*. Gland & Cambridge: IUCN.

Reeves, R. R. & Gales, N. J. (2006). Realities of baiji conservation. *Conservation Biology* 20: 626–8.

Turvey, S. T., Barrett, L. A., Braulik, G. T. & Wang, D. (2006). Implementing the recovery programme for the Critically Endangered Yangtze River dolphin. *Oryx* 40: 258–9.

Turvey, S. T., Pitman, R. L., Taylor, B. L., Barlow, J., Akamatsu, T., Barrett, L. A., Zhao, X., Reeves, R. R., Stewart, B. S., Wang, K., Wei, Z., Zhang, X., Pusser, L. T., Richlen, M., Brandon, J. R. & Wang, D. (2007). First human-caused extinction of a cetacean species? *Biology Letters* 3: 537–40.

Wang, D., Zhang, X., Wang, K., Wei, Z., Würsig, B., Braulik, G. T. & Ellis, S. (2006). Conservation of the baiji: no simple solution. *Conservation Biology* 20: 623–5.

Wang, K., Wang, D., Zhang, X., Pfluger, A. & Barrett, L. (2006). Range-wide Yangtze freshwater dolphin expedition: the last chance to see baiji? *Environmental Science and Pollution Research* 13: 418–24.

Yang, G., Bruford, M. W., Wei, F. & Zhou K. (2006). Conservation options for the baiji: time for realism? *Conservation Biology* 20: 620–2.

Zhang, X., Wang, D., Liu, R., Wei, Z., Hua, Y., Wang, Y., Chen, Z. & Wang, L. (2003). The Yangtze River dolphin or baiji (*Lipotes vexillifer*): population status and conservation issues in the Yangtze River, China. *Aquatic Conservation: Marine and Freshwater Ecosystems* 13: 51–64.

Zhou, K., Ellis, S., Leatherwood, S., Bruford, M. & Seal, U. S. (eds.) (1994). *Baiji population and habitat viability assessment report*. Apple Valley, Minnesota: IUCN/SSC Conservation Breeding Specialist Group.

Zhou, K., Sun, J., Gao, A. & Würsig, B. (1998). Baiji (*Lipotes vexillifer*) in the lower Yangtze River: movements, numbers threats and conservation needs. *Aquatic Mammals* 24: 123–32.

Zhou, K. & Wang, X. (1994). Brief review of passive fishing gear and incidental catches of small cetaceans in Chinese waters. *Report of the International Whaling Commission, Special Issue* 15: 347–54.

Zhou, K. & Zhang, X. (1991). *Baiji: the Yangtze River dolphin and other endangered animals of China*. Washington, DC: Stone Wall Press.

Further information about the history of China's environmental problems is given in:

Elvin, M. (2004). *The retreat of the elephants: an environmental history of China*. New Haven and London: Yale University Press.

Shapiro, J. (2001). *Mao's war against nature: politics and the environment in revolutionary China*. Cambridge: Cambridge University Press.

Further information about other successful and unsuccessful species recovery programmes can be found in:

Butler, D. & Merton, D. (1992). *The black robin: saving the world's most endangered bird*. Oxford: Oxford University Press.

Clark, T. W. (1997). *Averting extinction*. New Haven and London: Yale University Press.

Flueck, W. T. & Smith-Flueck, J. M. (2006). Predicaments of endangered huemul deer, *Hippocamelus bisulcus*, in Argentina: a review. *European Journal of Wildlife Research* 52: 69–80.

Groombridge, J. J., Massey, J. G., Bruch, J. C., Malcolm, T., Brosius, C. N., Okada, M. M., Sparklin, B., Fretz, J. S. & VanderWerf, E. A. (2004). An attempt to recover the po'ouli by translocation and an appraisal of recovery strategy for bird species of extreme rarity. *Biological Conservation* 118: 365–75.

May, R. M. (1986). The cautionary tale of the black-footed ferret. *Nature* 320: 13–14.

Phillipps, W. J. (1963). *The book of the huia*. Christchurch, New Zealand: Whitcombe and Tombs.

Rabinowitz, A. (1995). Helping a species go extinct: the Sumatran rhino in Borneo. *Conservation Biology* 9: 482–8.

Schaller, G. B. (1993). *The last panda*. Chicago: University of Chicago Press.

Snyder, N. F. R. & Snyder, H. (2000). *The California condor: a saga of natural history and conservation*. Princeton: Princeton University Press.

VanderWerf, E. A., Groombridge, J. J., Fretz, J. S. & Swinnerton, K. J. (2006). Decision analysis to guide recovery of the po'ouli, a critically endangered Hawaiian honeycreeper. *Biological Conservation* 129: 383–92.

Notes

~

Most of the information presented in this book is derived either from the many books and papers already listed as suggested reading, or from my personal experiences with baiji conservation. However, several passages, points, and quotes given in the preceding chapters require further referencing.

CHAPTER 1

1. *Investigations on Cetacea* **10**: 336 (1979).
2. Winchester, S. *The river at the centre of the world: a journey up the Yangtze, and back in Chinese time.* London: Penguin, 101 (1998 edn.).
3. *Smithsonian Miscellaneous Collections* **68**(9): 1 (1918).
4. Pope, C. *China's animal frontier.* New York: The Viking Press, 177–8 (1940).
5. The year that Charles Hoy shot his baiji is sometimes given in the scientific literature as 1916 instead of 1914, but Hoy himself reported the event as having taken place 'in the winter of 1914' (*The China Journal of Science and Arts* **1**: 154), and I'm assuming that he would probably know best.
6. *Smithsonian Miscellaneous Collections* **68**(9): 1 (1918); *The China Journal of Science & Arts* **1**: 157 (1923).
7. *The China Journal of Science & Arts* **1**: 155 (1923).
8. Ibid.
9. Johnson, C. *Australia's mammal extinctions: a 50 000 year history.* Melbourne: Cambridge University Press, 174 (2006).
10. *Australian Zoologist* **31**: 558 (2001).
11. *China Journal of Science & Arts* **1**: 163 (1923).
12. Pope, C. *China's animal frontier.* New York: The Viking Press, 177 (1940).
13. *Biochemical Genetics* **43**: 307–20 (2005).
14. *Proceedings of the National Academy of Sciences of the United States of America* **97**: 11343–11347 (2000), **98**: 7384–7389 (2001); *Proceedings of the Royal Society of London, Series B* **268**, 549–56 (2001); *Molecular Phylogenetics and Evolution* **37**, 743–50 (2005).
15. Pope, C. *China's animal frontier.* New York: The Viking Press, 181 (1940).

CHAPTER 2

1. Beck, B. & Wemmer, C. *The biology and management of an extinct species: Père David's deer*. Park Ridge, New Jersey: Noyes Publications, 5 (1983).
2. Pope, C. *China's animal frontier*. New York: The Viking Press, 180 (1940).
3. Winchester, S. *The river at the centre of the world: a journey up the Yangtze, and back in Chinese time*. London: Penguin, 102 (1998 edn.).
4. *The China Journal of Science & Arts* 1: 155 (1923).
5. *Investigations on Cetacea* 10: 346 (1979).
6. Ibid. 346.
7. Ibid. 343.
8. Ibid. 348.
9. Pope, C. *China's animal frontier*. New York: The Viking Press, 181 (1940).
10. Winchester, S. *The river at the centre of the world: a journey up the Yangtze, and back in Chinese time*. London: Penguin, 102 (1998 edn.).
11. Ibid. 103–4.
12. Adams, D. & Carwardine, M. *Last chance to see*. London: Pan, 203 (1991 edn.).
13. Zhou, K. & Zhang, X. *Baiji: the Yangtze River dolphin and other endangered animals of China*. Washington, DC: Stone Wall Press, 32 (1991).
14. http://www.zmnh.com/ShowArticle.asp?ArticleID=1194
15. Pope, C. *China's animal frontier*. New York: The Viking Press, 178 (1940).
16. Zhou, K. & Zhang, X. *Baiji: the Yangtze River dolphin and other endangered animals of China*. Washington, DC: Stone Wall Press, 47 (1991).
17. Adams, D. & Carwardine, M. *Last chance to see*. London: Pan, 158 (1991 edn.).
18. Winchester, S. *The river at the centre of the world: a journey up the Yangtze, and back in Chinese time*. London: Penguin, 101–3 (1998 edn.).

CHAPTER 3

1. *Investigations on Cetacea* 10: 349 (1979).
2. Zhou, K. & Zhang, X. *Baiji: the Yangtze River dolphin and other endangered animals of China*. Washington, DC: Stone Wall Press, 39–40 (1991).
3. Winchester, S. *The river at the centre of the world: a journey up the Yangtze, and back in Chinese time*. London: Penguin, 103–4 (1998 edn.).
4. *China Law Digest* 4(1): 'Wang Canfa: Environmental Protection Law professor' (2008): http://www.chinalawdigest.com/1179d.htm
5. Based on unpublished interview data from February to April 2008 Yangtze fishermen interview survey (S. T. Turvey and L. A. Barrett).
6. Adams, D. & Carwardine, M. *Last chance to see*. London: Pan, 203 (1991 edn.).

7. *Investigations on Cetacea* 10: 349 (1979).
8. Wei, Z. *Save the Yangtze River's endangered animals: we are all the Yangtze's children.* Wuhan: Hubei Children's Press (2005). In Chinese; quote translated by Alf Hickey.
9. *Occasional Papers of the IUCN Species Survival Commission (SSC)* 3: 147 (1989).
10. Zhou, K. & Zhang, X. *Baiji: the Yangtze River dolphin and other endangered animals of China.* Washington, DC: Stone Wall Press, 70 (1991).
11. Ibid. 58.
12. Ibid. 59.
13. Adams, D. & Carwardine, M. *Last chance to see.* London: Pan, 162 (1991 edn.).
14. Ibid. 168.
15. *Occasional Papers of the IUCN Species Survival Commission (SSC)* 3: 22 (1989); Zhou, K. *et al.* (eds.) *Baiji population and habitat viability assessment report.* Apple Valley: IUCN/SSC Conservation Breeding Specialist Group, 127 (1994).
16. *Occasional Papers of the IUCN Species Survival Commission (SSC)* 3: 22 (1989).

CHAPTER 4

1. *Aquatic Conservation: Marine and Freshwater Ecosystems* 15: 106 (2005).
2. *Occasional Papers of the IUCN Species Survival Commission (SSC)* 3: 6 (1989).
3. Ibid. 6.
4. *Aquatic Conservation: Marine and Freshwater Ecosystems* 15: 106 (2005).
5. *Occasional Papers of the IUCN Species Survival Commission (SSC)* 23: 83 (2000).
6. Zhou, K. *et al.* (eds.) *Baiji population and habitat viability assessment report.* Apple Valley: IUCN/SSC Conservation Breeding Specialist Group, 75 (1994).
7. Ibid. 24.
8. *IBI Reports* 8: 12 (1998).
9. Zhou, K. *et al.* (eds.) *Baiji population and habitat viability assessment report.* Apple Valley: IUCN/SSC Conservation Breeding Specialist Group, 177–8 (1994).
10. *Aquatic Conservation: Marine and Freshwater Ecosystems* 15: 107 (2005).
11. *The Wall Street Journal*, 6 December 2006 (http://www.pulitzer.org/year/2007/international-reporting/works/wsjintnlo8.html).
12. *Occasional Papers of the IUCN Species Survival Commission (SSC)* 23: 52 (2000).
13. Ibid. vi.

CHAPTER 5

1. Jones, S. *Almost like a whale: The Origin of Species updated*. London: Doubleday, 283 (1999).
2. Stonehouse, B. *Sea mammals of the world*. Harmondsworth: Penguin, 82 (1985).
3. Flannery, T. & Schouten, P. *A gap in nature: discovering the world's extinct animals*. London: William Heinemann, xxii (2001).
4. See Reeves *et al.* (2003), Zhang *et al.* (2003), Braulik *et al.* (2005) (reference details given above).
5. *Report of the workshop on conservation of the baiji and Yangtze finless porpoise*. Gland: World Conservation Union, 9 (2005).
6. http://www.celb.org/xp/CELB/news-events/press_releases/12042004.xml
7. http://www.baiji.org/fileadmin/pdf/2203_release_swim05.pdf
8. *The Wall Street Journal*, 6 December 2006 (http://www.pulitzer.org/year/2007/international-reporting/works/wsjintnl08.html).
9. *Occasional Papers of the IUCN Species Survival Commission (SSC)* 3: 150–6 (1989).
10. Zhou, K. *et al.* (eds.) *Baiji population and habitat viability assessment report*. Apple Valley: IUCN/SSC Conservation Breeding Specialist Group, 121–42, 147–8 (1994).
11. Myers, N. *The sinking ark: a new look at the problem of disappearing species*. Oxford: Pergamon Press, 43 (1979). See also *Ibis* **137**: S173–S180 (1995).
12. *The Journal of Animal Ecology* **63**: 215–44 (1994).
13. *Conservation Biology* **9**: 487 (1995).
14. http://web.conservation.org/xp/frontlines/species/06030506.xml; see also *Frontlines* (Spring 2005 issue), p. 3 (http://learning.conservation.org/portal/server.pt/gateway/PTARGS_0_126385_106450_0_0_18/ci_5ffl_5f10.pdf).
15. http://www.panda.org/about_wwf/what_we_do/freshwater/publications/index.cfm? uNewsID=21901
16. http://www.wwfchina.org/english/loca.php?loca=120 (wording formerly also at http://www.wwfchina.org/english/sub_loca.php?loca=25&sub=87).
17. WWF HSBC Yangtze Programme newsletter 4: October–December 2004 (http://www.wwfchina.org/english/downloads/hsbc/Oct.pdf).

CHAPTER 6

1. Soulé, M. E. *Conservation biology: the science of scarcity and diversity*. Sunderland, MA: Sinauer Associates, 1–12 (1986).
2. Butler, D. & Merton, D. *The black robin: saving the world's most endangered bird*. Oxford: Oxford University Press, 251 (1992).
3. *Conservation Biology* **20**: 621 (2006).

4. Ibid. **10**: 921 (1996).
5. *Science* **289**: 2289 (2000).
6. *Conservation Biology* **10**: 921–2 (1996).
7. Tagline for WWF-HSBC Yangtze Programme newsletter, available for download at http://www.wwfchina.org/english/sub_loca.php?loca= 16&sub=91
8. http://www.wwfchina.org/english/loca.php?loca=176
9. http://www.hsbccommittochange.com/environment/hsbc-case-studies/ water/hsbc-wwf-china/index.aspx
10. Nielsen, D. *Condor: to the brink and back—the life and times of one giant bird*. New York: HarperCollins, 147 (2006).
11. Snyder, N. F. R. & Snyder, H. *The California condor: a saga of natural history and conservation*. Princeton: Princeton University Press, 96 (2000).
12. Nielsen, D. *Condor: to the brink and back—the life and times of one giant bird*. New York: HarperCollins, 13 (2006).
13. *Aquatic Conservation: Marine and Freshwater Ecosystems* **15**: 107 (2005).
14. Snyder, N. F. R. & Snyder, H. *The California condor: a saga of natural history and conservation*. Princeton: Princeton University Press, 370 (2000).
15. *Nature* **320**: 13–14 (1986).
16. *Social Studies of Science* **17**: 3–33 (1987).
17. *Biological Conservation* **129**: 390 (2006).
18. Ibid. **118**: 373 (2004).
19. Ibid. **118**: 373 (2004), **129**: 391 (2006).

CHAPTER 7

1. *Conservation of the Yangtze River dolphin: emergency implementation meeting. Final report.* (2006) (unpublished; available at http://www.baiji. org/fileadmin/pdf/EmergencyBaijiImplementationMeetingreport.pdf).
2. *Conservation Biology* **9**: 482–8 (1995).
3. *Biological Conservation* **118**: 365–75 (2004).
4. *Nature* **436**: 14–16 (2005); *Science* **320**: 44–5 (2008).
5. BBC News website (Science/Nature), 27 June 2006 (http://news.bbc.co. uk/2/hi/science/nature/5122074.stm).
6. Letter from Laura Stansfield (Captivity Officer, Whale and Dolphin Conservation Society), 30 June 2006.
7. http://www.wdcs.org/dan.news.nsf/webnews/DDC3A29B4902C4278 02568CC 003357BF (originally uploaded on 26 July 2002; no longer available on WDCS website, but text still accessible at http://pets. groups.yahoo.com/group/world-altnews- net/message/1495 as of 14 April 2008).
8. *Nature* **440**: 1096–7 (2006).
9. Ibid. **440**: 1097 (2006).

CHAPTER 9

1. *Science* 320: 175 (2008).
2. *Proceedings of the National Academy of Sciences of the United States of America* 104: 15162–15167 (2007).
3. *Science* 301: 508–10 (2003).
4. Steller, G. W. *Journal of a voyage with Bering, 1741–1742.* Stanford: Stanford University Press, 134 (1988).
5. Ibid. 134.
6. Ibid. 163–4.
7. Ibid. 162.
8. *University of California Publications in Geological Sciences* 118: 164 (1978).
9. *Biology Letters* 2: 94–7 (2006).
10. *Marine Mammal Science* 23: 976–83 (2007).
11. Allen, G. M. *Extinct and vanishing mammals of the Western Hemisphere with the marine, species of all the oceans,* 453 (1942).
12. Ibid.
13. *Marine Mammal Science* 19: 300 (2003).
14. *Science* 319: 1184–5 (2008).
15. http://www.baiji.org/expeditions/1/shanghai.html;www.baiji.org/fileadmin/pdf/1206_release_YFDE.pdf
16. *Science* 314: 1860 (2006).

CHAPTER 10

1. Archer, M. (ed). *Carnivorous marsupials.* Mosman: Royal Zoological Society of New South Wales, 233–6 (1982).
2. *Ecological Economics* 45: 271–9 (2003).
3. *New Scientist,* 24 April 1986: 44–7.
4. Xinhua News Agency, 19 August 2007 (http://www.chinadaily.com.cn/china/2007-08/29/content_6066263.htm); television interview with Zeng Yujiang (http://www.reuters.com/news/video/videoStory? videoId=65164).
5. Xinhua News Agency, 19 August 2007 (http://www.chinadaily.com.cn/china/2007-08/29/content_6066263.htm).
6. Ibid.
7. National Geographic News, 31 August 2007 (http://news.nationalgeographic.com/news/2007/08/070831-baiji-dolphin.html).
8. baiji.org Foundation website, 31 August 2007 (http://www.baiji.org/in-depth/baiji/overview.html).
9. Xinhua News Agency, 19 August 2007 (http://www.chinadaily.com.cn/china/2007-08/29/content_6066263.htm).

CHAPTER 11

1. *Conservation Biology* 20: 626 (2006).
2. Butler, D. & Merton, D. *The black robin: saving the world's most endangered bird.* Oxford: Oxford University Press, 251 (1992).
3. *Biological Conservation* 118: 373 (2004).
4. *Asian Marine Biology* 14: 1–4 (1997).
5. *Conservation Biology* 21: 1654.
6. Xinhua News Agency, 12 January 2007 (http://www.china.org.cn/english/environment/195880.htm).
7. *Science* 302: 1149–50 (2003).
8. BirdLife International, 13 April 2005 (http://www.birdlife.org/news/news/2005/04/baers_pochard.html).
9. *Biological Conservation* 103: 93–102 (2002).
10. *Oryx* 40: 378–9 (2006).
11. http://www.bjreview.cn/EN/05-04-e/Nation-2005-4(b).htm
12. *Oryx* 40: 378–9 (2006).

Acknowledgements

~

A lthough this story has featured more than its fair share of characters who are not particularly deserving of commemoration, many people have provided me with invaluable assistance during my involvement with the baiji saga over the past few years, and deserve my sincere gratitude. First and foremost, Leigh Barrett has been a consistent source of comradeship, inspiration, and support, as well as an active driving force in our various frustrated attempts to generate any interest from the wider world in baiji conservation. Furthermore, without her help I would not have been able to participate in the 2006 baiji survey. Leigh: my heartfelt thanks.

Several people at the Zoological Society of London are more than worthy of mention. Georgina Mace, my first boss at the Institute of Zoology, generously gave me free rein to pursue my passion for baiji conservation in addition to my 'official' work on historical mammal extinctions. Carly Waterman, Jonathan Baillie, and all of my other colleagues in ZSL's EDGE of Existence team have provided unwavering support throughout my involvement with the baiji. Special thanks must also go to Alice Henchley, the best press officer in the world. My time at ZSL has been funded by the Leverhulme Trust and the Natural Environment Research Council (NERC).

I must thank the many international conservationists and cetacean biologists, especially Randy Reeves and Gill Braulik, for allowing me to join them in helping to try to establish an international recovery programme for the baiji at the eleventh hour. In particular, Jim McBain without a doubt went the proverbial extra mile to try to provide as much logistical support for the project as possible. I particularly wish to acknowledge the Chinese researchers who facilitated my involvement in the project and provided considerable information on cetacean conservation efforts in the Yangtze, notably Wang Ding, Zhang Xianfeng, and Hao Yujiang at the Institute of Hydrobiology in Wuhan, and Zhou Kaiya at Nanjing Normal University. Bill Perrin, Bob Brownell, Toshio Kasuya, Tom Jefferson, Nick Gales, Bernd Würsig, Tony Martin, and Suzanne Gendron provided invaluable insights into the history of international involvement with the baiji when I spoke with them at the 17th Biennial Conference on the Biology of Marine Mammals in December 2007; funding for this trip was provided by the Royal Society, and I also wish to thank Rob Ingle and Pernille Stallemo for hosting me during my stay in Cape Town.

My involvement in the 2006 baiji survey was made as enjoyable as the circumstances permitted by the camaraderie of the other participants, and in addition to the people already mentioned above, I wish to give special mention here to Bob Pitman, Todd Pusser, Michael Richlen, John Brandon, Brent Stewart, Tom Akamatsu, Kotoe Sasamori, Barb Taylor, Alf Hickey, Zhao Xiujiang, and Dong Shouyue for keeping me entertained. Funding for my return trip to China was provided by the Marine Mammal Commission, Ocean Park Conservation Foundation Hong Kong, People's Trust for Endangered Species, and the EDGE of Existence programme; I must give special thanks to Wang Xianyan, Zhang Xinqiao, and particularly Huang Yadong for being such a great team and providing me with such amusement during the writing of the final chapters of this book.

Many other people have also helped me out in other invaluable ways. In particular, Paul Jepson provided crucial information on the impacts of pollutants on cetaceans, and Zoe Smith helped with some tricky Chinese transliteration from old scientific papers that used their own unique re-imaginings of the Wade-Giles system. Special thanks must go to my parents, Bob and Kaija Turvey, to my brother William, and to my friends, especially Menis Koundouros,

Kate McClune, and Claire Risley, for always being there for me. I also owe Latha Menon at Oxford University Press a huge debt of gratitude for giving me such support to write this story: I hope it's the book you were expecting.

Finally, my apologies to everyone whom I haven't had enough time for over the past few years, because of my involvement both with the baiji saga and then with the writing of this book (you know who you are); I know that there's so much water so close to home. I'll try harder in the future; I promise.

About the Author

~

S amuel Turvey was born in Lohja, Finland, and was educated at Bristol Grammar School and St John's College, Oxford. He received a D.Phil. in Chinese palaeontology in 2002, and currently works as a Research Fellow at the Zoological Society of London. He lives in north London.

Index

~

DATE DUE

BRODART, CO.   Cat. No. 23-221-003